MW00330874

The Hemmings Book of

BUICKS

ISBN 0-917808-78-9
Library of Congress Card Number: 2001092944

One of a series of Hemmings Motor News Collector-Car Books. Other books in the series include:
The Hemmings Motor News Book of Cadillacs; The Hemmings Motor News Book of Chrysler Performance Cars; The Hemmings Motor News Book of Corvettes; The Hemmings Motor News Book of Hudsons; The Hemmings Motor News Book of Mustangs; The Hemmings Book of Oldsmobiles; The Hemmings Motor News Book of Packards; The Hemmings Book of Postwar Chevrolets; The Hemmings Motor News Book of Postwar Fords; The Hemmings Book of Prewar Fords; The Hemmings Motor News Book of Pontiacs; The Hemmings Motor News Book of Studebakers.

Hemmings Motor News
Collector Car Publications and Marketplaces
1-800-CAR-HERE (227-4373)
www.hemmings.com

The Hemmings Book of

BUICKS

Editor-In-Chief
Terry Ehrich

Editor
Richard A. Lentinello

Designer
Nancy Bianco

Cover photo by David Gooley: 1955 Buick Riviera

This book compiles driveReports which have appeared in *Hemmings Motor News*'s *Special Interest Autos* magazine (SIA) over the past 30 years. The editors at *Hemmings Motor News* express their gratitude to the following writers, photographers, and artists who made this book possible through their many fine contributions to *Special Interest Autos* magazine:

Terry Boyce	John F. Katz	Jim Tanji
Arch Brown	Michael Lamm	John G. Tennyson
David Gooley	Rick Lenz	Russ von Sauers
Tim Howley	Vince Manocchi	Josiah Work
Bud Juneau	David Newhardt	Vince Wright

We are also grateful to David Brownell, Michael Lamm, and Rich Taylor, the editors under whose guidance these driveReports were written and published. We thank Buick Motor Division, GM Design Staff, and GM Styling, who have graciously contributed photographs to *Special Interest Autos* magazine and this book.

CONTENTS

Special Interest Autos (SIA) magazine's back issues are referred to in this book by issue number. If in stock, copies may be purchased directly from Hemmings Motor News at 800-227-4373, ext. 550 or at www.hemmings.com/gifts.

DEPRESSION-BRED BEAUTY

drive report

1932 BUICK 60

by Josiah Work
photos by Bud Juneau

THE year 1932 wasn't a good one for anybody in the automobile business — or any other business, for that matter. It was a particularly bad time for Buick, whose total production came to a scant 41,522 automobiles. That's less than half the previous year's already dismal figure, and it represents an 84.4 percent tumble compared to 1926, the division's high-water mark up to that point (see sidebar, page 6). Having fought its way back from sixth place in 1928 to third in 1930, Buick had slipped to fourth in '31, from which it plummeted igno-miniously to seventh rank in 1932. Not since 1906 had Buick occupied so lowly a position.

Nor were prospects any brighter for 1933, and in the corporate offices there

was commencing to be serious talk of possibly liquidating the Buick Division. How ironic! For years, Buick had been General Motors' most profitable division, and here it was, evidently on the verge of extinction.

One of the anomalies of the automobile business — and perhaps of most manufacturing enterprises — is that hard times tend to act as a spur, and outstanding products are often the result. This was certainly the case with Buick, for the company's Depression-bred models were particularly memorable. For one thing, engineering had

made substantial advances. Buick's traditional six-cylinder engines had been replaced in 1931 by three brand new straight-eights. The multiple-disc clutch had been superseded in the Series 50 and 60 by the single-plate type. Internal expanding brakes had finally been adopted. And for 1932 the styling was strikingly beautiful, but we'll come to that in a moment.

As they had during 1931 (see *SIA* #41), the 1932 Buicks came in four distinct sizes. The price and volume leader was the Series 50, offered in eight body styles. The engine for this nimble little car had been enlarged from 220.7 to 230.4 cubic inches, raising its horsepower from 77 to 82.5. With prices ranging from $935 to $1,155 — about $100 lower than their 1931 counterparts —

Driving Impressions

Our knowledge is sketchy concerning the early history of our driveReport Buick. It was first sold in New York, to a woman who then drove it to Arizona. It remained in her service there until about 1940, when she put the car in storage.

Many years later the phaeton was taken out of storage and parked in a field, where it was covered by an old parachute. Eventually it was discovered by Walt Plunkett, a Tucson collector, who traced the owner through the car's license number. At that point — some time in the late 1970s — the lady was in a rest home, and getting the title released to Plunkett proved to be a complicated and time-consuming undertaking.

The car didn't look very good when Walt Plunkett finally acquired it. There was a great deal of surface rust, and of course the top, seats, tires, etc, were rotten. But except for the Wizard Control, which had been removed, it was complete. It had few dents and very little wood rot, making the Buick an ideal candidate for restoration.

Plunkett ironed out the sheet metal, stripped and painted the body (black with red pinstriping, as original), and replaced the few pieces of rotted wood, as well as the broken spring leaf. The seats were reupholstered in black leather with tan piping — again, as original, and Naugahyde took the place of the factory-installed imitation leather on the door panels. A new canvas top was fitted, and all brightwork was replated.

The cylinder head was cracked in two places, and there was deep rust in two of the cylinders. Plunkett sleeved the damaged cylinders, fitted new piston rings and installed a rebuilt head. The main and rod bearings were found to be within allowable tolerances, and the steering gear and suspension, apart from the one broken spring leaf, were all in excellent shape.

In 1987, Walt Plunkett advertised the Buick in *Hemmings Motor News*. But when Ralph Roper, an Auburn, California, watchmaker and Buick collector, called, Plunkett hung up on him. There had been too many bogus phone calls, evidently. But Ralph called back, and this time Walt took him seriously. The telephone conversation led to Roper's flight to Tucson, where he found Plunkett's description of the Buick to be entirely accurate, "warts and all." A deal was struck, and the phaeton was shipped to Auburn.

The odometer registered 54,639 miles when Walt Plunkett acquired the car, 56,808 by the time Ralph and Helen Roper bought it. At the start of our driveReport session the numbers read 57,928. And according to papers in the Ropers' possession, these figures represent the actual mileage logged by the phaeton — an average of about 80 miles a month over the car's lifetime!

The sidecurtains were missing when the Ropers bought the phaeton. The wrong grease seals had been installed, with predictable results, and there was insufficient oil in the transmission. Fortunately, Ralph had a pattern for the curtains; so new ones were made, along with a new top boot. The grease seals were replaced, as was the brake lining, and Ralph rodded out the radiator, "just to be sure."

Evidently the cylinder head had been improperly torqued, for the gasket blew during the Buick's first out-of-town trip. Ralph attended to that problem, and while he was about it he overhauled the carburetor, installed new spark plugs and a manifold gasket. Calling on his skills as a watchmaker, he fabricated replacements for three missing parts in the eight-day dashboard clock.

There is no adjustment for the front seat in this Buick phaeton. Fortunately for us, it was located with tall drivers in mind; so we found the position to be just right. The seats are supportive and comfortable, both front and rear.

We found the Buick to be a comparatively easy car to drive. Steering is heavy, yes, but not excessively so, especially for a car of this vintage. The clutch requires only light pedal pressure. Shifts are easy despite fairly long throws. The synchronizers do their job well, and second gear is remarkably quiet. Brakes are more effective than we expected, though they take quite a bit of pedal pressure — and would take even more, had Ralph not installed relatively soft linings.

Cornering is fairly flat and the ride is generally comfortable, but we did find more choppiness than we had expected. There's an incredible amount of low-end torque, so it's easy to take off from rest in second gear. The city of Auburn is built on a hillside, providing ample opportunity for us to test the Buick's climbing ability, which proved to be excellent. And thanks to all that torque, on level ground the Buick will idle along happily in top gear.

The Ropers recently drove the phaeton over Donner Summit (elevation 7,239 feet) to Truckee, a trip on which the car performed flawlessly, they report. On the freeway it cruises easily at 55 to 60 miles an hour, and it will do 80 if pushed.

We've always admired the 1932 Buicks, mainly because of their stunning good looks. But now, having driven this lovely phaeton for ourselves, we have to respect its performance, as well.

1932 BUICK

Above: *1932 was perhaps the pinnacle year of the decade for great looking cars from every manufacturer, and certainly Buick contributed with their handsome front-end styling.* **Below left:** *Headlamps and sidelamps are graceful and well-detailed.* **Below right:** *Radiator cap proudly displays the number of cylinders down below.*

these automobiles represented truly outstanding values. Not since the four-cylinder models of 1922-24 had any Buick been priced so reasonably.

Just how much the 1932 Buick buyer got for his money can be seen by comparing the Model 57 Sedan with its 1929 counterpart:

	1929	1932
Price	$1,320	$995
Wheelbase	115.75"	114.75"
Shipping weight (lb.)	3,630	3,450
Engine	6-cylinder	Straight 8
Displacement (cu. in.)	239.1	230.4
Hp/rpm	74/2,800	82.5/33,200
Torque/rpm	172/1,200	200/1,600
Compression ratio	4.30:1	4.75:1
Hp/c.i.d.	.309	.358
Weight/hp	49.05 lb.	40.83 lb.

And we're not even taking into account, here, the many chassis improvements that had taken place over that three-year period.

Buick's next most popular line was the Series 60, exemplified by our driveReport car. In this instance there were seven body styles, with prices ranging from $1,250 for the business coupe to $1,390 for the Model 65 sport phaeton pictured on these pages. Production of the latter was limited to 79 units as far

1932 Buick Table of Prices, Weights and Production

	Price	Shipping Weight	Production Domestic	Production Export	Total
Series 50, 114.75" Wheelbase					
Model 55 sport phaeton	$1,155	3,270 pounds	69	37	106
Model 56 business coupe	$935	3,305 pounds	1,726		1,726
Model 56C convertible coupe	$1,080	3,335 pounds	630	13	643
Model 56S sport coupe	$1,040	3,395 pounds	1,905	9	1,914
Model 57 sedan	$995	3,450 pounds	10,803		10,803
Model 57S special sedan	$1,080	3,510 pounds	9,766	175	9,941
Model 58 victoria coupe	$1,060	3,420 pounds	2,194	2	2,196
Model 58C convertible phaeton	$1,080	3,425 pounds	380	20	400
Bare chassis	N/a	N/a	504	140	644
Series 60, 118" Wheelbase					
Model 65 sport phaeton	$1,390	3,795 pounds	79	24	103
Model 66 business coupe	$1,250	3,795 pounds	1,726		1,726
Model 66C convertible coupe	$1,310	3,795 pounds	450	2	452
Model 66S sport coupe	$1,270	3,860 pounds	1,678	6	1,684
Model 67 sedan	$1,310	3,980 pounds	9,013	47	9,060
Model 68 victoria coupe	$1,290	3,875 pounds	1,514		1,514
Model 68C convertible phaeton	$1,310	3,880 pounds	366	16	382
Bare chassis	N/a	N/a	372	36	408
Series 80, 126" Wheelbase					
Model 86 victoria coupe	$1,540	4,335 pounds	1,800		1,800
Model 87 sedan	$1,570	4,450 pounds	4,089		4,089
Series 90, 134" Wheelbase					
Model 90 sedan, 7-passenger	$1,955	4,657 pounds	1,368	19	1,387
Model 90L limousine, 7-passenger	$2,055	4,810 pounds	164	26	190
Model 91 club sedan, 5-passenger	$1,820	4,620 pounds	2,237	1	2,238
Model 95 sport phaeton, 7-passenger	$1,675	4,470 pounds	131	15	146
Model 96 victoria coupe	$1,785	4,460 pounds	1,460		1,460
Model 96C convertible coupe	$1,805	4,460 pounds	289		289
Model 96S country club coupe	$1,740	4,470 pounds	586		586
Model 97 sedan, 5-passenger	$1,805	4,565 pounds	1,485		1,485

as the domestic market was concerned, by far the lowest of any style in the series, yet this car actually outsold its less expensive Model 55 counterpart. The Series 60's wheelbase was unchanged at 118 inches, and 1931's 272.6-c.i.d., 90-horsepower engine was retained without major modification.

The wheelbases of the senior Buick models were stretched by two inches: to 126 inches for the Series 80, 134 for the huge Series 90. Both were powered by a 344.8-cubic-inch, 104-horsepower straight-eight that was only slightly smaller in displacement than the Cadillac V-8. Just two body styles were offered on the shorter wheelbase, while nine were available in the Series 90, with weights running as high as 4,810 pounds in the case of the limousine. (Fortunately for buyers of these heavier models, an optional high-compression cylinder head was available, raising the horsepower to 113.)

There were a number of interesting new features for 1932. Perhaps the most novel of these was a device called Wizard Control, which paired free-wheeling with an automatic clutch. Operated by means of a small button located on the floorboard, just to the left of the clutch, the mechanism worked like this: The driver depressed the Wizard Control button and took his/her foot off the accelerator. A vacuum was thus created, causing the clutch to release. The transmission was then shifted to the desired gear, and when the accelerator was applied the clutch re-engaged automatically. Successive shifts were made without the use of the clutch, simply by depressing the button and releasing the accelerator pedal.

Wizard Control might be thought of as an early step toward "shiftless" driving, pre-dating the automatic transmission by several years. No doubt it was convenient, but unfortunately it was every bit as complicated as it sounds. Buick continued to offer the contraption as late as

Buick Versus The Competition

No other automobile in our driveReport Buick's price category was built in the phaeton style. Therefore, the following table uses four-door sedans for purposes of comparison.

	Buick Series 60	Hudson Sterling	Hupmobile 222	Nash 1080 Special 8
Price, f.o.b.	$1,310	$1,295	$1,295	$1,320
Engine c.i.d.	272.6	254.4	261.5	260.8
Horsepower/rpm	96/3,200	101/3,600	93/3,200	100/3,400
Compression ratio	5.03:1	5.80:1	5.40:1	5.25:1
Valve configuration	Ohv	L-head	L-head	Ohv
Main bearings	5	5	5	9
Lubrication system	Pressure	Splash	Pressure	Pressure
Brakes	Mechanical	Mechanical	Mechaical	Mechanical
Final drive	Spiral bevel	Spiral bevel	Hypoid	Spiral bevel
Ratio	4.54:1	4.64:1	4.36:1	4.43:1
Torque medium	Torque tube	Springs	Springs	Springs
Tire size	6.00/18	6.00/17	6.00/17	6.50/17
Wheelbase	118"	126"	122"	128"
Shipping weight	3,980 lb.	3,415 lb. (net)	3,580 lb.	3,870 lb.
Horsepower/c.i.d.	.330	.397	.356	.383
Lb./horsepower	42.2	33.8	38.5	38.7
Lb./c.i.d.	13.9	13.4	13.7	14.8

Above: Right-hand taillamp carried attractive enameled Buick emblem. **Below:** Series 65 sport phaeton was an unusual sight even when new. Only 103 were produced and 24 of them went overseas.

specifications

illustrations by Russell von Sauers, The Graphic Automobile Studio

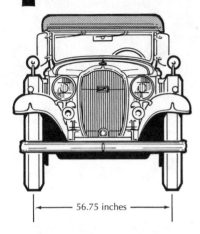

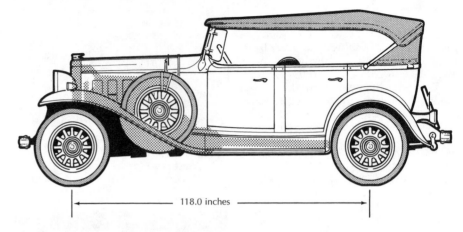

56.75 inches

118.0 inches

1932 Buick Model 65

Price	$1,390 f.o.b. factory, with standard equipment
Standard equipment, this model	Twin bugle horns, wind wings, dual taillamps
Options on dR car	6 wheels with sidemounted spares, white sidewall tires, trunk rack
Aftermarket equip.	Tire-mounted outside mirrors

ENGINE

Type	Valve-in-head straight 8
Bore x stroke	3.0625" x 4.625"
Displacement	272.6 cubic inches
Compression ratio	4.63:1
Horsepower @ rpm	90 @ 3,000
Torque @ rpm	200 @ 1,600
Taxable horsepower	30.02
Valve lifters	Mechanical
Main bearings	5
Fuel system	Marvel 1.3125" dual updraft carburetor, camshaft pump
Lubrication system	Pressure to main, connecting rod and camshaft bearings, and timing gear
Cooling system	Centrifugal pump
Exhaust system	Single
Electrical system	6-volt battery/coil

CLUTCH

Type	Single dry disc
Diameter	9.875"
Actuation	Mechanical, foot pedal

TRANSMISSION

Type	3-speed selective, synchronized 2nd and 3rd speeds
Control lever	Floor mounted
Ratios: 1st	2.89:1
2nd	1.74:1
3rd	1.00:1
Reverse	3.47:1

DIFFERENTIAL

Type	Spiral bevel
Ratio	4.27:1
Drive axles	3/4 floating

STEERING

Type	Jacox worm and roller
Ratio	17.0:1
Turns, lock-to-lock	3.25
Turning diameter	39' 6"

BRAKES

Type	4-wheel internal mechanical
Drum diameter	14"
Braking area	155.3 square inches

CONSTRUCTION

Type	Body-on-frame
Frame	Single drop; 7" channel iron, 6 cross members
Body	Steel over wood framing
Body style	Sport phaeton

SUSPENSION

Front	I-beam axle, 36.875" x 2" semi-elliptic 10-leaf springs
Rear	Rigid axle, 55.25" x 2.25" semi-elliptic 8-leaf springs
Shock absorbers	Lovejoy 2-way
Ride control	Manual
Wheels	Wood artillery type, de-mountable at hubs
Tires	6.00/18 4-ply, tube type

WEIGHTS AND MEASURES

Wheelbase	118"
Overall length	178"
Overall width	72"
Overall height	68.25"
Front track	56.75"
Rear track	57.8125"
Min. road clearance	8.25"
Weight	3,795 pounds

CAPACITIES

Crankcases	8 quarts
Cooling system	4 gallons
Fuel tank	19 gallons
Transmission	4 pints
Differential	7.5 pints

CALCULATED DATA

Hp per c.i.d.	.330
Weight per hp	42.2
Weight per c.i.d.	13.9
Weight per sq. in.	24.4 (brakes)

Crank hole is disguised by this shiny cover.

1932 BUICK

1934, but it was trouble-prone, and eventually it was abandoned. Evidently most owners disconnected the Wizard Control, and many of them removed it altogether.

Another interesting Buick feature in 1932 was its Ride-Control. Operated by means of a small lever on the left side of the steering column, this device permitted the driver to adjust shock absorber action to the road conditions. Six gradations were provided, ranging from #1 for smooth pavement to #6 for heavy bumps. It may be that the public failed to understand and make use of this potentially useful mechanism; in any case, it was abandoned after only one year.

A new transmission for 1932 featured a silent second speed, along with synchronized second and third gears. Perhaps "silent" represented a slight exaggeration, but at least the gearbox was very much quieter than its predecessors.

Styling, though still conservative, was fresh, new and very attractive. Windshields were given a smart, 10-degree rake, while outside visors were eliminated. The chrome-plated radiator grille was gracefully tapered toward the bottom, and hood doors — five on each side — replaced the previous louvers. Fenders were long and sweeping. Chrome-plated bugle horns hung beneath the headlamps, whose bullet shape was echoed by the small parking lamps that rode atop the front fenders. Artillery wheels with 12 wooden spokes were offered at no additional cost, for what proved to be the final time, but

Above left: Door handles are elegantly styled. *Right:* Dual sidemounted tires are factory accessories. *Below:* Big, puffy armrests are provided for rear seat passengers. *Bottom:* OHV straight eight packs enough punch to easily keep up with modern traffic.

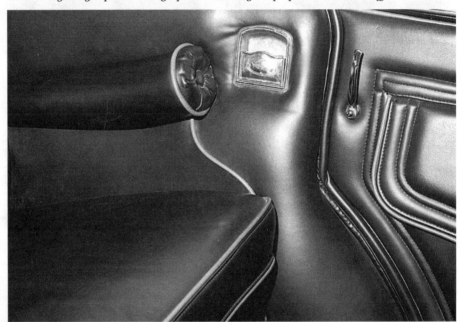

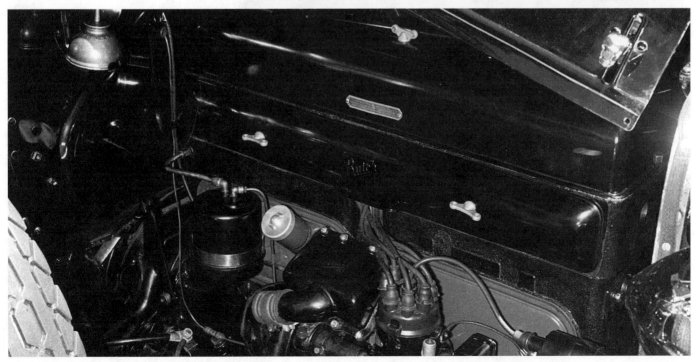

1932 BUICK

Above: Tool kit hides in this handy compartment in driver's door. **Below left:** Tonneau lights and robe rail are all part of the standard equipment. **Below right:** Movable air intakes are in bottom of hood.

most cars came equipped with painted wires. Dual sidemounted spare wheels, supplied as standard issue on the Series 90 cars, were an extra-cost option on the less expensive models.

Added to the 50 and 60 series were two particularly smart new models, a victoria coupe and a convertible phaeton — the latter a close-coupled two-door type. (There was also a Series 90 convertible phaeton, which came in a slightly different configuration.) The roadster, a Buick staple from the very beginning, was deleted, but the phaeton was retained for this one final season in the two smaller lines. (We're at a loss to explain why the four-door ragtop was continued while the two-seater was dropped from the line, for although production of the roadster was not great during 1930-31, it had far outsold the phaeton.)

But no matter how attractive the 1932 Buicks may have been, and despite the outstanding value they offered at what were remarkably reasonable prices, customers stayed away in droves. The Depression had the nation by the throat, and without exception all American automakers suffered a severe loss of sales. To some, the reduction was fatal. And among the remaining companies — and there were at least 30 of them, if the various corporate divisions were counted separately — only General Motors and Nash managed to eke out a profit for the year.

In response to the trouble, a major change took place in the GM front office during 1932, when Buick, Olds and Pontiac were combined, for both manufacturing and sales purposes, into a single organization known as B.O.P. The intent was to save as many dealers as possible from what appeared to be inevitable bankruptcy, by giving Buick dealers a lower-priced line of cars to add to their showrooms — and conversely, by providing Olds and Pontiac distributors with a more prestigious automobile. But brand loyalty was strong in those days, and the arrangement pleased nobody. The plan was abandoned after about a year and a half. (Interesting: What goes around, comes around. Today, although each division retains a degree of autonomy, one can find any number of dealers who handle more than one General Motors franchise.)

Surely it must have seemed that the automobile industry had hit bottom during 1932. But although 1933 saw substantial sales gains on the part of GM's Chevrolet, Pontiac and Oldsmobile Divisions, both Cadillac/LaSalle and

Critique

Like every other automobile that has ever been built, the '32 Buick had both its strong and weak points. Let's start with the good news.

• Styling. Harley Earl was in top form when the 1932 cars from General Motors were designed, for every one of them was a beauty. Compare the 1932 Buick with any of its competitors, or with Buicks of either earlier or later vintage, and it comes up winners every time.

• Performance. When a 60-year-old car, one that sold originally at a comparatively modest price, can keep up easily with modern freeway traffic and can climb hills with the best of them, somebody back then must have been doing something right.

• Quality. You see it in this car, everywhere you look. The Phaeton is stoutly built and nicely finished, in the Buick tradition.

• Ride. Despite some choppiness — probably inevitable, given that independent front suspension was still a couple of years in the future when this automobile was built — this is a comfortable car. The Ride Control feature may not have been entirely successful in its own time, but the idea appears to us to have been a sound one.

• And there are a number of welcome

touches of a minor nature. The fold-down armrest in the back seat; the ample rear leg room; the walnut-grained insert surrounding the dash panel, to cite just a few examples.

Still, as much as we like the Buick Phaeton, it does have a few shortcomings:

• The fixed-position front seat poses a real problem for short drivers, including co-owner Helen Roper, who uses two pillows when operating this car, according to her husband.

• And it takes a long stretch in order to reach the starter pedal, to the right and above the accelerator.

• If the top mechanism could be hidden from view in 1931, why must it be visible on the 1932 model?

• How come the updraft carburetor? Even Chevrolet had adopted a downdraft pot by 1932.

• And finally, wouldn't it have been nice if General Motors had seen fit to follow Chrysler's lead by adopting hydraulic brakes? Viewed with suspicion by many at first, juice brakes had long since proven their worth by the time our driveReport car was built. Yet Buick wouldn't employ them until 1936.

But perhaps we're nit-picking. Taken all in all, the 1932 Buick was — and is still — a great automobile.

Buick took a further drubbing that year. A dramatic turnaround would take place at Buick during 1934, under the leadership of a new general manager named Harlow H. Curtice, but of course that's a story in itself. ❑

Acknowledgments and Bibliography
Automobile Trade Journal, *August 1932*; Automotive Industries, *February 27, 1932*; Dammann, George H., Seventy Years of Buick; Dunham, Terry B. and Lawrence R. Gustin, The Buick: A Complete History; Heasley, Jerry, The Production Figure Book for US Cars; Kimes, Beverly Rae, "Wouldn't You Really Rather Be A Buick?" Automobile Quarterly, *Vol. VII, No. 1*; Langworth, Richard M. and Jan P. Norbye, Complete History of General Motors, 1908-1986; Motor, *January 1932*; Naul, G. Marshall (ed.), The Specification Book for US Cars, 1930-1969.
Our thanks to Dave Brown, Durham, California; Dan King, Auburn, California; National Automobile Museum, Reno, Nevada, Chuck Hilton, Executive Director. Special thanks to Ralph and Helen Roper, Auburn, California.

Left: *Woodgrained dash puts all the gauges right in front of driver.* **Above:** *Ride control was offered only in 1932 Buicks.*

Hard Times

By 1932, things looked bleak at Buick. In just three short years the division's production had tumbled from 196,104 to 41,522 cars, a drop of 78.8 percent.

Of course, the Depression was primarily to blame, for the competition found itself in precisely the same fix. Consider the record of some of the other makes in Buick's price class:

	1929	1932	Difference
Chrysler	92,034	25,291	-72.5%
Oldsmobile	101,579	21,933	-78.4%
Hupmobile	50,579	10,076	-80.1%
Nash	116,622	17,696	-84.8%

All of which must have been cold comfort to Buick's management.

It's not that traditional buyers of medium-priced cars were flocking to the less expensive makes, for even in that market, hard times had taken a similar toll. Taken together, by 1932 the "Low-Priced Three" — Chevrolet, Ford and Plymouth — had lost 74.1 percent of their 1929 volume.

Nor did the luxury marques fare any better. Over the same three-year period, Cadillac/LaSalle sales fell by 75.1 percent, while Packard took an 81.5 percent beating. Pierce-Arrow — a Studebaker subsidiary in those days — had its back to the wall; Marmon and Stutz were on the verge of collapse; Peerless was busy converting its factory into a brewery; and only the determination of Edsel Ford, together with the resources of the Ford Motor Company, were keeping Lincoln alive.

But the Depression wasn't the entire story by any means, for the start of Buick's troubles pre-dated by several years the coming of hard times.

Back in 1926, Buick had been riding high. Third in sales behind Ford and Chevrolet, it was by a wide margin the leading make in the medium-price field. But

Buick's management was ultra-conservative, and although the quality of the product was beyond reproach, in a number of respects the Buick was out of step with the times. Styling, for instance, was tall, angular and ungainly. Performance was ponderous and fuel consumption tended to be excessive. External contracting brakes — an exercise in sheer terror when they became wet — were retained at a time when the competition was turning to the internal expanding type.

Perhaps worst of all, while every other automobile except Dodge and the Model T Ford had adopted the standard SAE gearshift quadrant, Buick clung to a shift pattern that was the opposite of that most people had become accustomed to, thus:

Buick		SAE	
2	R	R	2
3	1	1	3

Competition, especially from Chrysler and Studebaker, was becoming increasingly stiff, and Buick sales slipped a little for 1927. The slip became a slide during 1928, leaving Buick production in sixth place. Still, there were signs of renewed life in Flint that year. The standard SAE shift quadrant was at last adopted, and a new, double-drop frame lowered the car's profile substantially. But the public remained unimpressed, for in some important respects Buick still seemed to be behind the times. Yet hopes were high for 1929, Buick's Silver Anniversary year. In celebration of the occasion, Harley Earl — who had come to General Motors as styling consultant for the 1927 LaSalle and had remained to establish GM's Art and Colour Section, the industry's first full-scale styling department — undertook to design a handsome new Buick. Unfortunately, while Earl was traveling in Europe, Buick's still-conserva-

tive engineering department had added five inches to the height of the new model while pulling the side panels in at the bottom. Bulging sides and a towering profile were the result, and the 1929 model became known, for good reason, as the Pregnant Buick (see SIA #56). Sales took another tumble, and at a time when the industry was setting new production records, Buick's volume dropped by an additional 13.1 percent.

The 1929 styling may have been Buick's most obvious problem, but it wasn't the only difficulty, by any means. The traditional three-quarter floating rear axle, for instance, was an obsolete design. So was the multiple-disc clutch, not to mention those miserable external brakes. There were two new Buick engines that year, but both were Sixes, at a time when the public's attention was focused upon Straight-Eights from Studebaker, Graham-Paige, Hupmobile and others. Even conservative Nash Motors had an eight-in-line in the works for 1930. Furthermore, the new 309-c.i.d. engine that powered the larger Series 121 and 129 Buicks proved to have an inordinate thirst.

By 1930, Buick had evidently come awake. Styling was slimmer and much more attractive. Engines were bored out to yield greater displacement and more horsepower, which of course resulted in improved performance. At long last, internal brakes were adopted. And on the drawing boards were four brand-new eights-in-line, scheduled to debut in late July as 1931 models (see SIA #41).

There should have been better days ahead for Buick. Should have been, but unfortunately, that's not the way events played out.

1938 Buick vs. 1938 LaSalle

Buick

Mention the name "Century" and you are sure to ignite the fire within most any Buick collector. Long before Olds engineers stuffed the hairy ohv V-8 Rocket engine into the Chevrolet-bodied model in 1949, creating the fabulous 88, Harlow Curtice had done the same thing to the Buick Special. That was in 1936. The lightweight Century, with the big Roadmaster engine, was offered from 1936 through 1942 and again from 1954 through 1958. While Buick Centurys of all years are much loved collectibles, the 1938 model is the most prized of all. The sport coupe has a particular fascination because it is the lightest weight of the Centurys. Many of these four-passenger coupes were hot rodded, so today one would be hard pressed to find a strictly stock Buick Century coupe from the 1937-38 era.

The 1936 model was truly the "resurrection" Buick, the brainchild of Harlow "Red" Curtice, who came over from AC to head up the ailing Buick Division in October 1933. Buick had started to fade with the 1929 plug ugly. Then came the Great Depression and the ghastly B.O.P., in which all Buick, Oldsmobile, and Pontiac sales and some manufacturing functions were consolidated. The number of exclusive Buick dealers shrank from 2,609 in 1927 to only 67 by the early spring of 1934. For 1934 and

by Tim Howley
photos by the author

1935 Buick offered interim models: light, cheap and not at all bad looking. Introduced in May 1934, some 63,000 were sold for that model year. While the figure was nothing to brag about, it was almost 50 percent better than that of 1933 and allowed Buick to break away from B.O.P.

The 1936 Buick was Harlow Curtice's all-new car. Soon after he arrived at Buick he paid a call on GM styling boss Harley Earl and asked him point blank, "what kind of a car do you drive, Harley?" Naturally the big man answered, "a Cadillac." Then Curtice went on to ask, "How about designing me a Buick with as much dash as a Cadillac, but make it different enough so that everybody will know it's a Buick from a block away."

In those days the styling of all GM cars was done at one place — the GM headquarters building in Detroit. There were three basic body shells — A, B, and C, or small, medium and large. Since differentiating any GM make from the others was referred to as "body politics," it took considerable ingenuity and per-

suasion for any division head to order a car that was significantly different from the others. Curtice possessed the special skills that got him a car that not only looked different from the pack but proclaimed that there had been a changing of the guard at Buick. The 1936 model was an instant success, with production reaching 168,596, compared to 53,249 for 1935.

Wisely, Curtice changed the model nomenclature from the meaningless Series numbers 40, 50, 60, and 90 to the "Special" for the 40, "Century" for the 60, "Roadmaster" for the 80, and "Limited" for the 90. The 50 Series was dropped. Century was a buzzword in the mid-thirties. It was associated with the Twentieth Century Limited streamliner train and the Century of Progress Chicago World's Fair. But not until 1938 did it stand for a Buick that would crack the 100 mph mark.

1936 Buicks were offered with two valve-in-head engines: the 233-c.i.d. straight eight continued from 1934-35 and the new Roadmaster and Limited 320 which was carried in the Century as well. The new engine was characterized by a short stroke, larger bearings, elimination of the infamous Buick oil cooler, and the addition of anolite aluminum pistons. One of the engine's more unusual features was a hollow rocker arm shaft with a water-cooled gauze filter.

Coolant from the block warmed the upstairs oil and helped keep down valve clatter after startup. This engine proved to be so powerful and reliable that it was retained essentially in its original form through 1952, with the horsepower gradually increasing from 120 to 170.

In addition to two engines replacing four, Buick cut down the expensive array of bodies from 25 to seven. Other new features for 1936 were a new frame for the Special and Century, all-steel "turret top," hydraulic brakes, and a new synchromesh transmission for the Century, Roadmaster, and Limited that was 36 pounds lighter than its predecessor. To quote SIA #46, "This gearbox had beautifully spaced ratios and would let the Century wind out to 42 in low and 66 mph in second (at 5,500 rpm)." This same gearbox with a few modifications was adapted by Cadillac and LaSalle beginning in 1937. Olds used it, too, but not until postwar years. Buick kept it until Dynaflow became standard equipment.

The landmark 1936 Buick pulled the fine old Buick dealer organization back together again. When the biggest Buick dealer in the country, Gus Southworth of Glidden Buick, New York, saw the 1936 cars he upped his order by 500 and cancelled his other franchises. By the end of 1936 nearly a thousand dealers were back in the fold as exclusively Buick stores.

For 1937 the Buick Century wheelbase went from 122 to 126 inches. The entire Buick line was restyled by Frank Hershey, recently recruited from the Murphy Body Company in Pasadena. The new bodies were considerably lower, wider, and longer, and had increased head room. There was a significant weight increase, 465 pounds, for example, in the Century sport coupe. The rumble seat remained in the convertible coupe, but in the sport coupe it was eliminated in favor of opera seats.

Obviously, a bigger, heavier car dictated a horsepower increase. The "Dynaflash" 320 engine got a horsepower boost from 120 to 130 through a new Aerobat carburetor (similar to the type used on aerobatic aircraft), and cam timing was revised. This was still not enough. For 1938 horsepower went up again to 141. This was accomplished with "turbulator pistons" which had a bump on the top designed to promote more efficient combustion as well as boost the compression ratio.

Styling changes for 1938 were minimal and were limited primarily to a more massive looking grille which appears to be a subtle copy of the 1936-37 Cord grille. The frame center section went from I beam to X member, and coil springs were added to the rear — an industry first. Since these coil springs were much softer and more resilient than the leaf springs, the shock

Above: LaSalle's graceful ornament had taken this form since 1934. Buick's hood jewelry is far less distinctive. Below: LaSalle fenders are more upright and formal-appearing than Buick's.

absorbers were made some four times the size of any others on the market. New clutch facings were designed for smoother operation. It is the engineering advances that make the 1938 Buick, particularly the Century, such a collector's favorite. From a styling standpoint, the '37 model is every bit as good looking; perhaps the grille is slightly better looking in the eyes of some.

In 1937 Buick production rose to 220,346, and the division moved up from seventh to sixth place in the industry. Although 1938 was a down year for all car makers, Buick was the hottest thing in the medium-higher-price class and secured a peak penetration of the US market at 8.8 percent, moving Buick up to fourth place in the industry, where it would remain through 1942. 1938 Buick production was 168,689.

LaSalle

You don't hear as much about Cadillac's Depression woes as Buick's. This may be because, with a 1930 production of some 17,000 Cadillacs and 15,000 LaSalles against nearly 182,000 Buicks, the venerable Cadillac Division did not have so far to fall. Nonetheless, fall the grand old dame did, to a low of 3,173 Cadillacs and 3,482 LaSalles for 1933. Sales figures did not become at all encouraging until the introduction of the 1936 models, of which 12,880 were Cadillacs and 13,004 were LaSalles. Still, Cadillac and LaSalle remained far behind Packard and Chrysler, and the new 1936 Lincoln-Zephyr became a formidable competitor for the LaSalle. It

can also be said with justification that the Buick Century was robbing LaSalle of buyers because the price differential was less than $100 after 1936.

Cadillac in the thirties is remembered for its many innovations: "Triple-Silent" Synchro-Mesh for 1932, that is, helical-cut gears at all three forward speeds; No-Draft Ventilation plus vacuum-assisted brakes for 1933; independent front suspension (shared with all other divisions) for 1934: and hydraulic brakes for all models, except the sixteens, for 1936, again shared with all other divisions. The thirties, too, was the era when Cadillac experimented with power steering, an automatic transmission, and the ohv V-8, which was not introduced until 1949. Cadillac was also a forerunner in styling, with Bill Mitchell's trend-setting 1938 Series 60 Special. (See SIA #62.)

The head of the Cadillac Division during these years of transition from limited-production Classics to mass-produced luxury cars was German-born Nicholas Dreystadt, who succeeded Lawrence Fisher in 1934. Unlike the colorful and publicity-seeking Harlow Curtice, Dreystadt preferred to work behind the scenes. He did not have to give a new image to an "old man's car" or bring a division out of a sales abyss. Both Cadillac and LaSalle were respected for their contemporary lines and stellar performance. They had not lost their market share. In fact they were gaining, relative to most other high-priced makes. Cadillac's and LaSalle's declining sales were related directly to the Depression, plus the fact that the wealthy did not

Above: LaSalle shares taillamp design with Cadillac; Buick's is better integrated into fender design. *Below:* LaSalle used Cadillac-style eggcrate grille; Buick's has 810 Cord overtones.

want to be seen driving around in expensive new machines while most Americans were going to the poorhouse in their old Fords and Chevrolets.

While the LaSalle never had quite the prestige of the Cadillac, it was a magnificent car. Remember, the 1927 LaSalle was the first US production car to be styled by a true automobile stylist, Harley Earl. With this car's success, Earl put together the industry's first styling studio, the GM Art & Colour Section.

LaSalle might have been dropped altogether for 1934, except for the persuasiveness of Harley Earl in high GM circles. As it turned out, the 1934 model had an Oldsmobile-derived L-head straight eight, and prices were slashed more than $800. What the make lost in prestige was made up for in styling. The 1934 LaSalle was a remarkable design achievement done by the highly creative Jules Agramonte. Its pencil-thin vertical grille was inspired by the Frontenac Ford race car. The biplane bumpers and half portholes were the latest in art deco trim. The styling and the L-head engine would remain through 1936.

The 1937 LaSalle was all new. Bodies were little different from the Cadillac Series 60, except for trim. The engine was a junior version of the Cadillac V-8. The 1937 LaSalle and Cadillac Series 60 were also designed by Bill Mitchell, who in later years succeeded Harley Earl as head of GM styling.

Recalling the 1937-38 models,

Mitchell told *SIA* in issue #18, "I came to General Motors in December 1935 and worked on the 1937 LaSalle just as a designer — and on the 1937 Buick and Cadillac, too. At that time they were all done in one room. And then I was put into competition on the 1938 Buick [presumably against Frank Hershey, whose design won]. Harley Earl used to hold styling competitions among the young designers to sharpen their ideas. Right after that they divided the cars into studios and named designers to head them. I was put in charge of Cadillac, and Paul Meyer was put in charge of LaSalle. When Meyer left and went to Briggs [Mfg. Co.], they gave me both Cadillac and LaSalle."

For 1937, LaSalle adapted the smaller, 322-c.i.d. version of the 346-c.i.d. Cadillac L-head V-8. This 322 engine was offered by Cadillac for 1936 only. Cadillac retained the 346 right up through 1948. The 322 was the only LaSalle powerplant from 1937 through 1940, the last year of production. For 1937-39 the horsepower was 125, raised to 130 for 1940.

The 322/346 represented GM's second attempt to cast and manufacture a monoblock V-8 on a mass production basis. The first had been the 1930-32 Oakland/Pontiac V-8. This time the attempt was so successful that Cadillac never seriously considered any other L-head V-8. Prior to 1936, the Cadillac V-8 block was a three-piece unit which

had no small number of problems due to temperature variations between the cast-iron block and the aluminum crankcase. Structurally, by 1936 they could make a much stronger and more reliable monoblock, and it was only 20 pounds heavier than the earlier engine. Two important innovations were introduced with the new 1936 engine — mass-produced hydraulic valve-lash adjusters and pressed-in piston pins. The new engine proved so satisfactory that the ohv V-12 and V-16 were dropped after 1937. Even the 1938-40 V-16 was of L-head design.

1938 LaSalle styling changes were minor, since 1937 had been the big year of change. The eggcrate grille was made two inches wider. The headlamps were nestled down flush with the fenders but were still not integrated into the fenders. The chevrons were deleted from the leading edge of the front fenders. Instead, there was now a triple streak from the center point of the headlamps to the bottom of the fenders. Interestingly enough, nowhere on the car does the name "LaSalle" appear, just the initials "LaS" on the hubcaps, centerpiece of the rear bumper, horn button, clutch and brake pedals. The vehicle identification number, mechanical components, and even the heater box are all identified as "Cadillac" or "Cadillac Division."

Two 1938 improvements worthy of note are the rear-hinged alligator hood and column-mounted gearshift.

The new body style and engine for 1937 took hold with the public. LaSalle production moved up to 32,000, nearly double that of 1936. 1937 was LaSalle's best year ever, with the make moving from nineteenth place to fifteenth place in the industry, a position they would enjoy until the very end. 1938 production dropped back down to 14,635. It is interesting to note that for the years 1936-40, LaSalle and Lincoln were about neck and neck in sales. Big Lincoln production was insignificant. The Lincoln-Zephyr and the LaSalle were after precisely the same market, with the junior Lincoln winning out only after Cadillac chose to drop the remarkable LaSalle for 1941.

Driving Impressions

For our purposes we wanted to compare 1938 models because 1938 represents the *crème de la crème* of Buicks and was also a very good year for LaSalle. We wanted to compare coupes because these would be the best performance models with the lightest bodies. But finding two nice coupes in California close enough to compare proved extremely difficult, and we can understand why. There were only 2,710 LaSalle coupes produced for 1938, even fewer Buick Century sport coupes: 2,030. Presuming a normal survival rate of one percent after this many years, that means there may be only 27 LaSalle coupes and 20 Buick Century sport coupes left in the entire country. (By the way, sport coupe is merely Buick nomenclature for the same car as the LaSalle coupe.)

The probability of finding Buick Century sport coupes is even less than that of finding LaSalles because these cars were hot-rodded at an early date.

We felt extremely fortunate when we found one in Ventura, California. The 320 engine has been slightly modified, and the interior is somewhat changed from the original. But the outward appearance is strictly stock. The car is owned by Gary Stafford, who has three other 1938 Buicks and is presently restoring a 1937 Buick Century convertible coupe. Our Buick comparison car can best be described as unrestored, modified as they were for drag racing in the late forties and early fifties.

The LaSalle is a ground-up restoration owned by Dave Collier, of Glendale, California, about 60 miles to the east of Ventura. Dave bought the car 25 years ago, then sold it to his brother, bought it back again six years later, and has only very recently completed the restoration. Dave is in the television production industry in Hollywood and has worked on many major television series and films. He is a lifelong Cadillac enthusiast and has owned many of these cars. But most recently he has pared his collection down mainly to the '38 coupe so that he could do a complete restoration.

Unfortunately, a direct performance comparison of the two cars could not be attempted for two reasons. The LaSalle is like a new car; the Buick is a somewhat mechanically tired old car and not stock. Moreover, in Southern California today it is hard to find a place where you can run a thorough road test in the sense that *Motor Trend* does it. So we can only look at the figures and speculate on how the two might have performed against each other had a comparison been done in 1938. That was long before the days of comparative tests, and even 0-60 mph figures are difficult to find from way back then.

Both cars have General Motors' all-steel B body, which offers the same passenger compartment dimensions. The Buick's two-inch-longer wheelbase (126 inches compared to LaSalle's 124 inches) is not at all apparent, as even the hoods of the two cars are precisely the same length. Actually, the LaSalle appears to be the longer of the two cars because its front fenders are six inches longer than the Buick's and the headlamps nestle down in the catwalk area, whereas the Buick headlamps stand upright on the traditional supports.

There are some other minor outside differences, but not many. The Buick has separate parking lamps. The Buick

Above: Engines on both cars nestle deep under their hoods and require a long reach for servicing anything but a carburetor. Below left: LaSalle dash is dominated by square and rectangular shapes. Below right: Buick uses a more circular and semicircular theme. Bottom: Despite the body shells, GM's clever styling gives the cars two very different appearances.

hood opens up from each side. The LaSalle hood is the new alligator style. The Buick gas filler cap is on the left, the LaSalle cap on the right. The Buick has all pot metal trim. The LaSalle was now beginning to use stainless steel trim, as was the Cadillac. At close inspection these cars have very much in common. For example, side-mounted tires were an extra-cost option on both makes.

The biggest interior similarity is the opera seats, which were standard equipment on the Buick, optional on the LaSalle. The seat bottoms fold down from the rear cowl area so that the two rear-seat passengers face each other. But the Buick Century offered the beautiful banjo steering wheel with a high-grade translucent plastic rim as standard equipment. In the LaSalle it was optional. The Buick Century's clock was standard, the LaSalle's was optional. The Buick dash has two ash trays, the LaSalle only has one. 1938 Buick Centurys had beautiful wood graining on the dash and window moldings. The

LaSalle dash and window moldings are painted a metallic beige.

The LaSalle coupe listed at $1,295, the Buick sport coupe at $1,226. What the LaSalle buyer got for another $69 was the Cadillac name and prestige, the same Fisher body, and an engine that was just not up to the Buick's standard of performance. If we want to be purely objective in the *Consumer Reports* sense, we would have to advise buyers that the Buick Century was quite a bit more car for a bit less money. Subjectively, however, we liked the frontal styling of the LaSalle a bit better.

But the LaSalle does have one safety/convenience feature we really like. Pull the headlamp knob all the way out for passing and the left light will go up to high beam to see down the road while the right light will go down to dim to prevent blinding the driver of the car you are passing. Both LaSalle and Cadillac had this neat little feature for about two years. By the way, the LaSalle parking lamps are carried in the upper portion of the headlamps.

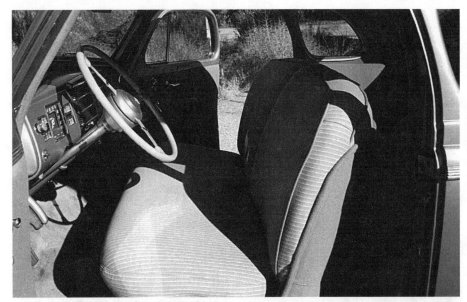

Above: Buick's speedo is marked for 10 mph greater top end than LaSalle's, but neither car will actually attain these numbers. **Below:** Door trim and materials on the two cars are totally different.

Both cars have very similar riding qualities, due to the virtually identical knee-action coil front springs and sway bars front and rear. Weights of the two cars are about the same: 3,745 pounds for the LaSalle, compared to 3,690 pounds for the Buick. Although the Buick went to rear coil springs, the LaSalle retained rear leaves. You might expect a difference in riding qualities. We didn't notice it. But then, why should we? Both these cars are coupes. Buick's rear coils were mainly for the comfort of the rear-seat passengers. Both of these cars have slow, heavy steering, which would have benefited much from power assist. It's a shame GM didn't put it on their big cars in the late thirties. They had already developed the technology.

The transmissions are similar but not quite identical. The real difference is that the LaSalle has a column-mounted gearshift, whereas the Buick gearshift is floor-mounted for one last year.

Coupled with its highly reliable, fast-shifting gearbox, the LaSalle 322 soon became a hot rodder's delight. In fact, one LaSalle so equipped was tested out on the Indianapolis Speedway in 1938. It was driven relentlessly for 500 miles at an average speed of 82 mph. The car was completely stock and, naturally, was a coupe, the lightest model in the LaSalle lineup save the convertible coupe.

A 1938 LaSalle coupe in perfect tune will come close to doing 100 mph, but probably will not pass the century mark; a 1938 Buick Century will, by about three mph. The LaSalle will go from zero to 60 in 15 to 16 seconds. The 1938 Buick Century should beat it by about two seconds, but we have yet to find any printed figures to document our suspicions.

Buick claimed that its 1938 Century models were the fastest US production cars on the road; certainly the Century was one of the industry's most powerful. It had 16 more horsepower than the LaSalle, 11 more even than the Cadillac. GM Proving Ground personnel punched one Century to a top speed of 103 mph, and acceleration was so strong that a 1938 Century sport coupe would hold a National Hot Rod Association class record for the next 25 years.

We ran across an interesting Buick Century ad in the March 20, 1937, issue of the *Saturday Evening Post*. Of course, this was for a 1937 model and a two-door sedan with sidemounts, a heavier and less aerodynamic car. The ad was primarily a reprint of an article written by one Don Short, automobile editor of the *New York Evening Journal*. He tested the car on the old Roosevelt Raceway, at Westbury, Long Island. Here is what he wrote:

"With my associate, Dave Preston, holding the stop watch, I 'gave her the gun' on the all-too brief three-quarter-mile straightaway. Those 130 mechanical horses under the hood did the trick in no uncertain terms, reaching 40 mph in eight seconds from a standing start, 60 in second gear in 16½ seconds, and 80 in high gear in 32¾ seconds. Incidentally, these tests were made in a pouring rain. Top speed on the straightaway was 86 mph."

With the 1937 and 1938 Century, Buick ushered in the high-performance era. These cars, especially the coupes, were so popular with hot rodders that they continued to appear on tracks well into the sixties. The 1937-38 LaSalle coupes were almost as popular, due primarily to their transmissions, which were often bolted up to modified Cadillac 346 engines and later Cadillac and Olds ohv V-8s. By the way, either the Buick or LaSalle gearbox of this era will bolt right up to the early postwar GM ohv V-8s.

They were both exciting cars, although very few remain for us to appreciate today. They represent not so much the end of the Classic era created by their fine art deco styling, but the beginning of the high-performance age.

A final comparison is the production figures — 14,635 LaSalles produced for 1938 compared to 19,287 Buick Centurys. The Century was the more popular of the two, but not because of the price or features. It was the popularity of the Buick touring sedan, 12,673 produced against 9,993 LaSalle touring sedans, plus Buick offered a fastback sports sedan in the Century series, with 1,516 produced. In the rare and desirable models the LaSalle sold a bit better: 855 convertible coupes against the Buick Century's 694, and 265 convertible sedans against the Buick Century's 219. The Buick Century outproduced the LaSalle in two-door sedans, 1,393 compared to 700. But LaSalle had a sunroof four-door sedan not offered in any Buick model. Only 72 were produced. ᐁ

Acknowledgments and Bibliography

1940 LaSalle convertible sedan, SIA #18, Aug.-Oct., 1973; *1934 LaSalle coupe,* SIA #40, May-July, 1977; *1936 Buick Century convertible coupe,* SIA #46, August, 1978; *1938 Cadillac 60 Special,* SIA #62, April 1981; "The Ubiquitous Buick," *Fortune Magazine,* November 1947; *1937 Buick Century editorial advertisement, Saturday Evening Post, March 20, 1937; Standard Catalog of American Cars, 1805-1942, Krause Publications; Encyclopedia of American Cars, 1930-1980.*

Special thanks to Gary Stafford, Ventura, California, and David Collier, Glendale, California, for furnishing the cars for our comparison Report.

Above and below: Tire and tool stowage and trunk space are also identical.

Above: LaSalle parking lamps are incorporated into headlamps, but Buick's are fender-mounted.

Specifications: '38 Buick Century and '38 LaSalle

	Buick	LaSalle
Price	$1,226	$1,295
Optional equipment	Radio, Appleton fog lamps, heater/defroster	Radio, wsw, opera seats, heater/defroster
Engine	Straight 8	L-head V-8
Bore x stroke	3 7/16" x 4 5/16"	3 3/8" x 4 1/2"
Displacement	320.2 cubic inches	322 cubic inches
Compression ratio	6.35:1	6.25:1
Horsepower @ rpm	141 @ 3,600	125 as 3,400
Torque @ rpm	269 @ 2,000	N/A
Taxable horsepower	37.8	36.45
Valve lifters	Solid	Hydraulic
Main bearings	5	3
Induction system	Marvel CD-2 or Stromberg AAV-2 dual downdraft 1 1/4"	Stromberg AAV-25 or Carter WDO 392s
Lubrication system	Pressure	Pressure
Exhaust system (original equipment)	Single	Single
Electrical system	6-volt	6-volt
Clutch	Single dry plate	Single dry plate
Outside diameter	11"	10.5"
Actuation	Mechanical, foot pedal	Mechanical, foot pedal
Transmission	3-speed selective; floor lever	3-speed selective; steering column lever
Ratios: 1st	2.39:1	2.39:1
2nd	153:1	1.53:1
3rd	1.00:1	1.00:1
Reverse	2.39:1	2.39:1
Differential	Hypoid	Hypoid
Ratio	3.90:1 standard; 3.60:1 this car	3.92:1
Drive axles	Semi-floating	Semi-floating
Torque medium	Torque tube	Hotchkiss
Turns, lock-to-lock	4.5	N/A
Brakes	4-wheel hydraulic, drum type	4-wheel hydraulic, drum type
Drum diameter	12"	12"
Swept area	181.4 square inches	N/A
Construction	Body-on-frame	Body-on-frame
Frame	Rigid girder X-type	
Body construction	All steel	All steel
Body type	Coupe	Coupe
Front suspension	Independent, 14 1/4" coil springs, sway eliminator	Independent, coil springs, sway eliminator
Rear suspension	Conventional axle, 19" coil springs, stabilizer	Conventional axle, semi-elliptic leaf springs, stabilizer
Shock absorbers	Delco double-acting, extra heavy duty	Delco double-acting
Wheels	Pressed steel, drop-center rims	Pressed steel, drop-center rims
Tires	7.00/15 4-ply	7.00/16 4-ply
Wheelbase	126"	124"
Overall length	203 9/16"	202.5"
Overall width	72.25"	N/A
Front track	58 5/16"	58"
Rear track	59.25"	59
Minimum road clearance	7.25"	N/A

They were great good friends, Harlow and Harley. Harlow Curtice ran Buick; Harley Earl was that towering, domineering head of General Motors Styling.

When they met in 1933, one of the first questions Curtice asked Earl was, "What kind of car do you drive, Harley?"

Earl said, "Cadillac."

"Then, how about designing me a Buick you'd like to drive yourself?"

Earl did, and it became the 1936 Buick, which included the first 100-mph Century. Overnight, Buick changed from an old doctor's car to a young doctor's car.

In 1937, Harley Earl designed his famous Y-Job, the sleek idea roadster that Buick craftsmen built for him in Flint in 1938. The Y-Job was definitely all Buick, although it might just as reasonably have become a Cadillac or Olds or Pontiac. But it did seem that Curtice was giving Earl freer rein than the other GM divisions, so Earl took more interest in Buick. And the Y-Job influenced Buick styling for many years afterward.

Harlow Curtice turned out to be one of GM's best businessmen—thoughtful, thorough, aggressive but easy to get along with, quality conscious, attuned to his dealers as well as to Buick buyers. He had pulled Buick up from a withering 43,247 sales in 1933 (the year he arrived) to 377,428 in 1941—and the wall chart had gone up in a straight line, not dipping even once. Curtice's good way of doing business and his correct decisions eventually led him to the General Motors presidency in 1953.

The case can be made that Curtice was trying during those prewar years to outdo Cadillac. He might have viewed it as a game but, if so, he surely knew that GM's bosses would never let Buick actually bump Cadillac. La Salle, yes, but Cadillac, no. Yet the evidence shows that Curtice was out to top Cadillac in every possible way: sales (which was easy), quality, styling, power, performance, and prestige (not so easy).

In 1936, Curtice handed Charles Chayne the division's top engineering spot, along with ample money, staff, and encouragement to upgrade Buick's mechanical side. Chayne had been with Lycoming and Marmon before arriving at Buick in 1930. His first major coup as Buick's chief engineer was the 1938 model: coil springs at all four corners, tube shocks, plus some rather dramatic changes in the upper half of the ohv Straight 8 (the lower half didn't need improvement).

For 1938, Chayne put squish into the big Buick 8. Squish meant a raised piston crown, domed combustion chamber, relocated valves and

1941 Buick Phaeton

spark plugs, and higher compression. The fuel/air mixture rushed into the cylinder at 250 mph, swirled around in a tight ball, then fired, burning more evenly than in a conventional flat combustion chamber. Buick's long-time adman Art Kudner dubbed this 1938 engine the Dynaflash 8 with a Turbulator piston.

For 1941, Compound Carburetion made the scene—two 2-barrel carburetors on a log manifold. The front carb operated full time; the rear one came in on hard acceleration. So, in normal driving, you theoretically got the economy of one carburetor and, when you needed full power, you got the added strength of one more. Kudner renamed this engine the Fireball 8.

But the 1941 Buick engine brought with it some grating embarrassments. It seems that, in pulling more horsepower from the big 8, Engineering got a little carried away. They raised the compression ratio from 6.6:1 to 7.0:1, which proved too high for that day's fuels, even with the revised Turbulator piston (now scooped on top). At the same time, Buick went to smaller, 10mm sparkplugs. Owners were soon complaining so much about ring and plug fouling that the factory supplied dealers with thicker head gaskets to lower compression and tools to machine out the plug holes to 14mm.

driveReport

Then, too, the twin carbs were hard to keep in tune, and they drank more gas than expected. Many owners switched back to the old single setup, especially during the war when gas was rationed. And if all that weren't enough, the 1941 engine's cylinder bores had been honed too smooth at the factory, and the rings wouldn't seat. Many dealers used to pour Bon Ami down the sparkplug holes as a quick fix. Others—more conservative—rebored the block.

All 1941 Buicks except the little Special came standard with Compound Carburetion. In the Century, Roadmaster, and Limited, this gave Buick the industry's highest horsepower that year: 165 at 3,800 rpm. It put Buick 15 horses above the Cad V-8, thus handed Curtice his power advantage. The lightweight 1941 Century, with its 3.6 or 3.9:1 rear axle, could walk away from any new Detroit product on the road. Tests at a major automaker's proving grounds showed that the Buick Roadmaster had 1941's highest top speed—101.9 mph. The Century was next-fastest at 101.1 mph. Then came the 1941 Buick Super at 97.9 mph, the Cadillac 62 at 95.2, and the Packard Super 8 at 95.0 mph. Through the gears from 5-60 mph, the following cars showed the best acceleration times for 1941: Buick Century, 11.46 sec.; Roadmaster, 11.84; Cadillac Series 63, 12.85; Cad 61, 12.95; and the Packard Super 8 (160 with overdrive), 13.05 sec. So Curtice certainly also had his performance advantage.

As for quality, 1941 Buicks were put together with great care and the best materials available. The difference in quality and workmanship between 1941 Buicks and 1941 Cadillacs was imperceptible. Roadmasters and Limiteds, of course, shared the big C and B bodies with Cadillac.

In the area of styling, Buick had its basic lines handed down to Chevrolet (as Cadillac had had to do in 1939 and continues to do even today). Of course, Buick also shared lines with other GM divisions—it had the "GM Look," and Warren Fitzgerald feels this helped, rather than hindered, Buick. "A Buick owner knew he had a Buick," says Fitz.

Curtice tried to boost Buick's prestige by offering a line of true coach-built models on the 1941 Limited chassis. These customs, built by Brunn, were to include towncars, landaus, broughams, and phaetons. The idea was to have dealers take orders, then make up specific cars for individual customers. But the buyers didn't materialize, so Brunn built very few custom Buicks, and Curtice finally put an end to the project after he got his wrists slapped for getting too uppity.

In 1941, Buick ranked fourth in total U. S. new-car sales, right behind Chevy, Ford, and Plymouth. Part of the reason was an excellent product; partly, too, an efficient and enthusiastic dealer organization. According to a FORTUNE analyst, writing in 1947, "Buick has considerably fewer dealers than any comparable manufacturer.... Even at its production peak in 1941, Buick held the number of its franchises down

Ornamental trunk medallion is mistaken by many for directional signal lamps. Actually, Buick's blinkers comprise lower half of taillights.

Only 312 Roadmaster phaetons were built in 1941 (plus 467 Super phaetons). Red leather interior looks smashing against black body.

LaMoine's parents converted dual carbs to single during WW-II. Big 8 gives 165 bhp—1941's highest. The dealers had to fix factory goofs.

to slightly under 3,000. Compare this with, for example, Ford Motor Co., which has something over 6,400 dealers. Accordingly, although Ford sold almost twice as many cars as Buick in 1941, a GM study shows that the average Buick dealer sold 126 new cars that year to the average Ford dealer's 83, and this, of course, despite considerable difference in price, and therefore dollar sales commission, between Buick and Ford. The average sales of a Buick dealer are, in fact, greater than the average for any other make of car. Chevrolet is nearest to it in that respect."

Buick for 1941 offered a number of interesting options. For example, the Super-Sonomatic radio had four international shortwave bands in addition to the standard band. The radio antenna on closed body styles was over the windshield crown, with a knob inside to raise and lower it. On open bodies, a fender-mounted antenna went up and down by vacuum.

There were a number of optional heaters to choose from, including underseat models and thermostatic controls to regulate hot water flow through the core. Other factory accessories of note: a stainless steel foot rest molding for the rear floor of sedans, a vacuum-pump windshield washer, EZI no-glare mirrors, and a No-Rol hillholder. This last, available since 1939, consisted of a hydraulic cylinder near the brake master cylinder. It had a check ball inside that, when the car was tilted (parked up a hill), covered an orifice and thus held on the brakes. By letting out the clutch though, the check ball moved away from the orifice and released the brakes.

Standard equipment included turn signals, map and glovebox lights, trunk illumination, and cigar lighter.

Keith LaMoine's parents bought this 1941 Roadmaster phaeton new in March of that year, and it hasn't been out of the family since. During the war, Keith's parents had the twin carbs taken off and a single put on, and that's how it still was when we drove it. The car has a little over 133,000 very careful miles on it, burns one quart of oil every 1,500 miles, has had one valve job (only major mechanical repair of its life), and is as tight and squeak-free today as it was 30 years ago. Now if that isn't saying something for Buick quality....

Keith, a cattle rancher with a 7,700-acre spread near Delano, California, took possession of the car in 1967, when his parents decided to sell it. Keith couldn't let them do that—it held too many memories. He'd used it on dates throughout high school, drove it to his senior prom, and had long considered it *his* car even when it wasn't.

The Buick needed very little to bring back to showroom freshness: new red leather on the seats (the door panels were fine), a new top, bumpers rechromed, and a new black paint job. Everything else was, and is, original. Even the dial faces and dashboard machine turning look mint.

We drove Keith's Roadmaster phaeton up into the foothills northeast of Stockton. It turned out to be a pleasure trip in every way—spring was just arriving; the Sierra, in the background, still had snow on them; the foothills were green, and the car performed flawlessly.

Starting comes by Buick's traditional accelerator press. The clutch engages smoothly, and the engine has enough low-rpm torque so you don't have to rev it or slip the clutch—just ease it out and take off. There's a bit of gear whine in low, but otherwise it's a very quiet car. We drove about 15 miles on the freeway, and at 65-70 mph there's no top flap or drumming. One complaint is poor rear visibility with the top

1941 Buick Spex at a Glance

Series	Whb.	Disp.	Bhp @ rpm.	Price range
Special, 40-A	118	248.0	115 @ 3,500*	$915-1,183
Special, 40-B	121	248.0	115 @ 3,500*	$935-1,463
Super, 50	121	248.0	125 @ 3,800	$1,031-1,555
Century, 60	126	320.2	165 @ 3,800	$1,195-1,288
Roadmaster, 70	126	320.2	165 @ 3,800	$1,282-1,775
Limited, 90	139	320.2	165 @ 3,800	$2,155-2,465

* Optional Compound Carburetion gives 125 bhp @ 3,800 rpm. In all other series, twin carbs are standard.

1941 Buick Body Styles

	4-dr sedan	2-dr sedanet	club cpe.	bus. cpe.	conv. cpe.	4-dr conv.	stn. wag.	4-34. limo
Special, 40-A	X		X	X	X			
Special, 40-B	X	X					X	
Super, 50	X		X	X	X	X		
Century, 60	X	X		X				
Roadmaster, 70	X		X			X		
Limited, 90*	X							X

* Limited series includes 4-dr., 7-pass. sedan and formal sedan, plus custom body styles by Brunn.

Keith stops at an old filling station in Lockeford, California, during our driveReport. These pumps have been in service continually since 1924.

Owner's manual is one of the most thorough we've seen, covers everything from repairs to theory. It stows in special kick-panel pocket.

PHOTO: GM STYLING

Lamps in front seatback light when right rear door is open—discourages stepping into traffic.

Earl (left) and Curtice worked closely, were good friends, set the course for Buick, later for GM.

Two-level trunk loses space to spare and lowered top. License lamp lights trunk with parkers on.

Manual top folds easily and flat. Car has been in LaMoine family since new, is mostly original.

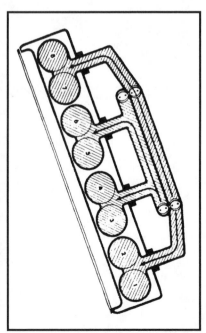

Front 2 barrels of Compound Carburetion work all the time; rear 2 cut in on hard acceleration.

Keith sets central roof pillar. Fit is so good that window glass matches channels perfectly.

21

Moderate cornering shows moderate lean, good stability. Roadmasters were the fastest U.S. cars made in 1941, according to proving grounds tests.

Hood hinges from either side, and with both releases unlatched, the hood is easily removed.

Steering rim stands on spring steel spokes radiating from attractive Lucite center medallion.

The 1941 Century and Roadmaster also topped all other U.S. cars that year in acceleration.

up, same as with the 1940 Cadillac convertible sedan we tested two issues ago. These two cars, of course, share basically identical bodies.

Cornering feels predictable and solid, with no tendency to plow or slide at slightly above normal speeds. There is some lean, and steering is slow by today's standards, but that's expected.

Acceleration impressed us as amazingly brisk for so heavy a car. And it cruises effortlessly at freeway speeds, getting about 13 mpg at a steady 70 mph. The ride is smooth, but with some minor jiggling on concrete. On unpaved roads, the coil springs lap up bumps with ease, and there's no problem at all with wander or sudden shifts of direction due to tar strips or potholes.

The Roadmaster has great seats—firm, yet supremely comfortable and fairly straight-backed. There's a fold-down armrest for rear passengers, plus a robe cord, and an amount of leg room that you simply don't find in today's cars.

We put about 150 miles on the car that day, stopping often to snap pictures. We'd had hamburgers at noon at a small restaurant in Clements, filled up the tank at a 1924 gas station in Lockeford about three that afternoon, then slowly wended our way back to Stockton through fruit orchards in full bloom. In the good company of Keith LaMoine and a 1941 Buick, what better way to spend a gorgeous spring day? ☜

Grateful thanks to Keith LaMoine, Delano, California; Dave Gosler, Buick Motor Div., Flint, Michigan; Warren Fitzgerald, GM Styling, Warren, Michigan; Charles Chayne, Pebble Beach, California; Earl D. Beauchamp, Jr.. CHVA, 71 Lucky Rd., Severn, Maryland; W. W. Ningard, Baltimore. Maryland; and to the Buick Club of America, Box 853, Garden Grove, California.

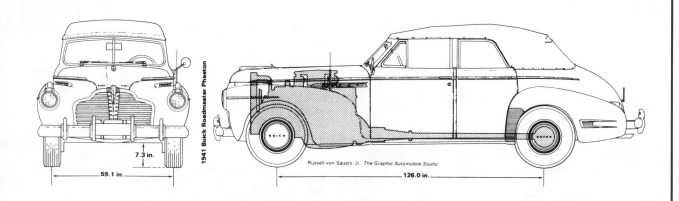

1941 Buick Roadmaster Phaeton

7.3 in.

59.1 in.

Russell von Sauers Jr The Graphic Automobile Studio

126.0 in.

SPECIFICATIONS
1941 BUICK ROADMASTER MODEL 71-C CONV. PHAETON

Price when new............$1,775 f.o.b., Flint, MI (1941).

Current valuation*........Xlnt., $4,455; gd., $2,625.

Options ....Radio, heater, whitewall tires.

ENGINE
Type ....Ohv. in-line 8, water-cooled, cast-iron
..................................block, 5 mains, full pressure lubrication.
Bore & stroke ....3.4375 x 4.3125 in.
Displacement...........320.2 cid.
Max. bhp @ rpm ......165 @ 3,800.
Max. torque @ rpm ..278 @ 2,200.
Compression ratio....7.0:1.
Induction system......2 downdraft 2-bbl carbs, mechanical fuel
..................................pump.
Exhaust system........Cast-iron manifold, single muffler.
Electrical system......6-volt battery/coil.

CLUTCH
Type ....Single dry plate, woven asbestos lining.
Diameter ....10.5 in.
Actuation.................Mechanical, foot pedal.

TRANSMISSION
Type ....3-speed manual, column lever, synchro-
..................................mesh second and high.
Ratios: 1st ....2.39:1.
       2nd...............1.53:1.
       3rd................1.00:1.
       Reverse.................2.53:1.

DIFFERENTIAL
Type ....Hypoid, spiral-bevel gears.
Ratio........................3.90:1.
Drive axles ....Semi-floating.

STEERING
Type ....Worm and ball nut
Turns, lock to lock....4.5
Ratio........................19.8:1
Turn circle ....43.5 ft.

BRAKES
Type ....4-wheel drums, hydraulic, internal
..................................expanding.
Drum diameter ....12 in.
Total swept area.......206.4 sq. in.

CHASSIS & BODY
Frame......................Channel-section steel, double dropped,
..................................central X-member.
Body construction....Steel.
Body style ....4-door, 5-pass. convertible phaeton,
..................................manual top.

SUSPENSION
Front ....Independent wishbones, coil springs,
..................................hydraulic lever shocks, anti-roll bar.
Rear ....Solid axle, coil springs, lever
..................................hydraulic shocks, radius rod and anti-
..................................sway bar.
Tires ....7.00 x 15, 4-ply, tube type.
Wheels ....Pressed steel, drop-center rims,
..................................lug-bolted.

WEIGHTS & MEASURES
Wheelbase ....126.0 in.
Overall length...........215.125 in.
Overall height...........59.75 in.
Overall width ....76.5 in.
Front track...............59.125 in.
Rear track ....62.125 in.
Ground clearance....7.3125 in.
Curb weight ....4,245 lb.

CAPACITIES
Crankcase...............8.0 qt.
Cooling system ....16.75 qt.
Fuel tank ....18.0 gal.

FUEL CONSUMPTION
Best..........................19.5 mpg.
Average...................13.8 mpg.

PERFORMANCE (from a manufacturer's 1941 tests):
5-60 mph..................11.84 sec.
Top speed ....101.9 mph.

*Courtesy **Antique Automobile Appraisal.**

Upper Middle Class "Class"

1948 Buick Roadmaster/ 1948 Chrysler New Yorker

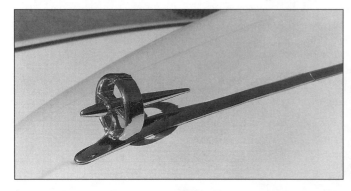

Originally published in Special Interest Autos #167, Sept.-Oct. 1998

by Arch Brown
photos and driving impressions by Bud Juneau

Above: *Buick grille exhibits traditional toothy grin, while Chrysler is composed of intricate series of rectangles. Both have plating of the highest quality.* **Below:** *Wheel cover treatments are similar.* **Bottom:** *Buick's coat of arms looks quite baronial. Chrysler's rosette has been revived on their new cars.*

THE postwar "seller's market" was commencing to fade a little by 1948, as America's automakers worked to catch up with the pent-up demand that had resulted from the nearly four years during which no new cars were built. Most dealers still had waiting lists, often with cash deposits in hand; but the wait wasn't as long as it had been during 1946-47, nor was it always necessary to accept as part of the deal a load of expensive accessories for which the buyer might or might not have any use.

Dealers were often criticized for "loading up" their new cars in this fashion; and resentment was not infrequently expressed when a customer was moved ahead, taking delivery of his (or her) new automobile ahead of someone whose name had been longer on the waiting list.

To be sure, unfair practices were not infrequent. But consider the situation from the dealers' perspective: Not only had they received virtually no cars during the four-year stretch from 1942 through 1945; even during the postwar years, production of passenger cars was far short of the prewar numbers. Consider Buick's record, for example:

Year	Production*
1940	310,995
1941	316,251
1942	16,601
1943	0
1944	0
1945	2,482
1946	156,080
1947	267,830
1948	275,504

(*Calendar year figures)

It wasn't until 1949 that Buick's production reached (and in fact exceeded) its prewar peak. The same was true throughout most of the industry; although two of the independents, Nash and Hudson, were able to exceed their pre-war output as early as 1946. So almost without exception, the dealers had endured several very lean years. And as for moving certain customers ahead on the waiting list, who could blame the dealer for rewarding a loyal customer of long standing, at the expense of a stranger?

Most American automakers were still serving up warmed-over prewar cars during the 1948 model year, there being little point in tooling up for new models while demand remained strong. This was certainly true of both Buick and Chrysler, represented here by their respective top-of-the-line 1948 convertible coupes.

In a number of respects these two cars are quite similar. Both are straight-eights, a configuration that the industry would abandon only a few years after these fine examples were built. Size, weight and engine displacement are also comparable, although the Buick has a distinct advantage in horsepower; and both engines are of long-stroke design. But there the similarity ends. The Chrysler is powered by an L-head engine, while the Buick uses its time-tested valve-in-head configuration. And while both cars are equipped with automatic transmissions (well, semi-automatic in the case of the Chrysler), the reader will note from Bud Juneau's driving impressions that the two units are totally dissimilar in both design and function.

The manufacturers had taken full advantage of the postwar seller's market, in which they could readily sell whatever they chose to build. With certain critical materials such as sheet steel in short supply, most automakers tended to adjust their production schedules so as to favor the more expensive (and thus more profitable) models. For example, during 1941 Chrysler's price-

leading Royal series accounted for 49.3 percent of the division's total output, but during the postwar period 1946-48, only 9.5 percent of new Chryslers were Royals. Meanwhile, production of the Windsor, Chrysler's upscale six-cylinder line, rose from 35.2 to 64.5 percent, while output of the company's various eight-cylinder series was increased from 15.5 to 24.8 percent of the total.

The situation at Buick was, if anything, even more dramatic. During the 1941 model run, the division built 240,742 of its moderately priced Specials, amounting to 64.3 percent of the season's total. But when production got under way again in 1946, exactly 3,000 Specials were produced, which translates to just under two percent of all new Buicks. Meanwhile the big, luxurious Roadmaster's share of the pie rose from 4.2 percent in 1941 to 20.7 percent in '46, while that of the Super series increased from 25.1 to 77.3 percent. As late as 1948, in fact, less than 12 percent of Buick's production was devoted to the once (and future) best-selling Special series.

There wasn't a lot of visible difference between the postwar Buick Road-

Above: *Both cars demonstrate the kind of handling that sacrificed roadability for ride. It's little wonder MG-TCs used to outrun them on twisty roads.*

masters and Chrysler New Yorkers and their 1942 counterparts. Both marques had been provided with the obligatory new grille, though that of the first post-war Buick hadn't changed much. Buick's Roadmaster and Super series, of course, had been totally redesigned for 1942, with sleek, swoopy lines and "air-foil" front fenders that swept across the doors and all the way to the leading edge of the rear fenders. This feature had been introduced on 1942's two-door types, but for 1946-48 it was extended to the sedans and estate wagons as well. Styling changes during the three immediate postwar years were minimal, though most people would agree that the 1947-48 grille was better looking than the 1946 design.

Chrysler, on the other hand, continued to make use of its 1941 body shell, though the front fenders were reworked for 1946 to blend subtly into the doors. A new grille was much bolder, and at the same time more attractive, than the somewhat dowdy 1942 version. But the cars were nearly three inches taller than the Buicks, in accordance with president K. T. Keller's declaration that he wanted to be able to wear his hat while driving or while riding in the back seat; and the overall effect was very conservative. And having settled upon this design, Chrysler made no styling changes whatever for 1947 or '48. In fact, these automobiles were carried over unchanged into early 1949 as that year's "first series" cars.

Mechanically, both the postwar New Yorkers and Roadmasters were changed significantly. At Chrysler, advertised horsepower was 135, down from 140 in the 1941-42 models. (This is not easy to explain, by the way, since the Stromberg AA-2 carburetor was unchanged and the compression ratio was actually increased, from 6.80:1 to 7.25:1.) But the most important difference was the adoption of the hydraulically operated M-5 semi-automatic transmission, replacing the trouble-prone, vacuum-powered "Vacamatic" of prewar days.

At Buick, the high-stepping but troublesome "compound carburetion" of 1941-42 was eliminated. Consisting of two carburetors with progressive linkage, this arrangement could be thought of as the precursor of the later four-barrel and multiple-pot setups. It helped provide the prewar Roadmaster engine with 165 horsepower, equal to that of the senior 1942 Packards and 15 bhp more than the contemporary Cadillacs. But on the downside, it was not easy to keep in proper tune; and owners complained that cars equipped with this feature required an inordinate amount of fuel. So for the postwar Roadmasters a two-barrel Stromberg AAV-267 carburetor was substituted, reducing the horsepower to 144.

When the 1948 model year opened, Chrysler had nothing new to offer. Nor did they need to make any changes, given the condition of the market. At Buick, however, when the 1948 Roadmasters were announced, prominent on the option list was Buick's first fully automatic transmission, the Dynaflow. Buick

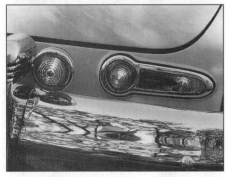

Above: Buick's hood accent also serves as release for left or right opening bonnet. Below: Chrysler model i.d. rides on the aft section of its hood. Bottom: Backup lights were factory adds-ons for Buick.

Specifications: 1948 Buick Roadmaster vs. Chrysler New Yorker

	Buick	Chrysler
Base price, conv. coupe	$2,837	$2,840
Standard equipment	Power top, seat, windows; clock, leather interior	Semi-automatic transmission with Fluid Drive; power top
Options on c/R car	Dynaflow, radio, twin heaters, wsw tires, backup lights	Highlander interior, radio, heater, windshield washers, wsw tires, fog lamps
Engine	Ohv straight 8	L-head straight 8
Bore x stroke	3.4375 inches x 3.3125 inches	3.25 inches x 4.875 inches
Displacement (cu. in.)	320.2	323.5
Compression ratio	6.90:1	6.70:1
Horsepower @ rpm	150 @ 3,600	135 @ 3,400
Torque @ rpm	276 @ 2,000	2708 @ 1,600
Taxable horsepower	37.8	33.8
Valve lifters	Mechanical	Mechanical
Main bearings	5	5
Carburetor	1.25 dual downdraft	1.25 dual downdraft
Lubrication system	Pressure	Pressure
Cooling system	Centrifugal pump	Centrifugal pump
Exhaust system	Single	Single
Electrical system	6-volt	6-volt
Clutch	n/a	Single dry disc
Diameter	---------	10 inches
Transmission	Dynaflow, torque converter automatic	M-5 4-sp semi-auto with fluid coupling
Ratios	1.82/1.00 (Rev. 1.82); max ratio at stall: 2.25	3.57/2.04/1.75/1.00 (Reverse 3.57)
Rear axle	Hypoid	Hypoid
Ratio	4.10:1	3.36:1
Drive axles	Semi-floating	Semi-floating
Torque medium	Torque tube	Rear springs
Steering	Ball bearing worm and nut	Worm and roller
Ratio	19.8	20.4
Turns of wheel, lock/lock	4.5	4.75
Turning diameter	42.5 feet	42.17 feet
Brakes	Hydraulic, drum	Hydraulic drum
Drum diameter	12 inches	12 inches
Effective area	207.5 square inches	189.2 square inches
Construction	Body-on-frame	Body-on-frame
Frame	Girder X-type	Ladder type
Body construction	All steel	All steel
Body type	Convertible coupe	Convertible coupe
Front suspension	Independent, coil springs	Independent, coil springs
Rear suspension	Rigid axle, coil springs	Rigid axle, semi-elliptical springs
Shock absorbers	2-way lever type	Double-acting hydraulic
Wheels	Steel disc	Steel disc
Tires	8.20/15 4-ply	8.20/15 4-ply
Wheelbase	129 inches	127.5 inches
Overall length	217.125 inches	216.75 inches
Overall width	78.625 inches	77.75 inches
Overall height (no load)	65.1406 inches	68 inches
Front track	59.125 inches	57.8125 inches
Rear track	62.1875 inches	61.5625 inches
Min. road clearance	7.7188 inches	8.75 inches
Shipping weight	4,315 pounds	4,332 pounds
Crankcase capacity	7 quarts	6 quarts
Cooling system	16.75 quarts	26 quarts
Fuel tank	19 gallons	20 gallons
Transmission	11 quarts	3 pints
Rear axle	3 pints	3.5 pints
Crankshaft revs per mile	2,952	2,749
Stroke/bore ratio	1.25:1	1.50:1
Horsepower per c.i.d.	.450	.412
Weight per hp	30 pounds	32.1 pounds
Weight per c.i.d.	13.5	13.4
Weight per sq. in. (brakes)	20.8	22.9

had eschewed GM's HydraMatic transmission, first introduced on the 1940 Oldsmobiles, because it wasn't entirely compatible with torque tube drive, a long-time Buick tradition. Experiments had shown that a jarring sensation was produced with every gear change. In contrast, Oldsmobile's (and Cadillac's) Hotchkiss drive had universal joints at either end of the driveshaft; and these tended to absorb much of the shock.

During the war, Buick had been building "Hellcat" tank destroyers; and these units were equipped with torque converter type automatic transmissions. Their smooth flow of power, with no shifting of gears, appeared to be ideal for use with Buick's torque tube drive; and of course this led to the development of the Dynaflow.

Some people complained, by the bye, that the Dynaflow permitted too much slippage; and indeed, Buick saw fit, first, to increase the compression ratio from 6.6:1 to 6.9:1, thus raising the horsepower of the Dynaflow-equipped

'48 Roadmasters from 144 to 150; and second, to equip those cars with hydraulic valve lifters, the better to stifle the clatter. But whatever the disadvantages may have been, the public loved the Dynaflow. Its availability was extended to the Super series in 1949 and to the Special a year later, by which time it would be fitted to about three-fourths of all new Buicks.

Our featured Buick Roadmaster is making its second appearance on the pages of this magazine, having shared honors with a Packard Super Eight in a comparison/Report published in *SIA* #116. Larry Klein bought this beauty in 1984 as a totally original, unrestored, 84,000-mile, one-owner, local car. It was in good shape mechanically, but there were dings and dents in the body, the paint was faded and worn, the upholstery was torn and there were holes in the top. In short, it needed a complete cosmetic restoration. With the exception of the leather upholstery, which was replaced by professionals, Larry did all the restoration work himself, including all body, paint, trim, glass, electrical components, rubber and so forth.

Klein never intended this car to be a concours winner; it's a "driver," and since the restoration it has covered several thousand miles on tours. Nevertheless, it has been shown from time to time and has taken a number of first- and second-place trophies. There are several fine automobiles in Larry's collection, but the Buick, he confesses, is a special favorite.

Our Chrysler New Yorker was purchased originally by a Seattle physician. We were amazed to learn that the doctor drove it for 41 years, though he evidently used it sparingly. It had logged only 82,000 miles when it was purchased, in 1989, by a relative of the current owner, Phil Jones, of Kentfield, California. It was still in reasonably good running order at that time, but Phil, who acquired it in 1990, spent four years on

Above: How many pounds of chromium plating are represented here? Buick nose is slightly lower than rival's. *Below:* It's two pedal motoring for postwar Buick owners whose cars have Dynaflow. Chrysler retained clutch for Fluid Drive shifting.

a complete restoration of the black beauty, farming out various parts of the job to specialists. The engine, for instance, was rebuilt by the Craft Machine Shop, of Santa Rosa; transmission/ fluid coupling/clutch by Healdsburg Transmission, of that city; paint by Farmer Brothers, of Ukiah, who took it all the way to the metal for a flawless

job. Along the way, the electrical system was re-wired; the brakes were completely rebuilt; the radiator was rodded out; the carpeting and the Highlander upholstery were replaced. One job remains, before Phil will consider the job complete: The front end needs work, as evidenced by a moderate amount of excess play in the wheel.

Like our comparisonReport Buick, this car is treated as a "driver," though the mileage is limited. Since the restoration, Phil has put nearly 4,000 miles on the Chrysler's clock. Even so, it has scored well on the concours circuit, having taken First Place trophies at the Santa Rosa and Stanford shows, and a Second (against fierce competition) at Silverado.

This car was Phil Jones's first restoration project. Evidently the job simply whetted his appetite, for he is now up to his elbows in the restoration of a 1947 Chrysler Town and Country sedan.

In a sense, these two fine automobiles could be said to have been "dated" from the time they were built; for within a year both marques would be totally restyled, and not long afterward their long-stroke straight-eights would be

1948 Buick Prices, Weights and Production

	Price	Weight	Production
Special, Series 40			
(121-inch w/b, 248.1 c.i.d., 110 hp)			
Sedan, 4-door	$1,809	3,705	14,051
Sedanet, 2-door	$1,735	3,635	11,176
Super, Series 50			
(124-inch w/b, 248.1 c.i.d., 115 hp)			
Sedan, 4-door	$2,087	3,855	53,447
Sedanet, 2-door	$1,987	3,770	33,819
Convertible coupe	$2,518	4,020	19,217
Estate wagon	$3,124	4,170	2,018
Roadmaster, Series 70			
(129-inch w/b, 320.2 c.i.d., 144 hp)			
Sedan, 4-door	$2,418	4,160	47,569
Sedanet, 2-door	$2,297	4,065	20,649
Convertible coupe	$2,837	4,315	11,503
Estate wagon	$3,433	4,460	350
Note: Production figures include cars built for export.			

Buick's trunk emblem looks like a light but it's not. Chrysler anticipated the third stoplight on new cars by a couple of decades.

replaced by modern, short-stroke V-8's. No matter; these are great cars, characterized by fine performance and exceptional comfort as well as good looks.

1948 Buick Roadmaster Convertible

As I settled into the driver's seat of the Buick, I was immediately struck by how far I was from the dashboard. The steering wheel is on a long, rather horizontal column that puts the wheel in your lap. You sit low, surrounded by the doors and dash, and the first point of interest is the gun sight hood ornament. This famous ornament, a direct influence of World War II themes, was often broken off of earlier models to be given as a bracelet to a girlfriend, but by 1948 had beefed-up mountings and added cross bars to avoid this bothersome pastime. The look over the long hood is impressive and fun, with the gun sight ornament leading the way. All of the plastic detail, steering wheel, shift knob, vent pulls, and so forth are black plastic for the first time, after many years of traditional ivory on Buicks.

There is no clutch pedal, this being the first year for Buick's new Dynaflow transmission, only available on Roadmasters, and the quadrant reads "Park, N, D, L, and R," in that order. This was the first transmission to use Park, a Buick invention. The step-on parking brake was another Buick first that was also adopted industry-wide. The ignition switch reads "Lock, On, and Off." If you remove the key in Lock position, then it cannot be turned on without the key, but if you remove the key in the On or Off position, then the car can be operated in those two positions without further use of the key. This would be handy in a parking garage where you did not

want to leave your keys. The starter is operated by pushing the accelerator pedal to the floor, and the big overhead valve straight eight roars to life and then settles down to a whisper quiet idle.

For normal driving, select the "D" position, release the brake by pulling a release button, and simply give it the gas. From zero to top speed with no perceivable shifts. It was a favorite with women drivers who marveled at its smoothness and predictability. For additional power, you could start out in Low range; this was not recommended for normal daily driving, but rather for rocking out of snow or sand. Incidentally, the Dynaflow was the first automatic that could be moved easily from forward

1946-48 Chrysler Prices, Weights and Production

	Price	Weight	Production
Royal Series			
(121.5-inch w/b, 250.6 c.i.d., 114 hp)			
Coupe, 3-passenger	$1,839	3,395	1,221
Club coupe, 6-passenger	$1,954	3,473	4,318
Sedan, 2-door, 6-passenger	$1,928	3,498	1,117
Sedan, 4-door, 6-passenger	$1,975	3,533	24,279
Chassis	n/a	n/a	1
Royal Series			
(139.5-inch w/b, 250.6 c.i.d., 114 hp)			
Sedan, 4-door, 8 passenger	$2,400	3,925	626
Limousine, 4-door, 8 passenger	$2,526	4,022	169
Total production, Royal Series:			31,731
Windsor Series			
(121.5-inch w/b, 250.6 c.i.d., 114 hp)			
Coupe, 3-passenger	$1,906	3,393	1,980
Club coupe, 6-passenger	$2,020	3,463	26,482
Convertible coupe	$2,434	3,693	11,200
Sedan, 2-door, 6-passenger	$2,009	3,508	4,034
Sedan, 4-door, 6-passenger	$2,041	3,528	161,139
Traveler, 4-door, 6-passenger	$2,183	3,610	4,182
Town & Country sedan	$2,880	3,957	3,994
Chassis	n/a	n/a	1
Windsor Series			
(139.5-inch w/b, 250.6 c.i.d., 114 hp)			
Sedan, 4-door, 8 passenger	$2,454	3,935	4,390
Limousine, 4-door, 8-passenger 2,581	$4,035	1,496	
Total production, Windsor Series:			218,898
Saratoga Series			
(127.5-inch w/b, 323.5 c.i.d., 135 hp)			
Coupe, 3-passenger	$2,190	3,817	74
Club coupe, 6-passenger	$2,290	3,930	765
Sedan, 2-door, 6-passenger	$2,279	3,900	155
Sedan, 4-door, 6-passenger	$2,316	3,972	4,611
Total production, Saratoga Series:			5,605
New Yorker Series			
(127.5-inch w/b, 323.5 c.i.d., 135 hp)			
Coupe, 3-passenger	$2,310	3,837	699
Club coupe, 6-passenger	$2,410	4,037	10,735
Convertible coupe	$2,840	4,132	3,000
Sedan, 2-door, 6-passenger	$2,399	3,932	545
Sedan, 4-door, 6-passenger	$2,436	3,987	52,036
Town & Country convertible	$3,420	4,332	9,368
Chassis	n/a	n/a	2
Town & Country hardtop	n/a	n/a	7
Town & Country sedan	n/a	n/a	100
Total production, New Yorker Series:			76,492
Crown Imperial Series			
(145.5-inch w/b, 323.5 c.i.d., 135 hp)			
Sedan, 4-door, 8-passenger	$4,712	4,865	650
Limousine, 4-door, 8-passenger	$4,817	4,875	750
Total production, Crown Imperial Series:			1,400
Total 1948 calendar year production:			119,137

NOTES: 1. Year-by-year breakdown of model year production figures is not available for this period. These production figures cover three years, 1946-47-48 and "first-series" 1949 cars.
2. 1948 prices are shown.

Buick's trunk lid is held up by elementary locking brace. Chrysler uses counterbalanced lid to keep trunk open.

to reverse while the car was still in motion, without a great, and possibly expensive clash of gears. I was pleasantly surprised at how quickly this large, heavy convertible accelerated, and by today's standards, in traffic, it was quite peppy and acceptable. The brakes are excellent, bringing the car down to a stop with very light pedal pressure and in a straight line.

The turn signal lever is to the right, near the shift lever, and this takes some getting used to, but is self canceling after your turn. Speaking of turning, there is some roll on a sharp turn, but this is to be expected on a coil spring suspension. This car was not designed nor intended for road racing, but rather for the softest possible boulevard ride, and in this, Buick succeeded. The top is raised and lowered by a hydraulic system with a pump under the hood, and this same system operates the power seat and front door windows, through power cylinders. All of this operates well, but owner Larry Klein reminded me that they are prone to leaking, and are one of the bigger headaches of cars so equipped. Once out on the open road, the ride is extremely smooth and pleasant, and not a sound or rattle comes from the body. The Roadmaster convertible was the "dream boat" of the Buick line; you look great being seen in it, and you feel great driving it. It was with regret that we ended our test drive, and handed the keys back to the owner.

1948 Chrysler New Yorker Convertible

The Chrysler has "chair-height seats" and you sit up nice and tall, with great lumbar support. The look over the very long hood is most impressive, and the smooth, winged ornament adds nicely to the effect. Since you are sitting up high,

Above and left: There's lots of flash on either dash. *Below:* Buick buried secondary gauges below driver's line of sight. Chrysler cluster is easier to scan. *Bottom:* Chrysler used flip-flop window cranks for a number of years. Claim was that they added safety as well as style to the interior

and close to the dash, you see more of the front fenders and have a good view of the pavement in front of the car.

These cars made use of the new miracle of plastic, with rich beautiful colors, and this maroon dash is in perfect original condition. The clutch pedal has "Safety Clutch" embossed on it and is quite small next to the normal-size brake pedal. This is for operation of the Fluid Drive, semi-automatic transmission. The shift lever looks normal for a stick shift car, but in fact, has no position where you normally would find low gear. To select low, you put the lever up and forward where you normally would find second gear. Reverse is in the normal up and back position. The clutch is used when selecting another shift position of the lever, but does not need to be used in normal driving. In the up-forward position, the car starts out in low, and if you let up on the accelerator, it will shift once to the next gear. You can return to a stop with use of the brake and do not

Above: *Both straight eights, but Buick uses traditional ohv layout and Chrysler sticks to its venerable flathead style.* **Below:** *Buick interior has high quality leather in a conservative pattern. Chrysler uses colorful plaid inserts with leather surrounds.*

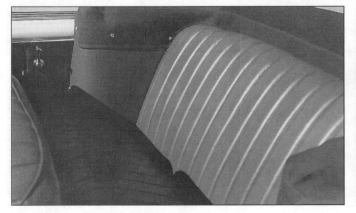

need to use the clutch. The fluid coupling allows you to merely give it the gas when you are ready to go and then let up when you are ready for it to shift. Put the lever in the down position, where you would find high gear in other cars, and it will take off in an intermediate gear and then shift to high gear when you are ready by letting off on the accelerator. It will also kick down to the previous gear for passing, if you floor the accelerator. In normal driving, brake and accelerator are all that are needed in the high range, and this takes much of the work out of driving. But in the high range, your acceleration can only be described as moderate, by any standards, and flooring the pedal doesn't change much, in off-the-line performance.

The ignition is turned on with a normal key lock with the right hand, and the car started by a push button to the left of the dash panel. The big Chrysler eight springs to life at the touch of the starter, and of interest is the left courtesy light, under the dash edge, blinking over the red painted emergency brake handle. This is a nice feature to avoid driving around with the emergency brake on, but that red brake handle is incongruous when viewed with the rest of the otherwise beautiful dash board. It is one of the oddities of this era Chrysler product, that enthusiasts relate to, and probably makes sense to the engineering mind, but is still jarring to the aesthetic senses. Be that as it may, when the brake is released, the light quits flashing.

I found the car to be quite peppy when started out in the low range and allowed to shift once by foot. In low speed driving in traffic, this was quite effective, with a shift to the high position once out on the road. The body is extremely tight for a convertible, with comfortable ride characteristics and very little roll on curves. It very much has the feel of a heavy, well built automobile, but the brakes take a little more than average foot pressure to bring this large, heavy convertible to a smooth straight stop.

Above: Buick hood opens either side; Chrysler uses alligator-type opening. *Below:* Radiators on either car contain more metal than an entire 1998 sub-compact's body. *Bottom:* Cloisonne crown is typical of quality touches in Chrysler's interior.

Once out on the open road, the ride is smooth, comfortable, and has a great feeling of luxury and quality. Not only is this Chrysler a pleasure to drive, but it is a winner in the "Longest Hood in the Neighborhood" contest. ⌖

Acknowledgments and Bibliography

Automotive Industries, *March 15, 1948; Dammann, George H.,* Seventy Years of Buick; *Dammann, George H.,* Seventy Years of Chrysler; *Dunham, Terry B. and Lawrence R. Gustin,* The Buick: A Complete History; *Gunnell, John,* Standard Catalog of American Cars 1946-1975; *Heasley, Jerry,* The Production Figure Book for US Cars; *Kimes, Beverly Rae, "Chrysler from the Airflow,"* Automobile Quarterly, *Vol. VII, No. 2; Langworth, Richard M.,* Encyclopedia of American Cars 1940-1970; *Langworth, Richard M., and Jan P. Norbye,* The Complete History of Chrysler Corporation, 1924-1985; *Norbye, Jan P. and Jim Dunne,* Buick: The Postwar Years.

Special thanks to Phil Jones, Kentfield, California; Larry Klein, Hillsborough, California. And we're grateful as well for the help of the late Richard H. Stout, of Delray Beach, Florida.

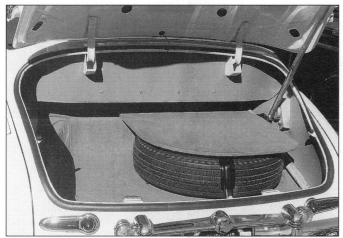

Top: Chrysler's clear plastic knobs were used into the fifties. *Above:* Trunk space in Buick is skimpier than Chrysler's. *Below:* Both cars are all curves in the back.

GM's Glamorous Threesome for 1953

Cadillac Eldorado, Buick Skylark, Oldsmobile Fiesta

by John G. Tennyson
photos by the author

A NEW president, the end of the Korean War, a time of new prosperity...that was the real beginning of the "fifties era" as we know it today. 1953 was, perhaps, a turning point in the United States, not only in peacetime and politics, but for American automobiles as well.

For most of Detroit, 1953 peacetime promised to be a better but not necessarily spectacular production year. Studebaker was completely redesigned, with striking new low-slung styling. But most cars from GM, Ford, Chrysler, Packard, Nash, Hudson and Kaiser-Willys were mild face-lifts of the previous year's models, albeit more attractively styled. Longer wheelbases, more glass, chrome and heavier grilles were featured. Buick finally introduced a new ohv V-8, several years after most other competitors had already abandoned the straight eight. Twelve-volt electrics were offered on some lines in order to handle a host of expanding accessories, like power windows, seats, and air conditioning. Power steering was now standard on some luxury models. Ford, Buick and Cadillac were celebrating 50 years of production.

What makes 1953 unique in American automobile lore, however, was the willingness of some manufacturers, particularly General Motors, to make available to the public what were originally prototype show cars.

It was probably not much of a gamble. GM had used roving Motorama car shows since 1949 to both tease and test the public with new designs for possible future production. In fact, many show cars were but modifications of existing production models.

Dream cars, such as the Buick "Y Job," had been the forte of GM designers, led by Harley Earl, since the 1930s. As early as World War II, Earl reputedly sought to design his cars after fighter aircraft, notably the P-38, the genesis of Cadillac's postwar fins. That plane's bubble-top canopy was also the inspiration for panoramic windshields on GM's early fifties' show cars. Hence, in view of their own history of design, GM's move from show car to production car was entirely logical.

At the 1952 Motoramas, there was a host of dream cars, many two-seater fiberglass sports models, such as the Buick Wildcat, Cadillac LeMans and Chevrolet Corvette. But there were also the larger all-steel variations of production cars, the half-roofed Pontiac Parisienne (see *SIA* #123), as well as the Oldsmobile Fiesta, Buick Skylark, and Cadillac Eldorado convertibles. Unlike previous Motorama show cars, the larger Olds, Buick and Cadillac models, and, of course, the Corvette, were actually brought into production. It was supposedly GM's response to the European sports cars, just starting to spark interest in the United States, but Corvette was the only one of the four which actually resembled a sports car. The other three convertibles were large, six-passenger customized luxury cars.

The ostensible occasion was the 50th Anniversary — at least for Buick and Cadillac. Olds — an older marque — joined in too. GM couldn't really expect to recoup its costs. Prices were far above those of even the highest priced standard Cadillac or Packard convertibles, aimed, perhaps, only for those of celebrity status. But like the show cars before them, GM's fabulous threesome were designed to bolster the prestige and sales of the regular lines, as well as whet the public's appetite for the future. Many of the features of the Motorama cars, the wraparound windshields, the full exposed rear wheels on Buicks, and the cut-down doors and belt-line "dip," were, indeed built into many 1954 and later GM production models.

GM's threesome chosen for this report belong to the Ramshead Collection, a private collection of two Sacramento, California, businessmen. All are white with red — and in the case of the Olds, orange-red — leather interiors.

Oldsmobile Fiesta

Of the three cars, the Olds, an older and mostly cosmetic restoration, is the rarest. The Fiesta has most of the same modifications, like the cut-down doors, of the other models. At a glance, however, except for the panoramic windshield, the Olds appears to be the least customized of the three.

The cowl had to be modified, as did the hood, to accept the new windshield. Top height was cut three inches from the Olds 98 convertible, and specially fabricated doors and a notable "dip" in the beltline, also characteristic of the Cadillac and Buick, were all part of the Fiesta's motif. The Fiesta was also fitted with special "spinner" hubcaps, which became a trademark on later Oldsmobiles and popular in the aftermarket as well.

On the outside, everything else was largely standard Olds: a huge chrome-bumper combination, with bumper guards built into the grille, a variation on other GM designs. The side treatment was massive, with rear fender skirts and upper portions of the rear fenders and trunk painted a contrasting color and separated from the lower body by a chrome sweepspear. The Ramshead car also sports the dealer-installed continental kit with extended bumper, giving the Fiesta an even longer and more customized look. Without the continental spare, Olds rear end styling is rather plain, in contrast to the rest of the car.

Mechanically, the 98's 303-c.i.d. V-8, a bored and stroked version of the "Rocket" engine first introduced in 1949, received special manifolding with a four-barrel carburetor and an increase in compression of 8.3:1 over the standard 8:1. However, at 170 horses, there was only a five-horsepower advantage over the Olds 98. A four-speed HydraMatic automatic transmission and a faster rear axle ratio were designed to keep the heavier 4,459 pound Fiesta within the acceptable range of expected Olds performance.

On the inside, the white leather upholstery with reddish-orange inserts is not the least subtle — looking like it might well belong in a circus. Almost every accessory available on lesser Olds models was standard on the Fiesta.

The price tag of $5,715 — some $700 more than the Skylark, and even $500 more than a Packard Caribbean convertible — was apparently just too steep for most people. After all, an Olds 98 convertible listed for only $2,963. With only 458 copies, the Fiesta convertible was dropped, and the most expensive Olds convertible for 1954 became the Olds 98 Starfire at $3,249. But then the Starfire was not a custom-built car.

Buick Skylark

The Skylark, even without the wraparound windshield common to the Olds and Cadillac, is perhaps the most customized looking of the three, though in reality the least. Using a Roadmaster body, the conventional windshield was lowered. The doors and mid-section were cut down like the others, but the mid-body "dip" was made to look more pronounced. What really gives the Skylark a more custom appearance, however, is the full wheel cut-out design of the rear fenders, a feature not common to the other special cars or to any other Buick at the time. The fully exposed wheels are further accentuated by an extension of the traditional Buick side body sweepspear. Instead of ending at the front of the rear wheel wells, as in previous Buicks, the sweepspear bounds up and around the wheel well and trails back to the taillamps on a horizontal plane parallel with the fender line. This styling feature was adopted on some 1954 production Buicks and lasted through 1957.

Additionally, the Kelsey-Hayes wire wheels give the Skylark a more sporty

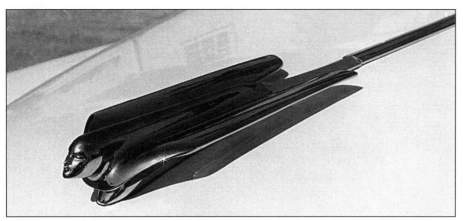

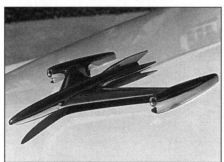

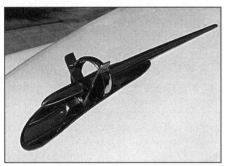

Above and below: *Three distinctive hood ornaments adorn the cars: Caddy's traditional flying lady; Buick's new-for-'53 split V for its V-8; Olds's familiar rocket.* **Bottom:** *Authentic wire wheels for the Eldo and Skylark, but Fiesta makes do with spinner caps.*

look than the Olds spinners, and the Skylark has several unique features, such as special badges ahead of the rear wheel cut-outs, a special Anniversary Edition emblem on the steering wheel hub, with a picture of a 1903 Buick and an inscription of the original owner's name, and an engine-turned appliqué on the face of the dash. The Skylark was also clean shaven, free of the traditional Buick "portholes" on the front fenders, but the Roadmaster insignias still remain on the front bumper and deck-lid.

New for 1953 was a Buick V-8 of 322 cubic inches, replacing the old straight eight, which Buick has used since the 1930s. The engine was one of the most efficient in the industry at the time, producing 188 horsepower with 8.5:1 compression. The smaller and lighter engine allowed Buick to chop six inches off the length of the '53 Roadmaster, as compared with previous models. The same basic block, with periodic increases in bore and other modifications, was used through 1969.

In addition to the new V-8, Buick modified its sluggish but smooth Dynaflow automatic transmission and came up with the so-called Twin-Turbine Dynaflow, to provide a 10 percent improvement in performance.

Like Olds, the Skylark came with a host of standard features, such as power steering, brakes, front seat and windows, a special "Selectronic" radio with foot control, and electric antenna. Seating is, of course, leather, with needlepoint style red carpeting and two-toned white seats with red pleated inserts and piping on our featured car, a colorful package not unlike the Olds.

The Ramshead Buick, a mostly original car with some mechanical and cosmetic refurbishing, was purchased in 1985 sight unseen from an Ohio man, who had owned and garaged the car since 1954, and whose wife had only used it for proverbial Sunday drives. So well maintained was the Buick, it could have been driven from Ohio to California.

The Skylark, the least costly of the

Comparison of Major Styling Features

Feature	Eldorado	Skylark	Fiesta
Windshield	Panoramic	Conventional but chopped	Panoramic
Vent windows	Frameless	Conventional	Frameless
Doors	Cut down	Cut down	Cut down
Quarters	Beltline "dip"	Beltline "dip"	Beltline "dip"
Distinguishing side treatment	Rear fender scoop	Full body sweepspear	Rear fender sweepspear
Rear fender	Skirted wheels	Exposed wheels	Skirted wheels
Wheels	Wire	Wire	Conventional spinner caps
Body color	Solid	Solid	Rear two-tone
Hood ornament	Flying goddess	Bombsight	Rocket ship
Boot cover	Hinged, flush-fitted metal	Snap-on conventional	Snap-on conventional

threesome, was still, at $5,000, more expensive than a $4,200 Cadillac 62 convertible. Some 1,690 were produced, and the Skylark was carried over for one more year, although on the shorter Special-Century chassis.

Cadillac Eldorado

The Eldorado was the most expensive American car in 1953. The custom convertible was the first of Cadillac's so-called "personal" production luxury cars. Based on the Series 62 convertible, the Eldo, like the Fiesta, came with Cadillac's first panoramic windshield, cut-down doors, and special leather interior. Colors were limited to white, ochre, red and blue.

Power steering, brakes, windows, front seat, underseat heater, signal-seeking radio, along with HydraMatic, wire wheels, a unique "Electro Vac" windshield wiper motor, which could be turned on to assist the vacuum wipers when needed, and almost every other conceivable amenity, were standard. The only accessory not available on the Eldo was air conditioning, and the price of the car was a whopping $7,750.

Unique to the Eldo, and not found on any of the other GM specialty cars, was a special metal boot cover, which fit flush with the body, giving a more streamlined appearance. The cover remains in position as a shelf when the top is up. To put down the top, a rear section, along with the small glass rear window, can be unfastened, and the hinged metal cover unlatched and pulled through the rear opening. The top can then be lowered, using a convenient switch next to the power window button above the left rear seat armrest. When the top is down, the hatch cover is lowered and locks back into place.

Every car was virtually hand built. The hood, doors, cowl, and dash had to be modified to accommodate the special wraparound windshield. The doors and rear quarters were cut down to give a more streamlined appearance, the top about three inches lower than the standard 62 convertible, on which the Eldo was based. The frame and suspension were beefed up to accept the extra weight, but the brakes and engine remained that of the regular 62 series.

The power plant, Cadillac's standard 331-c.i.d. V-8, with 210 horses, four-barrel carburetion and dual exhaust, coupled to a four-speed HydraMatic automatic transmission, made Cadillac the most powerful 1953 American car in terms of horsepower.

The Eldorado's special interiors include a padded leather dash and aluminum trim, which extend into the door panels. Front seats, custom made for the Eldo, were covered in rich pleated leather, available in solid or two-tone

All three cars are sportier than their regular production convertible counterparts, but Skylark appears to have the sportiest styling of the trio.

combinations. Some hardware, like the inside door handles, were purloined from Cadillac's limousine. Gold emblems grace the dash and door sills.

The '53 was the first in a long line of Eldorados, but few would match the custom-built character of the original.

Our featured Eldorado is a fairly new ground-up restoration of a nice original car and, with less than 500 miles on the odometer, drives and handles like brand new.

Similarities and Differences

The three GM Motorama production cars had much in common. They were all lowered convertibles, based on the top-of-the-line model, with cut-down doors, a full array of power accessories as standard equipment, special leather interiors and various custom touches, like special emblems and special wheels, to name a few.

But the three cars were also quite distinctive, while maintaining their badge

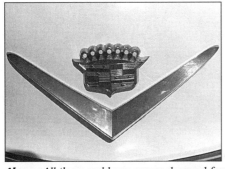
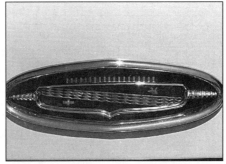
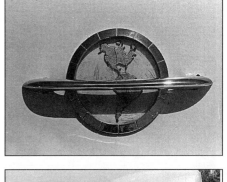

Above: All three emblems are unchanged from ordinary GM offerings. *Below:* Cad and Olds introduced wraparound windshields to the world, but Buick opted for slightly chopped stock unit. *Below right:* Buick's open wheel treatment looks more rakish than skirted rivals. *Facing page, top:* How many pounds of chrome do these cars carry? *Below:* All three trunks are nicely finished, but Eldo's, *top,* has a nearly custom-tailored appearance.

identities with standard models. The Olds and Cadillac had the new panoramic windshield, the Buick a conventional, though chopped windscreen. The Buick had full rear wheel cut-outs, while the Olds and Cadillac were skirted. The Olds had the only engine modified from the standard line — though only by five horses. The Cadillac was much heavier and somewhat larger than the Buick and Olds, the Buick the smallest and lightest of the three, though none of these cars was small by any means.

The Buick is thought by many to be the most attractive, and truest to the concept of the "sporty" car, which these limited-production convertibles were said to represent. This is no doubt due to the unique rear fenders and more pronounced beltline "dip." But the Buick is somewhat shorter than the others, and thus the interior seating position, particularly leg room for tall drivers, and head room with the top up, is more cramped. The Olds and Cadillac, while streamlined, seem somehow more massive and chrome-laden than the Buick. But then, the Buick does not feature the more dramatic panoramic windshield, frameless vent windows, or reworked cowl and custom padded dash of the others, nor does Buick's revised Dynaflow transmission compare as favorably to the performance offered by the Olds and Cadillac HydraMatic.

Of the three in the Ramshead Collection, the Cadillac is the best driver, probably because of its recent and extensive restoration. It's also the most luxurious and impressive of the three GM specialty convertibles, as well as more attractive than bulkier looking Eldorados of the mid and late fifties. The wraparound windshield and lowered doors give the Cadillac a sporty flair without altering the Cadillac "style." The metal boot cover provides a custom look, and the rich dash, gold emblems, and semi-bucket seats done in leather provide the luxury touch. Again, the Skylark appears to be the most distinctive, in comparison to standard Buicks, while the Fiesta, on the outside, seems the least changed from its basic Olds 98 counterpart.

Where are they now?

The threesome — The Eldorado, Skylark, and Fiesta — were a bold move,

1953 Comparison Specifications

	Cadillac Eldorado	Buick Skylark	Oldsmobile Fiesta
Price (f.o.b.	$7,750	$5,000	$5,715
Body style	2-dr, 6-pass. convert.	2-dr, 6-pass. convert.	2-dr, 6-pass. convert.
Chassis	Ladder frame, Central X member	Ladder frame Central X member	Ladder frame Central X member
Wheelbase	126.0 inches	121.5 inches	124.0 inches
Length	220.8 inches	207.6 inches	215.0 inches
Width	80.1 inches	79.9 inches	76.9 inches
Height	58.5 inches	N/A	N/A
Front track	59.1 inches	60.0 inches	59.0 inches
Rear track	63.1 inches	62.0 inches	59.0 inches
Weight	4,800 lb. (cw)	4,315 lb. (cw)	4,459 lb. (sw)
Engine	ohv V-8	ohv V-8	ohv V-8
Displacement	331 c.i.d.	322 c.i.d.	303 c.i.d.
Bore/stroke	3.813 x 3.625 inches	4.00 x 3.20 inches	3.75 x 3.44 inches
Compress.	8.25:1	8.5:1	8.3:1
Horsepower	210 @ 4,150 rpm	188 @ 4,000 rpm	170 @ 3,600 rpm
Torque	330 lb/ft @ 2,700 rpm	N/A	284 @ 1,800 rpm
Carb	4-bbl	4-bbl	4-bbl
Exhaust	Dual	Single	Single
Transmission	HydraMatic 4-speed	Dynaflow 2-speed	HydraMatic 4-speed
Rear axle	Hypoid	Hypoid	Hypoid
Ratio	3.77:1	N/A	3.42:1
Suspension	Front, independent, coil springs; rear, solid axle, leaf springs	Front, independent, coil springs; rear, solid axle, leaf springs	Front, independent, coil springs; rear, solid axle, leaf springs
Brakes	Hydraulic, power 4-wheel drum	Hydraulic, power 4-wheel drum	Hydraulic, power 4-wheel drum
Drums	12 inch	N/A	11 inch
Swept area	258 sq. in.	N/A	191.7 sq. in.
Steering	Recirculating ball power assist	Recirculating ball power assist	Recirculating ball power assist
Lock/lock	5 turns	N/A	5.5 turns
Tires	8.00x15 inches	8.00x15 inches	8.00x15 inches
# produced	532	1,690	458

but then the Chrysler Town and Country woodie sedans, convertibles and hard-tops, and Continental Mark II are also evidence that manufacturers were, per-haps, more willing to take chances with limited production specialty cars in those days. None of them lasted as semi-customs, and their names were later hijacked for other, and often rather mundane, production cars.

In the case of Olds, the Fiesta was

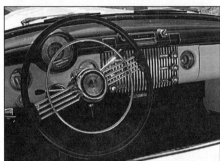

Above: All three dashes display an abundance of chrome. Below: And all three are motivated by V-8s ranging from 170 to 210 bhp.

Above: Metal boot gives Eldo very smooth, sleek appearance. Other cars use conventional vinyl covers.

dropped after only one year. The name later appeared on 1957-58 Oldsmobile station wagon offerings. The Skylark was continued through 1954 but on a smaller Special-Century chassis and, with even more dismal production (836) than in 1953, was not offered for 1955. The Skylark name was revived in 1961 as a sporty and more luxurious version of Buick's compact Special, and the Skylark continues today as Buick's compact two- and four-door model.

Through the years, the Eldorado has had a more successful career as a luxury line. In fact, until the Seville, the Eldo was the top-of-the-line Cadillac for more than 20 years. It was a dressed-up production line 62 convertible in 1954, with a strip of stainless metal on the lower rear fenders, and the price was dropped by $2,000. In 1955, unique shark-like fins set the Eldo apart from other Cadillacs. The Eldorado convertible became the Eldorado Biarritz in 1956, and a two-door hardtop Eldorado Seville was added to the line. An ultra-expensive custom Eldorado Brougham four-door was offered from '57 through '60 on a very limited basis. Eldorado convertibles were continued through 1966, but Eldorados in the sixties were almost indistinguishable from the standard Cadillac line. An all new "personal" front-wheel-drive two-door hardtop Eldorado was introduced in 1967, and the Eldorado convertible was re-introduced in 1971 and lasted through 1976. The first downsized 1979-1985 Eldorados were also attractive, and a limited number of reworked hardtops appeared as convertibles in the last few model years. After 1985, the Eldorado became a cookie-cutter compact with a luxury price, barely recognizable as a Cadillac.

Cadillac rear styling is quite graceful; Buick's sleek and modern for '53; Olds makes long even longer with accessory continental kit.

The 1992 and later models show more promise of reviving the standard.

The fabulous threesome from GM are truly unique, not only as one-year models, but in the fact they represent a special effort by one manufacturer to bring three separate customized cars to the market simultaneously — the kind of expensive effort that we shall probably not see repeated in our lifetimes. ❑

**by Terry Boyce
photos by the author**

Buick's pre-World War II Series 60 Century had given the prestige cars from Flint a performance image. The 1936-42 Century models, with their big 320-cubic-inch straight eights and small Special bodies had been among America's fastest production automobiles. But they were never volume sellers. When Buick reentered the automobile business after the war ended, in 1946, the Century was gone.

In a buyer's market, Buick was willing to coast on its reputation as a maker of big and fast cars. By 1950, though, a new interest in handling and performance was evident in the marketplace. Buick's engineers were developing a new V-8 that would be one of the best and most powerful engines in the industry. A totally new Special was already being planned for 1954. Combining the new powerplant and the new chassis/body would produce a car certainly worthy of the Century nameplate. Thus began, in 1954, Buick's second Century.

The new 1954 Series 60 Century shared the concurrent Special's totally redesigned, 122-inch wheelbase chas-515 and body. But, in place of the Special's rather small 26-cubic-inch V-8 (also new for '54) was the Roadmaster's big 4-barrel carbureted, 322-cubic-inch engine. Horsepower was rated at 200 with Dynaflow, 195 (due to a compression reduction) with manual transmission.

Buick's "vertical valve" V-8 for 1954 appeared nearly identical to the first production versions seen in 1953 Roadmasters and Supers. Only a redesigned air cleaner, with a lower profile to clear the wide, flat hood, caught the eye. But there were significant changes inside. Heads and pistons were revamped for 1954. Nearly half an inch had been shaved from the domed piston tops, while the head work created a smaller combustion chamber. More performance — the 1954 rating was up twelve horsepower — and elimination of the annoying pinging evidenced by some 1953 engines were the goals.

Backing the V-8 was either an optional Twin-Turbine Dynaflow or a manual three-speed transmission. Buick engineers had spent long hours coming up with a new rear power-team mount that would absolutely minimize vibration in the 1954 cars.

Careful attention to detail was also evident in the new car's front suspension. Automotive magazine writers had hardly gotten through their first corners in a new Century before they began to

1954 BUICK CENTURY ESTATE WAGON

rave about the new Buick's handling.

Characterized by long, unequal length A arms, the new suspension used parallel steering linkage and a new vertical steering knuckle to alter steering geometry with pleasing results.

Delco tube-type, direct-acting front shocks went into the 1954's front coil springs, breaking a long tradition of lever-type shocks all around. The heavy, antiquated design was retained on the rear axle for a few more years, however.

Even the tires were given extra consideration. They were of a new tread design, with a modified composition that made them softer and put more tread on the ground.

All these re-engineered components were attached to a new X-type frame that lowered the whole car, again improving handling through a lowered center of gravity. Egress was made easier, too, by the new Buick's lower stance.

Buick claimed the new cars had a "million dollar ride," but in truth many more dollars than that had been spent by chief engineer Verner Mathews and

his team during the 1954's development.

Mounted to the chassis was a new, spacious Fisher body that had a somewhat chopped off look The chrome-plated zinc grille, headlamp doors, and general taillamp designs gave the radically new styles some family resemblance to earlier Buicks. Continued, too, were the now famous Buick VentiPorts — or "portholes" on the front fenders. Like everything else, they were newly designed for 1954. Specials and Centurys would have three VentiPorts per front fender for 1954, while the larger Supers and Roadmasters got four. Evidently, Century customers complained, for in 1955 the 60 series would get four "holes" and the Super, with its two-barrel engine, would get the short grouping.

A major innovation on 1954 Buicks (and Oldsmobiles and Cadillacs sharing the new Fisher B-C bodies) was the Libbey-Owens-Ford panoramic windshield.

The wraparound style windshield was an outgrowth of L-O-F's World War II

Originally published in Special Interest Autos #83, Sept.-Oct. 1984

fighter plane canopy work. The first automotive appearance was on GM dream cars around 1950. Consumer research detected a strong public Interest in the windshield as used on Buick's 1951 xP-300 idea car. Early in 1951 GM's Harley Earl decided GM cars would have the windshield, but it took GM and ~O-F engineers months of research - much of it trial and error -to establish an optimum curvature that would not distort the driver's vision. The new windshields reached semi-production status on the cowls of the limited-run 1953 Olds Fiesta and Cadil-lac Eldorado (but not, curiously, on the 1953 Skylark).

Satisfied at last, the go-ahead was given to include the new glass in 1954 B and C-body GM styles. Even after production started, Buick engineers would remove a car at random from the assembly line to ghake, twist and otherwise torture-test the new windshield.

This ongoing testing was done even though the L-O-F glass had survived an "ultimate" test when two new 1954

Buicks were deliberately rolled at high speed. Neither suffered a broken windshield.

Elimination of the blind spots created by traditional windshield pillars was the panoramic windshield's main selling point: the accursed "dog leg" it created in the door opening was its least favorable feature - at least in the early years. Later, Detroit gave us too much of a good thing and the ever-larger panoramic glasses became increasingly distortion-prone.

Looking through the new windshield, almost all 1954 Buick drivers could see the front fenders for the first time in many a year. The flattened "plateau" of hood sheet metal and newly raised fender lines were responsible. Glancing in the rear view mirror drivers of average or taller height could readily see the bumps on the rear fenders, too. Customers who had complained about the lousy rear vision and invisible fenders of their late forties' Buick bloat boats must have cheered.

For the first time since 1941 Buick's

instrument panel was completely new. Controls were scattered about the panel, and most important, the headlamp switch was now to the left of the steering column - well out oflitfie baby boomer's reach.

The enormous black plastic steering wheel cranked through a reduced ratio in both manual and power-steered Buicks for 1954.

The Century driver peered through the steering wheel at matching speed-ometer and engine-monitoring round gauge clusters. (Supers~and Road-masters had a completely different instrument panel, with a horizontal "redliner" speedometer). The speedom-eter included Buick's traditional trip odometer (a subfle reminder that this was a "road car"). Arrayed on the lower, bulged lip of the panel were the heater/ defroster controls - vertical sliding levers and toggle switches that were distincfly "aircraft."

The least expected Century model was the new Estate wagon, a six-passenger, all-steel station wagon. Buick had been

BUICK'S SECOND CENTURY

1954 Buick Century

the last automaker to use wood in station wagon construction, in 1953, when the composite wood/steel Estate Wagons were either Roadmasters or Supers. For 1954, the Estate Wagon did a switch-about and became a Special/Century style. Boxy but low, the new body suited the Special/Century chassis well. Actual assembly of the Estate Wagons was done by Ionia Mfg. Co. (see sidebar, page 48) to Buick specifications. Interiors were Cordaveen, a durable synthetic, with carpeted floors and cargo area on both models. A small vestige of the glorious past was found in the wooden inner tailgate panel, finished off with chrome rub strips.

Apparently, all Estate Wagons were finished in two-tone color combinations, with a light roof panel and window surrounds over a medium or dark lower body.

Driving Impressions

We were anticipating sliding behind the big ebony steering wheel of John Galandak's 1954 Century Estate Wagon. After all, during the mid-seventies we had driven a '53 Skylark and '55 Century convertible thousands of miles. It would be familiar and nostalgic to drive the Estate Wagon, we thought.

But, we were surprised. It seemed strange—the steering wheel is so large, and so high. Harley Earl decided customers wanted to feel like they were driving a bus about this time, we guess. Anyway, it is totally unlike our newer cars to which we've (sadly) become accustomed. We did remember to turn the key straight up, and floor the accelerator to start the '54 Century. In true "nailhead" V-8 fashion, it roared to life almost before we heard the starter engage. We were momentarily confused by the shift quadrant for the Dynaflow. Park is at the top, reverse at the bottom. Once so familiar, now so quaint.

Out on the coastal highway near John's New Smyrna Beach, Florida, home, we recalled the word most associated with Buick's 1950s ride qualities: "billowy." The faster we drove, though, the firmer the suspension became. This Buick doesn't get comfortable until about 60 mph — a real road car in the old sense.

The engine's torque was stronger than we remembered. Our ears have become adept at judging car speed by rpm after shift points, but with Dynaflow you get no such audible hints. The engine is very quiet and there are no upshifts, unless you start in low and manually upshift. We kept glancing at the speedometer, trying to keep the car under the legal speed limit, but we were consistently surprised to find we'd glided into the 60-70 mph range without noticing it. Increasing throttle from any speed opens a beautifully smooth flow of power that is refreshing. "Step on it a bit, and it's right

out there," John agrees.

We were impressed with the optical quality of the original L-O-F panoramic windshield. GM and the manufacturer really did their homework on this piece of glass. distortion is nil.

The brake pedal sits lower and is wider than that of our '53 Skylark. Stopping power was obviously better, although this car has a bit of pulsation in the brake application. John blames it on the power booster, which seems a likely culprit. There was no sign of the disconcerting fade our '53 Skylark always suffered from — Buick had some widely publicized problems with soft drums and defective boosters in 1953, but the 1954 system was cured.

Going into a corner fairly fast, the Century leans more than our newer cars, but it is still impressive, especially compared to the 1953's handling. You'd have to drive both to appreciate what a super improvement the 1954 suspension and lower body made.

Ionia did a good job on the Estate Wagon body. Even after 30 years, the Cordaveen interior looks like new and there are no squeaks or rattles in this original car. Though it weighs 180 pounds more than a comparable Riviera hardtop, the Estate Wagon is nimble in a manner not associated with earlier station wagons.

Parking the Century, we could see the tops of all four fenders, a remarkable achievement by Ned Nickles and his stylists and so unlike earlier Buicks.

We agree with Walt Woron; the gauges are too small, but they are beautifully detailed and we like them anyway. A black panel with chrome CENTURY lettering divides the nacelles and reminds us of the prestige we're enjoying. We still get a kick, too, out of the needlessly complicated heater/defroster controls. Man, you can imagine you're feeding it to the big engines of a Constellation,

playing with those "aircraft" controls.

Our test Century seemed quite willing to head on down the coast for Key West, but we knew it was time to return to John's driveway. This car has yet to see 40,000 miles, and it is in truly outstanding condition. Only a respray of its original beige and white exterior colors was required to put it in the condition you see it here.

John Galandak obtained the pristine Estate Wagon nine years ago. As so often happens, it was through a casual conversation that he found this prize. He was engineering the installation of an air conditioning system in a prestigious Chicago apartment building when a chance mention of his old-car collection to a resident widow introduced the Buick into his life.

The lady and her husband had been the original developers of Aspen, Colorado. Buried beneath blankets in the garage of their Aspen estate was an old Buick station wagon, she told John. She wasn't sure of the year, but would call him with a detailed description the next time she was out there.

Finally, the long-awaited call came. The Buick had "Century" nameplates on its rear fenders, and a trio of portholes on the front fenders, a description that could only match a 1954 model, John knew. The mileage was just over 28,000. John purchased the car sight unseen, and flew to Colorado to close the deal. Since that time he has added about 10,000 miles to the speedometer; some of it when he took it to Buick's 75th Anniversary Celebration in Flint during 1978. When a retirement move brought the Galandaks to New Smyrna Beach, the Century Estate Wagon came with them — safe in the box of a U-Haul truck.

Buick's second Century lasted only five years, through the 1958 model year. Today any fifties' Century is a desired collector car, but it is the convertibles and Estate Wagons that are the rarest and most sought.

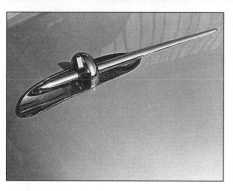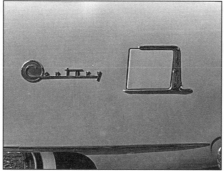

Facing page: Front end design was a refinement of 1953's cars. More teeth in grille, markedly lower hood line distinguish the '54 cars. **This page, left:** Deft treatment of sweepspear helps give wagon a long, low appearance. **Below left:** Indented "V" in a ring hood ornament first appeared in '53. **Below center:** Century model i.d. appears on rear fenders. **Below:** Distinctive teardrop-shaped headlight trim was inspired by 1951 XP-300 show car.

The Century Estate Wagon was General Motors' most expensive station wagon, listing for $3,470. (America's most expensive 1954 station wagon, though, was Chrysler's New Yorker Town & Country at $4,024.)

The basic Ionia body was used for 1955 and 1956 Estate Wagons as well. 1956 styles had fully opened rear wheel houses.

Buick introduced the Century and Special Estate Wagons along with their other new 1954 cars on January 2, 1954. Also in the Century line were a Riviera hardtop and a sedan. Interest in the new cars was spurred by a major feature on their design which appeared in *Life* magazine on January 18, 1954 (the Buick Design Chronology sidebar was drawn from this article).

Sales manager Alfred Belfie really stirred showroom traffic with an intensive "Spring Fashion Show" promotion that began on April 2. Stars of the show were the new Estate Wagons, and the Special and Century convertibles — the Special having been promised since January, and the Century a surprise replacement for the failing 1954 Skylark — which was built on the Century chassis in 1954.

More than 1.5 million Americans rode in Buick demonstrators during the two-week promotion, Belfie later claimed.

Motor Trend gave their February 1954 cover to the new Buicks, showing a mint green Skylark and a yellow Roadmaster — both equipped with chromed Kelsey-

1954 Buick Design Chronology

July 10, 1950: Buick Division executives formally request that Buick's design studio begin work on a major redesign for 1954. This gives stylists a head start on the normal minimal GM 21-month lead time to create a new car.

Autumn 1950: General Motors Consumer Research data, Buick owner and dealer comments, complaints and suggestions are reviewed. Specific design goals are drawn from these sources. Owners want more shoulder room, which will be accomplished by widening the body above the belt line. Complaints about the grille-ducted ventilation system are frequent — some type of new cowl ventilation system is desirable. The design staff adds their own objectives: The new car will be fresh from the road up, yet will retain Buick family characteristics; a new instrument panel design will replace the 1950-53 type which carries the theme first established by the 1941 models; a perking interest in sports-type cars should be reflected even in the Buick's style for 1954.

February 1951: Chief stylist Ned Nickles and his staff present first detailed idea sketches. During next 11 months more presentations will be made, as drawings are rejected, redone, changed, and shown again. The 1954 styling theme begins to emerge. A panoramic windshield is already included in the sketches, although much research remains to be done to ready it for production.

January 21, 1952: Harlow Curtice, GM's engineering policy committee, Buick management, and all concerned studios view and approve basic 1954 design. Trim details remain to be finalized.

February-April 1952: Following executive approval of full-size airbrush renditions, stylists begin building a clay mockup. An ongoing debate about the wraparound windshield's pillar design is settled at this point: In a split decision, it is ordered that B-body models will have slanted pillars, while the larger, C-body cars will have vertical pillars. The finished clay gives stylists their first chance to see how light plays on the design. An awkward "hump" appears in the roof line. Nickles shaves it down a fraction of an inch at a time — after removing three-eighths of an inch it looks right. General Manager Ivan Wiles objects to the proposed Skylark-like sweepspear body-side moldings. They are too expensive, he says. A compromise is apparently reached; they are redesigned and will be stamped stainless — and most will also be used on the 1955 models. The new cowl ventilation system, using a grid inlet, is approved.

August 1952: A sedan body is built, using new fiberglass materials. Chromium brightwork is simulated with foil. Corporate executives view this full-size model as it is towed around a track, giving them a preview of its road appearance. Enthusiasm is high. Plant manager Ed Ragsdale begins plans to add 19 more assembly stations to build the more complex 1954 Buicks. New tooling for the 1954 line is estimated at $45 million. Dies are ordered for production, while color specialists choose and name the 1954 colors, using the fiberglass mock-up to test potential combinations.

January 2, 1954: Buick showrooms reopen after the New Year's holiday with the 1954 Buicks on display for the first time.

specifications

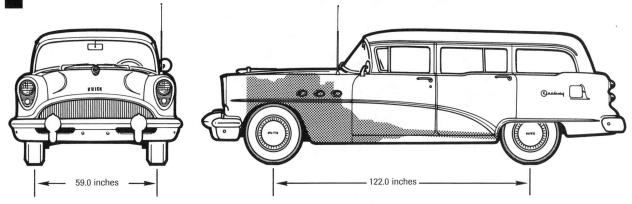

← 59.0 inches →

← 122.0 inches →

1954 Buick Century Model 69

Original price $3,470 base
Options on dR car Dynaflow automatic transmission, power steering, power brakes, Sonomatic radio, power antenna, full wheel covers, twin outside rear view mirrors, 7.60 x 15 whitewall tires, heater and defroster, gas door guard

ENGINE
Type	Overhead-valve V-8, cast-iron block
Bore x stroke	4 inches x 3.2 inches
Displacement	322 cubic inches
Horsepower @ rpm	195 @ 4,100 (200 w/Dynaflow)
Torque @ rpm	309 @ 2,400
Compression ratio	8.01:1 (8.5:1 w/Dynaflow)
Induction system	4-barrel Carter or Stromberg downdraft carburetor
Exhaust system	Cast-iron manifolds with cross over, single muffler and pipe to rear
Electrical system	12-volt Delco-Remy battery/coil

TRANSMISSION
Type	Automatic, torque converter with gears
Ratios: Drive	1 x Converter ratio
Low and reverse	1.82 x Converter ratio
Max. ratio to stall	2.45 @ 1,700 rpm

DIFFERENTIAL
Type	Hypoid
Ratio	3.9:1 (3.4:1 w/Dynaflow)
Drive axles	Semi-floating

STEERING
Type	Ball bearing worm and nut
Turning circle	43 feet
Turns lock-to-lock	4.5

BRAKES
Type	Hydraulic,
Size	12-inch diameter, front and rear
Total swept area	207.5 inches

CHASSIS & BODY
Frame type	X-type, steel girder
Body	4-door station wagon, all steel construction, built by Ionia Mfg. Co.

SUSPENSION
Front	Independent coil springs, unequal A-arms, direct-acting shock absorbers
Rear	Coil springs, axle torque taken by torque tube, lever-type shock absorbers
Tires	7.60 x 15
Wheels	15-inch welded steel discs

WEIGHTS AND MEASURES
Wheelbase	122 inches
Overall length	206.3 inches
Overall width	76.6 inches
Front track	59 inches
Rear track	59 inches
Shipping weight	3,975 pounds w/standard equipment; add 85 pounds for Dynaflow, 55 pounds for power brakes

PERFORMANCE
Top speed	105-112 mph
0-60 mph	10.6-12 seconds (starting in low range)
Quarter mile time	18.3 seconds
Fuel consumption	15.4 mpg average

(based on published 1954 Century sedan tests)

Even with tailgate down it's a rather high lift to put things into the back of the Buick compared to other wagons of the time.

Below: *Wagon body style carries two-tone color scheme especially well.* **Below center left:** *Hubcaps are of restrained design with traditional Buick block lettering.* **Below center:** *Big round instrument pods are typical Buick feature of the period. It's a long reach to the cigar lighter, and the clock is nearly impossible for the driver to check at a glance.* **Bottom:** *Century followed the tradition of its prewar models by stuffing a lot of power into a car of moderate weight. Bhp was 195, compared to heavier '54 Super's 182.*

1954 Buick Century

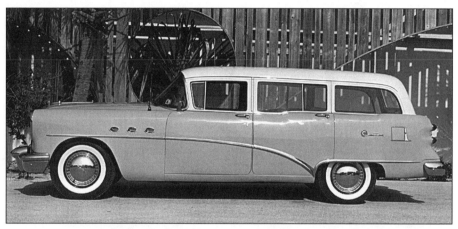

Hayes 40 spokers. (They were standard on the Skylark.)

Some press photos showed a Century Estate Wagon equipped with the beautiful, genuine wire wheels.

Don MacDonald gave *MT*'s initial impressions of the Century, under a headline reading, "Bombshells from Flint." He had high praise for the new Buick. Knocking off 0-60 times in less than 11 seconds proved that "Dynaflow's lack of acceleration is no longer a problem," he wrote.

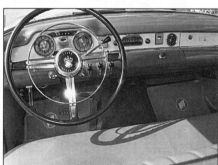

In the April issue, *MT*'s Walt Woron told of his experiences with a new Century sedan, confessing that at first he disliked its look, but that he found the styling grew on him. Like MacDonald, he found only one complaint with the new Buicks. Pushed "foolishly" fast into a corner, the Century tended to enter a four-wheel drift due to its inherent understeer. The rear end could come around suddenly with an inexperienced driver at the wheel. Again like MacDonald, Woron praised the Century's brakes. A new feature for 1954 was an electric motor that supplied power braking vacuum when the engine speed dropped below 300 rpm and manifold vacuum became unusable.

Woron put his Century on a chassis dyno and found 116 horsepower was getting to the road — representing 63 percent of the engine's brake horsepower — an impressive figure to Woron.

By November 1954, with the sight of a new Buick no longer unusual, *Motor Trend* decided the new Century wasn't "strange" looking after all and declared the model 61 "America's Best-Looking Sedan!"

Griff Borgeson, writing for *Motor Life*, was unabashedly impressed with the 1954 Century. "Wipe from your mind whatever impression you may have of

1954 Buick Century

Above: *Interior has loads of room for the family.* **Above right:** *Lift-up rear window is handy for long, awkward loads.* **Right:** *Spare hides out of the way under rear floor.* **Below:** *It's a good-looking wagon from about any angle.* **Bottom:** *'54 marked the last year for Buick's "toothy" grille theme.* **Bottom right:** *Very substantial bumper helps protect the rear from harm.*

the Buick automobile unless you've driven this year's line," he began his April 1954 article.

On one run, Borgeson's Century sedan had been clocked at 112.2 mph (with a two-way average of 107.5 mph). He found 60 miles per hour in 10.6 seconds. "Buoyant but wiry, big but nimble at all speeds," Borgeson wrote, concluding that all automotive enthusiasts should take a test drive, whether they were in the market or otherwise, "...not because the Buick has changed, but because it is one of the world's best cars." No wonder crowds gathered at dealerships that month.

The Century's performance, style, and praise spurred Buick towards the cherished number three automaker's title. Model year production would actually be less than 1953's total by 44,000 units — due to the short 1954 model year, which ran from January to November 19, 1954, when the new 1955 models were released. Century models accounted for 81,983, of which the Estate Wagon could contribute but 1,563 units, being the lowest production Century style of 1954. Still, Buick soundly whipped Plymouth with the 1954 models and rose to the coveted number three position on sales and production charts.

Considering their durability and fairly high production numbers, the 1954 Buicks have become rather uncommon today. Even the popular Riviera hardtops are seldom found, even at gatherings of Buick collectors. We only spotted one 1954 Buick among the dozens of Flint products seen at last October's Bulck-Olds-Pontiac show in Orlando, Florida. It was the gorgeous Century Estate Wagon seen in the accompanying photos — and used for this exclusive driveReport. ᐁ

Acknowledgments and Bibliography
Motor Trend, *February, April, Novem-ber 1954*; Motor Life, *April 1954*; Life, *January 18, 1954*; Automotive News Almanac *issues, 1954-1955*; The Buick: A Complete History, *Terry Dunham and Lawrence Gustin, Automobile Quarterly Publications, 1980*; Buick: The Postwar Years, *Jan Norbye and James Dunne, Motorbooks International, 1977*; NADA Used Car Guide, *July 1954*; Buick Magazine, *various 1954 issues*; 1954 Buick literature.

Special thanks to Mr. and Mrs. John Galandak, New Smyrna Beach, Florida, for the use of their 1954 Century Estate Wagon.

Ionia Mfg.

Buick's 1954 Estate Wagon bodies were built by Ionia Mfg. Co., a division of Mitchell Bentley Corp. Ionia was named after the small Michigan town — west of Flint, between Lansing and Grand Rapids — where its facility was. President of Mitchell-Bentley was Don R. Mitchell, born in Owosso, Michigan, in 1903. He started in the auto business in 1921, as sales manager of Weatherproof Body Co. in Coruna, Michigan. Director of the Ionia operation, and chairman of Mitchell-Bentley's board was Calvin P. Bentley (born 1883).

During 1954 Ionia advertised in trade journals that their customers included, in addition to Buick, these firms:

• **Packard.** Ionia Mfg. "...played a major role in restyling and redesigning the body of the 1954 Packard Caribbean, "producing the car's convertible top, seat cushions and other trim."

• **Studebaker.** Seat-cushion assemblies for Commander V-8 Starliner hardtops, Land Cruiser Sedans, and Conestoga station wagons were made by Ionia.

• **Dodge.** The fiberglass body of Dodge's Granada show car was built by Ionia, as were 1954 Suburban production station wagon bodies.

• **Nash.** Airflyte interiors used Ionia-assembled seat cushions, armrests, and sun visors.

Ionia built Mercury station wagon bodies for 1955, while continuing to produce the Buick Estate Wagon assemblies and doing work for many other makers. A prototype sample of a 1955 Oldsmobile station wagon was apparently built, but did not reach production. We have seen 1964 full-size Oldsmobile station wagons bearing Mitchell-Bentley body tags, though. Checking with information in 1984, no listings were in the Ionia directory for either Ionia Mfg. or Mitchell-Bentley.

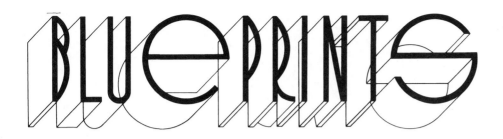

BLUEPRINTS

1941 Buick Century

by Bob Hovorka

They were troublesome cars: twin carburetors that required a love of things mechanical to keep in proper adjustment; a compression ratio that wasn't quite as happy with 80-octane gasoline as advertisements claimed; and a set of smaller spark plugs (Buick called them racing-car type) that fouled quickly at anything short of racing-car speeds.

But General Motors was not about to let such things stand in the way of a record-breaking year. Dealers fiddled with carburetors, slipped in thicker head gaskets, and rebored cylinder heads to accept standard-size spark plugs. They called it "The Best Buick Yet," and more than 370,000 left the factory before year's end, among them a sleek new Century.

Available as either four-door, business coupe, or Sedanet, the 1941 Century displayed a muscular physique long before such terms were applied to automobiles. Yet, there was nothing magical about it. Buick simply took a reworked Special body and stuffed it full of Roadmaster engine, "we believe, America's most powerful standard-production automobile engine."

Advertisements called it the Fireball Eight, and bragged about the way its specially contoured piston "rolls the fuel charge into the shape of a flattened ball that centers around the new, smaller, racing-car-type spark plug." With a heavy foot, a new Century could easily push the speedometer needle over its three-digit namesake. But there was more to a Buick than mere speed.

"For '41: Finest we've done! More ROOM — from longer, broader bodies; more POWER — from stepped-up Fireball engines; more COMFORT — from softer, steadier ride; more VALUE — any way you measure it!"

All hype? Part hype? Buick said, "It's hard to picture the new 1941 Buicks fairly with old adjectives," and quipped, "...when you see Buick, you've seen the best of the bunch."

Originally published in Special Interest Autos #161, Sept.-Oct. 1997

1957 Buick Special

A Better Buick?

by Tim Howley
photos by the author

NINETEEN FIFTY-SEVEN is generally regarded as one of Buick's lesser years, with lousy styling and engineering, production problems, and dismal sales. In fact, Buick did so poorly in 1957 that it fell from third place in the industry in 1955-56 to a poor fourth, then down to fifth in 1958. Buick's 20-year success run was over. Armed with 40 years of bad rumors about the 1957 Buick, we went out and found a very original 1957 Buick Special. What we discovered is a car that is head and shoulders above the hearsay, and well may be the best of all fifties Buicks.

In the fifties the flamboyant Buick was the epitome of American automobiles, and in 1957 it was mostly new—new styling, new chassis, new engine, and new balljoint front suspension. Same old Dynaflow, same old four-coil suspension, which were no bad things. Buick was more interested in ride than roadability, and air-suspension—to come in 1958—would fit a lot better into coil housings than smaller leaf-spring areas. The velvet Dynaflow was a major reason why Buick was so popular during this period.

In the Special and Century, which shared the same body and frame, the chassis was 122 inches and the overall length was 208.4 inches, a 3.4-inch inrease over 1956. In the Super and Roadmaster, the chassis was 127.5 inches and the overall length was 215.3 inches, a whopping 10.3-inch increase over 1956.

About the only thing the 1957 Buick had in common with the 1956 was 15-inch tires. The fresh new styling came out best on the Riviera hardtops, which today are arguably the best-styled Buick

hardtops of the decade, even in the Special line. 1957 Buick Special and Century bodies were 1.2 inches narrower than in 1956 and were 4 inches lower, with no sacrifice in head room. The steering wheel snugs up closer to the driver's lap, and the swept-back windshield gives the driver a false illusion of being closer to the road.

1957 brought bigger engines all across the board. The 322-c.i.d., ohv V-8, which had served Buick well since 1953, was replaced with a bored-out and much advanced 363.5-c.i.d. version for all models. Its 3.4-inch stroke and 4.125-inch bore was the shortest stroke and widest bore of the big V-8s in the industry at the time. In the Special, this engine developed 250 horsepower, in all other models 300. The 300-horsepower engines, with their 10:1 compression ratios, require 98 octane fuel, meaning they need octane booster with today's anemic fuels. The Special,

9.5:1 compression ratio with Dynaflow, 8:1 with manual transmission, and two-barrel carburetor, will run fine on today's premium fuels. The 1957 Buick Special should equal the 1956 Century in performance. All 1957 Buick engines breathe easier than 1956s. Venturi area was increased 30 percent, intake manifold area 36 percent, exhaust manifold area 15 percent, exhaust valves plus 9 percent and intake valves plus 15 percent. Those familiar with vapor lock in earlier Buicks will appreciate the cooler location of the inverted fuel pump. Engine mounts were carefully repositioned to points of minimum vibration.

Dynaflow was standard on all models except the Special. This was changed very little from 1956. The bulky but trouble-free torque tube drive was retained. It is amazing that Buick was able to get the height of their cars down in 1957 without increasing the size of the drive tunnel. An additional U-joint, located just forward of the differential provided for the low drive train tunnel.

Much attention was paid to details in the colorful interiors. The instrument panel was brought up to current safety standards with fully recessed knobs, and standard padding on all models but the Special. An interesting version of the "Redliner" speedometer, instead of flowing across the panel, popped up in little segments as your

1957 Buick Special

speed increased. The top of the panel is easily removable for service access. Windshield wipers and washer controls were moved to a convenient spot adjacent to the driver's left hand. Combination heater air-conditioner controls to the driver's right were redesigned to be more complicated.

As all cars got bigger and heavier in the late fifties, they became notorious for brake fade. 1957 Buicks, which stopped about as well as the Queen Mary, had only 192.7 square inches of brake swept area, far too little for a car with Buick's weight and performance. Lining life was short and fade (brake failure due to overheating) was the norm. In 1958 Buick's brakes would go from just about the worst in the industry to nearly the best. This would be due to the use of finned aluminum drums, more lining area and greatly improved design.

At the beginning of this article we pointed out that with the 1957 model, everything at Buick went downhill. The car's gross misfortunes really began with Harley Earl's 1955 Park Avenue show car,

which set the design themes for the 1957 Cadillac, Buick and Oldsmobile, and in 1958 were carried over into Pontiac and Chevrolet. Harlow Curtice, who for years had picked winners, somehow got hooked on these 1957 design proposals, approving them enthusiastically. When the 1957 Buick, Cadillac and Oldsmobile were designed, GM was totally unaware of the 1957 Chrysler designs. When top GM stylists finally saw the Chrysler products in a storage lot, panic set in and the 1959 GM cars were totally redesigned.

Styling for the 1957 Buick was linked closely to two Buick show cars

of the time, the Centurion and the Wildcat III.

Buick, which had been riding high in 1955, saw a sales slump in '56 due to quality control problems and declining sales for the industry. Then came the '57 which turned off the buyers right and left. General Motors president Harlow Curtice is said to have loved the '57 Buick. Dealers were less enthusiastic. Lack of sales soured them on the design completely. In retrospect, the '57 Buick was a good design, but it was not perceived as such in 1957. The model year was further marred by a bad reputation for the mechanics and assembly. A strong case could be made that the 1957 Buick suffered from the division's poorest quality control ever. This was because, with sky-rocketing sales in 1955 and 1956, Buick could not maintain quality control. Quality control began to fall down in 1955, got worse in 1956 and reached its bottom in 1957-58. The poor guy who got blamed for it all at Buick was Ed Ragsdale, a 34-year veteran of Buick engineering, and Buick manufacturing manager since 1949. He just happened to be in the wrong place at the wrong time. In 1956 he was made Buick division head, succeeding Curtis and

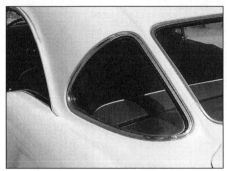

*Facing page, top: Grille design shows continuity from previous years. **Bottom:** Hood ornament was updated. **This page, top left:** Fuel filler lid was part of bumper. **Above left:** Triple rear window treatment was breakthrough from wraparound style. **Above:** The '57 Buick still favors a soft ride over taut handling. **Below:** Wheelbase looks a lot longer than 10 feet, 2 inches.*

Ivan Wiles, two tough acts to follow. By this time both the '57 and '58 designs were "locked in." A mild recession was looming and the import attack was on.

Buick's problems were only beginning in 1957. Buick's peak year of production in the fifties was 1955 at 737,035, a banner year for the industry. Buick production dropped to 635,158 in 1956, which was not as good a year for the industry as 1955. Production dropped further to 404,049 in 1957, due to the economy in general and Buick's growing poor reputation in particular. Production dropped even further in 1958 to 240,659, and Buick fell from fourth place in the industry to fifth. Things got no better in 1959 with completely new models and even a disowning of the old Buick surnames. Even though production was up to 284,248, Buick moved down to seventh place. Harlow Curtice, head of GM, retired in 1958, Harley Earl retired at the end of 1959. Ragsdale,

without allies, was out once the 1959 models proved to be another bomb. Ned Nickles got the blame for the '57-'58 Buick designs, but he survived. Buick's great years as a car were far from over, but holding third or fourth place in the industry was now beyond the Buick division's wildest dreams.

Driving Impressions

The car featured is a mostly original 1957 Buick Special owned by Doug Nurse, of Fallbrook, California. It is a 69,000-mile Arizona car, which was always garaged. Doug is the second owner. As far as the present owner knows, the engine has never been rebuilt. Even though the car is a Special, it has the quality and detail of a far more expensive car, and certainly is not lacking in chrome and stainless inside and out. The most striking feature of this car is the exterior two-tone

color, a light pinkish-beige with pale turquoise below the distinctive Riviera Sweptspear. This color combination was not popular in 1957. Today it is extremely contemporary, especially in southern California.

If you have driven a 1956 Buick you will find that the 1957's ride is definitely superior. It is firmer, and the new balljoint front suspension design cuts braking dive considerably. Buick's front end was greatly reworked for 1957 to improve handling and eliminate erratic braking. The silk-smooth Dynaflow was arguably the smoothest transmission in the industry at the time, and still impresses us after 40 years. New Variable Pitch Dynaflow was standard on the Roadmaster, Super and Century, but not the Special.

Here's what *Motor Trend* said in road testing a 1957 Buick Century. "Buick's highway handling, greatly favored by some, is too mushy for us. On bad dips

specifications

illustrations by Russell von Sauers, The Graphic Automobile Studio

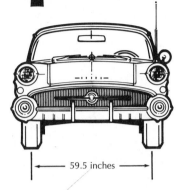
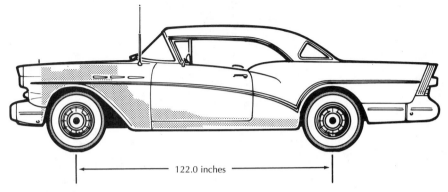

59.5 inches

122.0 inches

1957 Buick Special Series 40 Riviera two-door hardtop

Base price	$2,704
Price as equipped	Approximately $3,300
Std. Special equipment	Red-line speedometer, trip mileage indicator, glovebox lamp, dual horns, directional lights, dual sunshades
Options on dR car	Dynaflow, power brakes, front bumper guards, carpeted floors, padded instrument panel, outside rearview mirror on driver's side, seat belts, Sonomatic radio, electric clock, backup lights, white sidewall tires

ENGINE

Type	Ohv V-8
Bore x stroke	4.125 inches x 3.4 inches
Displacement	363.5 cubic inches
Compression ratio	9.5:1
Horsepower @ rpm	250 @ 4,400
Max. torque @ rpm	380 @ 2,400
Main bearings	5
Induction system	Stromberg or Carter 2-bbl down-draft carb.
Ignition system	12-volt
Fuel system	Camshaft-driven vacuum pump
Exhaust system	Single
Valves	Hydraulic lifters, mechanically adjustable

TRANSMISSION

Type	Automatic variable-pitch Dynaflow 2-speed planetary gearset with torque converter
Ratios: 1st	1.82:1
2nd	1.00:1
Reverse	1.82:1
Max. ratio at stall	310 @ 1,500

DIFFERENTIAL

Type	Hypoid
Ratio	3.07:1
Drive axles	Semi-floating

STEERING

Type	Saginaw recirculating ball nut, power assisted
Turns lock-to-lock	5.0
Ratios	17.5:1 gear; 19.7:1 overall
Turning circle	43.2 feet

BRAKES

Type	4-wheel hydraulic, power assisted, cast-iron drums
Drum diameter	12 inches
Effective area	192.7 square inches

CHASSIS & BODY

Construction	Body-on-frame
Frame	Channel section with K member
Body	All steel
Body style	2-door hardtop

SUSPENSION

Front	Independent ball-joint type, coil springs, double-acting shock absorbers, direct type, ride stabilizer
Rear	Coil springs, double-acting shock absorbers, direct type
Tires	7.10 x 15 four-ply tubeless

WEIGHTS AND MEASURES

Wheelbase	122 inches
Overall length	208.5 inches
Overall width	74.8 inches
Overall height	58 inches
Front track	59.5 inches
Rear track	59 inches
Curb weight	3,956 pounds

INTERIOR MEASUREMENTS

Head room	35.5 inches
Leg room (front)	43.5 inches
Hip room	62.6 inches
Shoulder room	56.9 inches

CAPACITIES

Crankcase	5 quarts (with filter)
Cooling system	18 quarts
Fuel tank	20 gallons
Transmission	22 pints

PERFORMANCE

Top speed	110 mph
Acceleration: 0-60 mph	9.6 seconds
30-50 mph	4.1 seconds
40-60 mph	5.0 seconds
50-80 mph	11 seconds
Standing 1/4 mile	17.1 seconds/80.5 mph
Fuel mileage	10.3 in traffic, 11.1 average

Source: *Motor Trend*, for a 1956 Buick Century

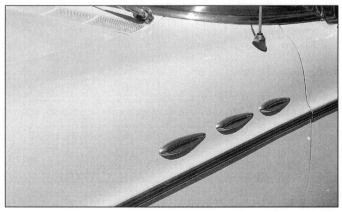

1957 Buick Special

it loses its head, coming out with a great bounding and wallowing that could mean trouble. Sharp curves mean discomfort, mental and physical, for the driver... Wind gusts and high crowns have practically no effect on your smooth progress. Jerk the wheel sharply and the car will find its previous course as though it had an automatic pilot, even if you're on a rough road. When Buick licks its marshmallow handling and its shakes, it will be a car for even more makes to worry about....

"Buick still rides like a pillow, soft and floating.... Stiffer shocks would make connoisseurs happier and would perhaps please even soft-ride lovers."

Surprisingly, *MT* did not find the 300-horsepower 1957 Century as hot as the 236-horsepower '56. Zero to 60 time was down to 10.1 seconds from 9.6 in 1956. They did, however, find an improvement in passing speeds. And, as *Motor Life* noted, "Practically no other make equipped with an automatic transmission will attain a true 60 mph, with the selector level held in low all the way." This publication attained a 0-60 time of 8.7 seconds using low and drive, 9.3 seconds using drive alone, still not as good as their 1956 Buick Century figures.

Brakes were still the big criticism: 192.7 square inches of brake swept area were simply not enough, even in the Special. *MT* found brake fade on the fourth hard stop. Swerving to the left or right was also noted after many stops.

So why did the 1957 Buick fare so poorly in the marketplace?

As we said at the beginning of this article, the flamboyant Buick was the epitome of American automobiles in the fifties. Buick built its entire advertising

Facing page: Wraparound windshields first appeared on Buicks in 1954; "ventiports," now simply chrome accents, came out in 1949. **Above:** *Special doesn't lack for dig. It could crack zero to 60 in under 11 seconds.* **Below:** *Dipped beltline was developed from GM show cars like the LeSabre.*

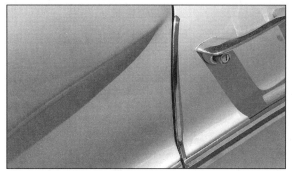

and marketing strategy on the theory that for a little more money, the Ford, Chevy and Plymouth buyer could move up to a Buick Special. Unfortunately, at the very time of the 1957 Buick's introduction a new counter car move was shaping up. That was to the Volkswagen and other small imports. Buick, which for years had stood as the American dream, suddenly became the height of all that was wrong with American cars—big, flamboyant, dripping with chrome, gas guzzling etc. But Buick was not alone in being rejected en masse. The 1958 Edsel, built to the same ideals, fell for all the same reasons as the 1957 Buick. The all-new 1957 Plymouth also proved formidable competition for the 1957 Buick Special—and Century.

Buick Riviera History

Hardtops, the darlings of the fifties, began with the 1949 Buick Riviera. This was a mid-year introduction, soon followed by the 1949 Cadillac Coupe de Ville and 1949 Oldsmobile 98 Holiday. In 1949, the Riviera was only available in the Roadmaster series. The distinctive Sweptspear was not available on the very earliest models, it was adapted during the 1949 model year.

According to the often told story, Sarah Ragsdale, wife of Buick's manufacturing manager Ed Ragsdale, always drove a convertible but never lowered the top. Hence, Ragsdale encouraged the production development of a convertible with a permanent top welded to it. The actual design development came from Buick's chief designer, Ned Nickles, who as early as 1945 was developing hardtops independent of Ragsdale. Independent of GM, Chrysler in 1946 built seven Town & Country hardtops. In 1949, Kaiser offered the Virginian four-door hardtop. So who's to say where the idea originated?

What's important is that Buick's fore-sighted division head, Harlow "Red" Curtice, pushed the hardtop concept into mass production during the 1949 model year. Chrysler quickly followed with hardtops for Chrysler, DeSoto and Dodge in 1950, Plymouth in 1951. Studebaker and Hudson had hardtops in 1951. Ford was a hardtop latecomer, introducing the body style in Ford only in mid 1951, then in Mercury and Lincoln in 1952.

Buick expanded the Riviera hardtop concept to the Super in the Special in 1951. From 1951 on, the Riviera's Sweptspear was used loosely on all Buick models. In 1959 the Riviera name and the Sweptspear disappeared. The Riviera returned in 1963 as a new personal luxury Buick to compete with the Thunderbird.

Going back to the fifties, by 1955 nearly one third of the automobiles produced in this country were hardtops. The hardtop concept continued to dominate the industry until federal safety requirements and the emergence of utility vehicles made the impractical but fun-loving hardtop obsolete.

*Above left and right: Interior is fairly conservative for mid-fifties design. **Below:** V-8 is rated at 250 bhp. **Right:** Dash design is a riot of rectangles and circles.*

Acknowledgments and Bibliography

Dunham, Terry B. and Lawrence R. Gustin, The Buick: A Complete history; Lodge, Jim, "Road Test, '56 Buick Special and Century," Motor Trend, June 1956; "1957 Buick Century Road Test," Motor Life, February, 1957; Molson, Pete, "Driving the Hot 3," Motor Trend, February 1957; Norbye, Jan P. and Jim Dunne, Buick: The Postwar Years; Krause Publications, Standard Catalog of Buick, 1903-1990.

Special thanks to Doug Nurse, Fallbrook, California, for furnishing our driveReport car.

Fifties Buick Special Popularity

In the fifties the Buick Special nearly dominated the price range just above Ford, Chevrolet and Plymouth. In 1950 the Special engine was the 248-c.i.d., overhead-valve straight eight, an engine unique to the Special. In 1951 and 1952 the Special shared the 263.3-c.i.d., straight eight with the Buick Super. In 1953, when other Buick models received a 322-c.i.d., ohv V-8, the Special retained the 263.3-c.i.d. straight eight. But always, the Special only had a three-speed manual transmission as standard equipment, Dynaflow being an option. In 1954 the Special received a 264-c.i.d., ohv V-8, and in 1956 it received a detuned version of the 322-c.i.d. V-8. In 1957-58, the Special shared the 363.5-c.i.d. V-8 with the Super and Roadmaster.

In 1957, Buick produced 220,242 Specials, more than half of the division's total production. This was more than the combined production of the Mercury Monterey and DeSoto Firesweep. Of all Buick's 22 1957 models, the Special two-door hardtop was the most popular, with 64,425 produced, more than even the Buick Special four-door sedan. Feeling the sting of declining sales, Buick introduced a whole new generation of cars for 1959: LeSabre, Invicta, Electra and Electra 225, ending the Special, Super and Roadmaster era. But for 22 years, 1936-1958, the Special was the main reason why Buick was able to give Ford, Chevrolet and Plymouth major competition.

1957 Buick Special

In addition, Buick quality reached its lowest point in 1957, as we noted earlier. If Buick couldn't get its factory act together with the 1956 models, which were now three-year-old designs, then how could there be any improvement with such a radically new car as the '57? While Buick dealers worked overtime to correct the construction flaws of 1957 Buicks, the word got around fast that the 1957 Buick was a car to be avoided like Adlai Stevenson for President. The truth is that the 1957 Buick was a great car once the bugs were worked out, and Stevenson would have been a great President had he resoled his shoes. Given the tenor of the times, neither the 1957 Buick or Stevenson had a chance. ᐅ

*Above right: Taillamps are refinement of '55-'56 design. **Above:** Speedo is ribbon-style.*

Color Gallery

Photograph by Bud Juneau

1920 Model K-44 Roadster
For 1920, Buick had six models to chose from. All rode on a 124-inch wheelbase with wood-spoke wheels and were powered by a 60hp, 242 cu.in., in-line six-cylinder engine. A total of 19,000 Roadsters were built this year and cost $1,495. A front bumper and spotlight were options.

Photograph by Bud Juneau

1932 Series 60 Sport Phaeton
Buick freshened up its lineup for 1932 with new styling that included raked windshield and tapered grille. Hood doors replaced the side louvers. The 90hp, 272.6-cu.in. in-line eight was retained but was fitted with a new 3-speed gearbox. Only 79 Series 60 Sport Phaetons were built this year and cost $1,390.

1936 Special Business Coupe
Turret-top bodies and fresh new styling were some of the 1936 Buick's features. An improved independent front suspension and alloy pistons were some of its mechanical hallmarks. Priced at $765, the Special Business Coupe, with 93hp, 233 in-line eight, was the most affordable Buick in 1932.

Photograph by Bud Juneau

1937 Century Sport Coupe
With an official test speed of over 100 mph, the 1937 Century lived up to its name. Its 320-cu.in. straight-eight made 130hp; its chassis stretched to 126-inches, and new styling treatment included a lower body and revised grille. Buick sold 2,840 Century Sport Coupes, which had a sticker price of $1,187.

Photograph by Bud Juneau

1948 Roadmaster Estate Wagon
With only 350 models built, the $3,433 Roadmaster Estate Wagon, with upper wood paneling, was the rarest of all 1948 Buicks. A 144hp, 320.2-cu.in. Straight Eight was standard power for all Roadmasters, but custom trim and cloth upholstery with leather bolsters were optional.

Photograph by Jim Tanji

1949 Roadmaster Riviera Hardtop Coupe
Considered to be the first domestic production hardtop, the 1949 Roadmaster Riviera, sans B-pillar, had all-new styling, shorter, 126-inch wheelbase, and the venerable 320 straight eight for power. At $3,203, the Riviera hardtop coupe was the most expensive Buick this year.

Photograph by David Gooley

1955 Riviera

Restyled sheet metal from the previous year included a revised nose, tastefully restrained grille treatment, and sleeker quarter panels. The 1955 Buick Roadmaster used a 236hp, 322 cu.in. V-8 engine and Dynaflow-drive automatic transmission as standard equipment.

Photograph by Tim Howley

1957 Special

The 1957 Buick had a wider and lower body, while three ventiports on each front fender were cues of the base-model Special. Standard power was a new, 250hp, 364-cu.in. V-8, and Dynaflow drive was a $220 option. With more than 64,000 sold, the hardtop coupe was the best-selling Special this year.

Photograph by Bud Juneau

1957 Century Caballero

Found in the Century line, the 4-door Caballero station wagon used a high-compression, 364-cu.in. V-8 that made 300hp. Its 4,498-pound overall weight was just two pounds lighter than the Roadmaster convertible. Total 1957 Caballero output was 10,186; they were priced at $3,830.

Photograph by Terry Boyce

1958 Limited convertible

For 1958, Buick, restyled its cars with bulkier bodies, quad headlights, and lots of chrome. The top model was the Limited, which measured 227 inches, bumper to bumper. It had 12 vertical louvers in the rear fenders, cloth and leather interior, and used a 300hp, 364-cu.in. V-8 for power.

Photograph by Rick Lenz

Photograph by David Newhardt

1962 Wildcat

As part of the Invicta line, the Wildcat Sports Coupe had a long, low body, with bucket seats, console, tachometer, and dual exhaust as standard equipment. A 325hp, 401-cu.in. V-8 and Dual Range Turbo Drive automatic transmission were used in this, Buick's high-performance offering for 1962.

1964 Wildcat

Liberally trimmed with brightwork, the 4,000-lb. Wildcat was more of a high-speed highway cruiser by 1964. Top-performance engine was the optional 360hp 425-cu.in. V-8 with two four-barrel carburetors. With a $3,200 price tag, 22,900 Wildcat Sport Coupes were sold this year.

Photograph by David Newhardt

1965 Riviera GS

With hide-away headlights and cleaner rear-deck styling, the Riviera was the most unique offering from Buick in 1965. Cars ordered with the Gran Sport option came with a 360hp, dual-quad, 425-cu.in. V-8, Super Turbine transmission, dual exhaust, and positive-traction rear axle.

Photograph by David Gooley

1965 Electra

The Electra received a new grille and revised rear-end styling for 1965. Its rear-wheel skirts and ribbed lower-body molding were retained from the previous year. Standard features included a 325hp, 401-cu.in. V-8, Super Turbine transmission, power steering, power brakes, and many other amenities.

Photograph by Robert Gross

1967 GS 340

Sharing the same body as the GS 400, the one-year-only GS 340 had a smaller engine and offered more balanced performance. Available in either silver or white, with red side stripes, fewer than 3,700 were built; a 260hp, 340-cu.in. V-8 engine and Super Turbine 300 automatic came standard.

Photograph by Richard Lentinello

1972 GSX

Based on the intermediate Skylark, the high-performance GSX came equipped with a 225hp, 455-cu.in. V-8, though an optional Stage 1 version that made 270hp was available. A four-speed manual transmission was optional. Of the 8,500 Gran Sports built this year, only 44 were GSXs.

Paragon of Excess

by Terry Boyce
photos by the author

1958 Buick Limited

Perhaps no car better epitomizes the grandiose use of chrome for chrome's sake than the 1958 Buick Limited. Some parts of the car look as though the shiny stuff was slathered on with a trowel. Grille is composed of 160 .75-inch chrome squares. Accessory continental kit is ultimate gild-the-lily touch.

MORE THAN any other products, the optimistic excess of the fifties was reflected by the big American cars of 1958. Garish, impractical, gadget-laden, they would be remembered as symbols of the improvident attitudes characterizing those times.

The auto industry had been enjoying good times. The year 1955 had been the best ever, and there seemed to be no place to go but up. But sales fell off in 1956. Then, in 1957, came another downturn.

Detroit was worried. They turned to those commercial sociologists, their marketing people, for guidance. Market research indicated buyers were on a plateau. Top-of-the-line models weren't far enough out of reach any more. The industry had upgraded their customers beyond the furthest advancement offered by the product. According to Vance Packard, in his book *The Status Seekers*, the Institute for Motivational Research was still saying as late as 1958 that the auto industry's opportunities might "...lie in the direction of more elegance and exclusiveness."

The obvious solution was to extend

the product up the socioeconomic ladder a rung or two, opening profitable new vistas. The marketing research reading was false, the treatment faulty. But before anyone could correct it we had cars like the 1958 Edsel and the 1958 Buick Limited in our midst.

General Motors heartily endorsed the concept of pushing their products upwards. All of their lines but Oldsmobile were capped with new models during 1957-1958. Chevrolet brought out the Impala to succeed the Bel Air in 1958. Pontiac made their Bonneville into a new luxury series. Buick split the Roadmaster line into two series for 1957, then drove the point home with the Limited in 1958. Cadillac, searching for summits beyond the previously charted limits of status, continued with their Eldorado Broughams.

The Edsel, of course, would become the most famous flop of 1958. But neither it nor the rest of the U.S. car offerings could compete with the 1958 Buick Limited for our title, Paragon of Excess.

The Limited was perhaps the biggest, most chromed, and most corpulent of them all. It was created by the same expediency Olds had used to thrust their 98 into the lower reaches of the luxury market: by extending the rear deck (size equals dollars equals status) and by using exclusive brightwork.

To stretch the 1958 Buick Roadmaster 75 was definite overkill. The 75, at 219 inches overall, already had plenty of metal overhanging its 127.5-inch wheelbase. Buick's stylists, under Ned Nickles, extended the Roadmaster's deck eight inches without altering the wheelbase. The resulting behemoth ran

a tape out to 227 inches, giving the customer a car that could only be nosed out in this dimension by another great whale of the fifties, the '58 Lincoln.

The speeding-bullet motif adorning the sides of lesser '58 Buicks was replaced with three sets of fake louvers on the Limited's flanks. Special trim on the rear deck included a finely detailed metalized Buick crest, one of the Limited's few touches reminiscent of its pre-World War II ancestors. (Buick's 1958 literature did not allude to the new Limited's distinguished predecessors, incidentally, which is unfortunate, for the Limited indeed had a proud namesake in the 1936-1942 models.)

Taillights, mounted in the vertical "Tail Towers," as Buick called their tail fins, were given chrome grilles on the Limited, which was also the only Buick to have full chrome gravel shields between rear wheel wells and bumper. The Limited's frontal sheet metal was shared with other 1958 Buicks, as was the brightwork. The grille was made up of 160¾-inch chrome squares. It was the most influential styling on the car. Imitations, usually fashioned from drawer pulls, adorned numerous "show customs" for years to come. The massive front end looked best on the Limited, where it was more proportionately correct, than on smaller series Buicks.

Nobody could accuse the stylists of any 1958 big car of tying their brightwork together in an integrated design. On the Buick, the 1958 version of their sweepspear was a nice touch, flowing out of the headlamp bezel down to the rear wheel opening. The nearly closed rear wheel houses were greatly revised from the wide open spaces of 1955-1957, and they added to the overweight look of the 1958 cars.

Gone in 1958 were the famous Buick VentiPorts, or "portholes," that had identified Buicks for nine years. Perhaps it was felt they were excessive. By personal insistence of Ed Ragsdale, Buick's General Manager, the 1958 cars retained 15-inch wheels in a time when nearly all the competition was shifting to 14-inchers. The wheels on all 1958

Buicks were finished in bright red as a standard color, a colorful but old-timey touch.

The 1958 Buick large sales catalog, at 36 pages and measuring 14 x 11 inches, was excessive itself. Strangely, it promoted the cars as being lighter and more graceful through the use of aluminum. Still, it bragged about the car's size: "...this big, bold, buoyant B-58 Buick...is literally born out of more aviation principles, starting with its extensive new use of aluminum throughout, than any car before."

The slogan for 1958 was, "The Air-Born B-58 Buick," which in the case of cars equipped with Air-Poise suspension was a literal statement (see sidebar, p.71).

Everything on the '58s looked heavier. The bumpers were fattened to grotesque proportions (the rear bumper was touted as the industry's largest). Only the front bumper guards looked curiously dainty; they were absolutely little sisters compared to the Marilyn Monroes on contemporary Cadillacs.

Inside the Limited and Roadmaster 75, it was the living room on wheels approach taken a step beyond. Even the door panels were upholstered, right to the windows. Chrome was everywhere, slathered across the dash and trim panels in streaks. Limited convertibles were trimmed in Cape Buffalo grain top quality leather, available in four solid and three two-tone combinations.

The Limited, "proudly presented and proudly possessed," came in three models: the four-door Riviera, Model 750; the two-door Riviera, Model 755; and the convertible, Model 756. Down the ladder at Buick in 1958, in order of declining price tags, was the Roadmaster 75 (there was no plain Roadmaster In '58), the Super, Century, and Special.

A fully equipped Limited convertible could cost almost double the base price for the lowliest Special. With Air-Poise on nearly every car, few if any Limiteds listed out for less than $5,000. A host of power accessories was standard on the Roadmaster 75 and Limited (see specifi-

Limited's taillamps have chrome accents. Angle of lamps and the chrome combine to make them nigh-impossible to see if you're following in a taller vehicle. **Right:** *Disparate styling ideas mark front end. It's a potpourri of circles, squares, horizontal lines.*

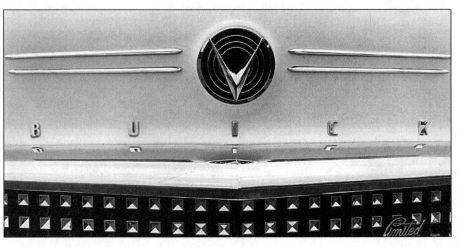

cations). The Limited buyer could add air conditioning, Sonomatic, or Wonder Bar radio (with power antenna extra), Autronic Eye headlight dimmer, E-Z-Eye glass, and a Perimeter heater (an extra heater assembly under the front seat) as options.

Buick was beating three drums on the mechanical side in 1958. Two of the year's heavily promoted innovations turned out to be turkeys. One was a genuine improvement. The turkeys were Air-Poise Suspension and Flight Pitch Dynaflow. The improvement was the aluminum brake drums, standard on all models except the Special, where they were optional at extra cost.

Air-Poise was a pressurized air suspension system using air bags in place of coil steel springs. It was a disaster, as it was on all the other GM car lines, and didn't survive the year in its original form (see sidebar, p.71).

Flight Pitch Dynaflow would be eventually developed into the reliable Triple Turbine Buick transmission, but the original 1958 version qualifies as a turkey. The Flight Pitch sounded like it slipped more than the original 1948 Dynaflow. Gas consumption, especially in city driving, was terrible, giving expensive testimony that the slippage was more than sound.

Flight Pitch was standard on the Limited and Roadmaster 75, and available optionally on other series. *Buick Magazine* described how it worked in this way:

"Flight Pitch Dynaflow is a triple-turbine unit with an infinite number of positions for the variable stator blades. Three converter turbines share the job of transmitting torque. Each turbine adds to the driving force with the smooth transition from starting to normal vehicle speed that is a Buick trademark.

"As you accelerate, the first turbine starts you in motion. As the power is increased, the first turbine gradually distributes the load to the second turbine, and this gradual transition continues to the third turbine as engine and car speed level off."

The first and second turbines freewheeled at cruising speed, but cut back in if the throttle was applied. There were "literally a million ways to switch the pitch" of the stators in the three turbines.

"There has never been performance like you get with the new Flight Pitch Dynaflow," *Buick Magazine* promised.

Don Francisco, testing a pair of 1958 Buicks for *Motor Trend*, sort of agreed. He wrote, "The first impression I got when I stepped on the throttle...was one of extreme slippage...engine speed went up with throttle movement, but the car didn't accelerate as it should have. To get the car moving fast enough to

Above: *Chrome sweepspear helps to further emphasize the gargantuan length of the Limited. All '58 Buicks shared the sweepspear, but only Limited carried special rear fender inserts consisting of twelve vertical chrome spears on each side.* **Below:** *Combo spotlight/mirror follows wraparound windshield styling.*

keep up with normal traffic it was necessary to push the throttle to the floor, where the converter ratio changed to a still lower pitch...acceleration to pass another car was out of the question without shoving the throttle to the floor."

Francisco found the Variable-Pitch twin-turbine Dynaflow, standard on Century and Super models, optional on the Special, to be much more responsive.

The one talking point Buick salesmen had in 1958 which was really good news for the customer was the vastly improved brakes. Buick brakes were well known for their lack of stamina in the mid-1950s. Although the immediate predecessors of the B-58 had fairly good brakes, the bad publicity was something Buick felt they had to overcome. This they did with some fine binders for 1958.

Buick's famous aluminum brakes were developed under engineers Frank Daley and Charles D. Holton. The aluminum drums, used on the front assemblies only, used a pearlite iron

liner for contact with the brake shoes. A total of 45 cooling fins spaced radially around the drum, rising to about 1/3-inch height at the flared rim of the drum, helped dissipate heat build-up.

The aluminum drums were first offered on the 1957 Roadmaster 75.

How good were they in 1958? Don Francisco had this to say about Buick's brakes, in *Motor Trend*: "The stopping ability of the brakes was excellent under normal conditions." That might not sound extravagant, but it was virtually

specifications

Illustrations by Russ von Sauers, The Graphic Automobile Studio

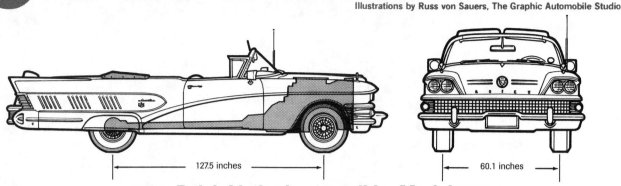

127.5 inches   60.1 inches

1958 Buick Limited convertible, Model 756

Price when new	$4,663 f.o.b. factory	**DIFFERENTIAL**	
Std. equip.	Flight Pitch Dynaflow, carb-uretor, dual exhausts, power steering, power brakes, elec-tric windows, 6-way power seat, glare-proof rear view mirror, speed safety buzzer, electric clock, padded instru-ment panel cover, trip mile-age indicator, windshield washers, foam-backed car-peting, backup lights, Deluxe wheel covers, Lucite paint	Type	Conventional
		Ratio	3.23:1
		Drive axles	Semi-floating, hypoid gears

DIFFERENTIAL
Type — Conventional
Ratio — 3.23:1
Drive axles — Semi-floating, hypoid gears

STEERING
Type — Recirculating ball nut, power assisted, overall ratio 19.7:1
Turns lock-to-lock — 4.0
Turn circle — 42 feet

BRAKES
Type — 4-wheel hydraulic, air-cooled aluminum drums on front, cast-iron on rear, 12-inch diameter, power assisted, step-on parking brake

CHASSIS & BODY
Frame — Rigid I-beam center cross-member, channel-type side-rails, 5 crossmembers
Body construction — Welded steel body
Body style — 6-pass. convertible coupe

SUSPENSION
Front — Coil springs, double-acting shock absorbers, direct type, ride stabilizer

ENGINE
Type — High-compression, ohv V-8
Bore x stroke — 4.125 inches x 3.4 inches
Displacement — 364 cubic inches
Max. bhp @ rpm — 300 @ 4,600
Max. torque @ rpm — 400 @ 3,200
Compression ratio — 10.0:1
Induction system — One 4-barrel carb
Exhaust system — "Y" manifolds to dual ex-haust mufflers an resonators
Electrical system — 12-volt battery/coil

TRANSMISSION
Type — Fully automatic, torque con-verter, three turbines
Max. torque ratio stall — 4.5 @ 3,200

Rear — Coil springs, sway control by radius rod, double acting shock absorbers, direct type
Tires — 8.00 x 15, 4-ply, tubeless
Wheels — 15 x 6 steel disc, five-lug bolts

WEIGHTS AND MEASURES
Wheelbase — 127.5 inches
Overall length — 227.1 inches
Overall width — 79.8 inches
Front track — 60.1 inches
Rear track — 61.0 inches
Shipping weight — 4,691 pounds

CAPACITIES
Crankcase — 6 quarts (with filter)
Cooling system — 18 quarts
Fuel tank — 20 gallons, anti-rust fuel line

FUEL CONSUMPTION
Best — 18 mpg.
Average — 10-12 mpg.
Required octane — Premium

---

the nicest thing Francisco had to say about the 1958 Buicks. The aluminum drums really worked to prevent brake fade. Francisco found that both the B-58s he drove could make more than a dozen full panic stops before serious fade set in. Most cars of the time lost their brakes by the sixth stop.

Buick hungrily pursued publicity for their new brakes, and they got it. NASCAR gave Buick a first-ever safety award for the 1958 brake system. Bill France said, in presenting the award, "We put these brakes through as diffi-cult a test as we could devise on the courses here at Daytona Beach, and they were outstanding. We drove the cars from standstill to 60 mph, slammed on the brakes in a 'panic' stop, then drove on again, getting up to 60 mph as quickly as possible so there was no chance of the brakes cooling off. The

Buick was able to repeat this tough maneuver *176* times—and still had safe brakes.

Sports Car Illustrated said Buick's brakes were the "...best brakes on a Detroit sedan by far...they are conserv-atively a 100 percent improvement over conventional Detroit brakes."

Praise was also forthcoming from

Extremely long rear fender line on the Limiteds makes the front end seem some-what stubby by comparison.

Motor Life for the aluminum brakes. Although the magazines pointed it out, nowhere in Buick's 1958 sales literature did it mention the aluminum drums were on the front wheels only. The 1958 Buicks got finned but still cast-iron drums on the rear, too.

Under the hood, 1958 Buicks were hardly changed from the year before. Ed Ragsdale mentioned a new generator in his springtime *Buick Magazine* article and there was frequent talk of an im-proved electrical system in sales litera-ture. The first Rochester four-barrel carbs made their debut atop the 300 hp, two-barrel version of the same engine. (For a complete review of Buick engines in the mid-1950s, see *SIA #47*, Buick Goes to V-8 Power.)

Without any real news in the engine compartment, and right in the middle of the horsepower race, Buick's promotional people must have felt cheated, and felt moved to overcompensate with hype. How else can we charitably explain the B12000?

That's right, the B12000 (no comma, please) B-58 V-8 engine; Among the excesses of 1958, we have what surely will remain the world's only auto engine with a five-digit factory identification. Buick explained: "This spectacular V-8 engine takes its name—B 12000—from the fact that it develops a thrust of 12,000 pounds behind every piston as it is fired." The designation had the ring of an aircraft engine's name, following through on the B-58 theme. Buick outdid even the DV32 Stutz (an eight with four valves per cylinder) with the B12000.

The 300-horsepower Buick V-8 was fettered by the Flight Pitch in the Limited but it could still move the smaller series cars at more than 110 mph. Even the Limited convertible, which neared the two-and-a-half ton mark at the curb, could exceed 100mph, given enough road.

Who were the men responsible for the 1958 Buicks? We've already mentioned Ned Nickles and Ed Ragsdale. Nickles was made Buick's Chief Designer under Harley Earl's central management in 1945. His coups at Buick are famous— the VentiPorts of 1949, the 1953 Skylark, and many more. He directed the styling of all Buicks of the fifties, finally being transferred to Corporate Advanced Styling by Bill Mitchell in 1961. Mitchell had succeeded Harley Earl in 1958 as Vice President in charge of Styling, for GM.

Edward T. Ragsdale was Buick's General Manager during the development and release of the 1958 Buicks. He had been with Buick since 1923, coming to the firm from Buffalo, New York, where he had been a body designer for Pierce-Arrow. His rise through Buick's ranks was steady. In 1935 he became a body engineer, moving to the Assistant Chief Engineer for Bodies post in 1939. (Ragsdale was responsible for Buick's Brunn custom body program in 1940-1941—see *SIA #51*.) He became General Manufacturing Manager at Buick in 1949, then reached the zenith of his promotions when he was appointed General Manager in 1956.

Ragsdale's arrival coincided with the beginning of the end of Buick's winning streak in the mid-1950s. He inherited a number of quality-control problems and an aging, bewildered management staff seeking new directions with uncertainty. Ed Ragsdale had laid the groundwork for Buick's recovery when he retired in the spring of 1959, but the culminating years of his career had been marred by the rough times at Buick in 1957 and 1958.

Flight Pitch Dynaflow and Air-Poise

Above: Buick's wallowy air suspension, great length, and weight combine to give Limiteds mushy, tire-screeching cornering ability. It's a real handful even at low speeds. ***Below left:*** You were expecting restraint on the inside? Again, a dazzling show of chrome surrounds ribbon speedometer, full set of gauges. There's nothing subtle about the Limited dashboard. ***Below right:*** Limited identification abounds on rear fenders, shown here, as well as on grille, trunk, dashboard.

were unfortunate developments occurring during the short tenure of Oliver K. Kelley as Buick's Chief Engineer. Kelley was a native of Finland, born in 1902. He came to the United States in 1921, obtained a technical education, and joined Cadillac in 1927. He was transferred to the corporate engineering staff in the early 1930s, where he quickly developed a reputation for his advanced ideas about automatic transmissions.

Kelley might well be called the father of Dynaflow drive. The original 1948 unit sprang directly from his work for General Motors Advanced Engineering. In August 1957 Kelley became Buick's Chief Engineer, succeeding Verner P. Matthews, who retired. Kelley's work with GM Engineering had been largely involved with the evolution of Dynaflow,

and his first priority at Buick was the implementation of the triple-turbine transmission that was introduced, prematurely, as the 1958 Flight Pitch Dynaflow.

Jan Norbye, writing in *Buick–the Postwar Years*, described Kelley as "an engineer's engineer, but his bent was not the administrative work that a divisional chief engineer gets so easily bogged down in. He was not happy when he was separated from the actual hardware or from the drawing board. He had no experience in manufacturing, and could not get used to the Buick timetable, where all the engineering must be finished at the start of the year if production is to begin in August. He was used to working five years or more away from an actual production schedule, and that

During 1958 Buick sponsored the Wells Fargo TV show. To publicize this fact they ran up a special "Wells Fargo" Limited convertible for the series' star, Dale Robertson.

was his main problem at Buick. He made it his most important task at Buick to find a man for his own office so he could return to the Engineering Staff."

It took Kelley two years to find that man, who was Lowell A Kintigh. Kelley turned the reins over to him in December 1959, returning to Advanced Engineering for the Corporation.

The year 1958 was a transitional one for Buick. Harley Earl retired that year. Buick's stylists had been busy settling themselves into the new GM Tech Center while they were finishing up the 1958 design in early 1957. By 1958 they were deep into a completely new styling concept for 1959-1960.

Buick's management ranks were in upheaval, too. By introduction time for the 1959 models, E.C. Kennard, Sales Manager at Buick in the late 1950s, could write that the successors to the B-58s were products of "a new Buick team." Ed Ragsdale, preparing to hand over the top divisional post to Edward D. Rollert, wrote of the changing scene at Buick also, pointing out that the average age in Buick management was 48. The new spirit at Buick disdained the past, so much so that Buick discarded all their old model designations for 1959. Thus, although 1959 mockups carried Limited insignia as late as mid-1957, there would be no more Limiteds after 1958 until the name was resurrected once again for luxury Electra 225s in the 1970s.

Most recently the Limited nameplate has been affixed to the 1980 Skylark Limited, a diminutive luxury Buick for these times. The latest Limited isn't much longer overall than the wheelbase of the 1958 Limited.

Buick was reaching toward the future in other areas during 1958. Despite the predictions of the market research wizards, small cars were coming into their first American vogue. Buick hedged their bets with the importation of Opel Rekords at the rate of 1,000 per month for sale by Buick dealers during that year.

Buick engineers quickly latched onto some of the new Opels for use as test chassis for a new, small aluminum V-8 they were developing for Buick's compact 1961 Special.

The R&D activity couldn't do anything for the 1958 models, though, and the year was a sales disaster. Production was 241,892, down from 405,086 in 1957, which had been a whopping 25 percent nosedive from 1956. The Limited lived up to its name in terms of sales, accounting for only 7,436 cars in 1958—5,571 four-door Rivieras, 1,026 Riviera two-doors, and 839 convertibles.

Market penetration fell to 5.7 percent during the year as Buick tumbled further away from the number three sales slot it had firmly occupied just a few

Top: The Limited convertible's upholstery was extra-plush and made from the finest top-grain leather hides. Above: driveReport car has had 1953 Skylark wheels mounted; production wheel covers were same as used on other series Buicks. Below: "Eyelid" treatment over the quad headlights was a characteristic of '58 Buicks. Fender ornaments were standard throughout Buick line-up in '58.

years before. By the end of the year Buick traded places with Oldsmobile, to rate fifth in sales. A number of Buick dealers, accustomed to the fat years of the first decade after the war, began slipping away.

Some historians claim that 1958 was as bad or worse than 1933 for Buick. This isn't altogether valid, though, for unlike that disastrous Depression year, there was no talk around the GM board room about putting Buick to sleep in 1958.

Driving Impressions

Our driveReport Limited convertible belongs to Aaron Krueger, a young jukebox service man from Wausau, Wisconsin. While we were photographing his big white Buick, Aaron told us about its

history. "The car was purchased new in Green Bay, Wisconsin, by a man from Clintonville, who traded it on a '59. Then, that year the Buick dealer's daughter got married, and he gave this car as a wedding present. They had it until July 4, 1976, when I bought it."

Aaron's Limited convertible carries body number 838, making it the second from last Limited convertible built. Built as a white car, the Limited was painted black, then red, by the previous owners. It was apparently used little in winter and had virtually no rust damage when Aaron acquired it. He had it repainted the original white.

The speedometer was out of the car, broken at 73,000 miles, when Aaron bought it. He estimates it has about 100,000 miles on it now. The red leather interior remains in excellent condition. The original engine and transmission have required little beyond normal maintenance, although the transmission is leaky. It has obviously been a well-maintained car all of its life.

A number of accessories have been added to the Limited since 1976. Chromed fender skirts, dual spotlight-mirrors, a set of 1953 Skylark wire wheels, and a tissue dispenser, to name a few. All are trivial compared to the addition of a Hollywood Accessories continental kit. This appendage to the rear of the Limited is absolutely overwhelming. The Limited measures 19½ feet long with the kit.

We drove the Limited on an overcast and chilly day. We kept the top up on the road, although we lowered it briefly during our photo session.

The first thing that struck us as we slid behind the Limited's big steering wheel was how high we seemed to be, compared to a '57 Buick. We used to have a '57 Roadmaster convertible; in it you nestled down between the rounded tops of the front fenders. Aaron says that the '58 sets higher than the '57 Buick—and it's quite a bit higher than a '58 Olds 98 convertible, too.

Not only does it seem higher, but the car seems narrower. This illusion is caused by the curvature of the hood and nearly invisible front fenders. In fact, the '58 Limited is 1.5 inches wider than a '57 Roadmaster.

Moving into traffic in this land yacht isn't fun. A Pinto trying to squeeze by on the right as we were cutting across lanes for a freeway entrance was as unsettling as being chased by a small yapping dog. We were always conscious of that tremendous overhang aft of the rear wheels.

We were surprised to find the rear fender tops clearly visible in the rear view mirror. The fins, or "towers," were something of an asset, then, in parking the giant Buick. The front fenders have individual bomb-sight ornaments, which also serve as useful guides.

Moving out on the freeway, the Limited felt like it lagged behind the responsive V-8 propelling it. The "nail head" Buicks had some pretty progressive cam timing to compensate for their somewhat small valves, and they were high-revving motors. But the Flight Pitch transmission wasn't able to keep up.

Taking the big Limited up to a cruising speed just over 55, the engine settled into a steady drone. We had prepared ourselves for the Flight Pitch, but still we unconsciously looked at the shift quadrant to see if we were running in an intermediate gear. Nope, it was right there in Drive. Aaron's Limited has a little noisier exhaust system than stock, so we were acutely aware of the engine's noise as we tensed for the overdue shift that would never come.

Flooring the throttle produced a wonderful winding moan from the exhaust, which changed pitch as the carb's secondaries cut in, but the only real feeling of acceleration was visual, as the trees began to speed by faster in our peripheral vision. The slippage in the transmission is very evident during acceleration, and is an obvious factor in the wide variance in mileage between town and highway driving.

The Limited we tested, like all the others that we know of, has been converted from Air-Poise air bags to coil springs. It still has a very soft, billowy ride. At one point we turned up a road toward a very rough stretch. The bumps passed unnoticed beneath our wheels. The air suspension system must have been soft way past the point of overkill if it was softer than the ride on this Limited. We didn't corner too fast, as even moderate speeds, 15 to 20 mph, produced plenty of tire squeal. Although Buick made quite a bit out of their larger stabilizer bar in their 1958 literature, the prospect of the Limited's big tail coming around in a fast turn is enough to keep even the most adventurous driver's foot light on the throttle.

At low speeds this Limited shakes quite a bit. Our test car had some uneven tires, perhaps from its winter slumber. The car seemed especially loose at 30 mph. Above 50 on the freeway there was a surprise. The Limited stopped its dancing and leveled out in a smooth glide, changing almost magically into a very solid, tight machine.

Buick's truly big mechanical news in '58 was their long overdue improvement in the brake system. Our test Limited had the famous aluminum front drums. They functioned as well as their publicity would indicate, bringing the two-ton-and-then-some cruiser down with ease.

The Limited's steering wheel is large, but it gives excellent vision through its spokes to the instruments, which are mounted high on the dash. Buick liked to fool around with speedometers in the Fifties—the '58 Limited has one of those

Air-Poise Suspension

Air suspension Systems were certainly nothing new in 1958 (see *SIA* #17, Air Suspension History), but that was the year Detroit decided the world was ready to ride on air.

The buying public, however, didn't warmly embrace this supposed revolution in suspension systems. Enthusiasm for the bags collapsed quicker than a Cadillac with a ruptured bellows. By 1959 the excitement was almost gone. The handful of surviving air suspension systems amounted to little more than load levelers in their revised designs. Only Cadillac stuck it out, using air suspension on some models through 1960.

Buick jumped right on the GM air suspension wagon; it fit right into their "Air Born" theme for 1958. Their closed system was named Air-Poise. *Buick Magazine* welcomed air suspension with gusto. An article showing a Super floating in the clouds crooned: "You travel on four cylinders of air instead of four coil springs, and the result is satin-smoothness on boulevards and equal smoothness over back country roads. The laws of gravity and centrifugal force are literally pushed aside in this new concept of ride engineering."

It was really a fairly simple system. A small two-cylinder compressor, mounted on the left front of the engine and driving off a belt, pressurized a tank resting between the front frame horns at 290 pounds. The tank, in turn, kept 100 pounds of air pressure in the four rubber bellows supporting the car. Standard shock absorbers were used.

A knob on the instrument panel could raise the car as much as 5.5 inches at the touch of a finger. This was useful for removing hubcaps, or for lifting the Buick over places it really didn't belong anyway without dragging its skirts.

Don Francisco's *Motor Trend* test of a '58 Super with Air-Poise should have killed it right there. He could find absolutely no advantage to the system, and plenty of disadvantages. On even semi-rough roads, Francisco's test car vibrated badly. "On one of the concrete freeways in the Los Angeles area, wheel movements became so bad at the limit of 55 mph that the entire car and the legs of its passengers were vibrating," he wrote. The steering wheel shook so badly that the horn sounded itself a few times.

Out on the open desert road, Francisco found Air-Poise to be very mushy. As the car rose from small dips it would "wallow like a small boat in the surf," he said. It bottomed out hard on the frame in larger dips. Francisco was surprised, and no doubt relieved, to find the suspension handled on par with the coil-spring Century he also drove on tight turns.

By the time Francisco was preparing his article for the May 1958 *Motor Trend*, leakage in the air suspension systems was already "a common problem."

The suspension systems leaked air from the factory, in many cases, due to loose fittings. Ruptured bellows were the next causes of dismay for already dissatisfied owners. Slow leaks were compensated for by the compressor while running, but when stopped overnight, the vehicle would sink to its knees like the original low-rider, if the system leaked.

By mid-year it was evident that Buick had cooled its ardor for air suspension. The splashy copy for Air-Poise at the beginning of the year was quietly tucked away. What little promotional space was given to air suspension referred to it simply as "Air Ride."

For 1959 Buick had a new Air Ride, greatly revised and downplayed. Introducing the 1959s, O.K. Kelley wrote, "Air Ride, introduced last year, has probably undergone the most revolutionary revision. This year's Air Ride combines coil springing with ride stabilizer for the front wheels, and air cylinders with automatic load compensation for the rear wheels."

Buick was keeping a little air in their suspension systems just in case buyers, in their fickle way, decided it was the wave of the future after all. Such was not the case, of course, and by the end of 1959 air suspension had breathed its last at Buick.

helix jobs that gives the impression of a line of fluid spurting across the instrument face during acceleration. It is "highly inaccurate" and rather unsteady in its old age.

The turn-signal indicators on the 1958 Buicks resembled cat's eye marbles. The big green orbs light up brilliantly in time, with a distinct click from the switch. Our remarks about the signals reminded Aaron of a problem he's discovered with the Limited. It seems that drivers of vans and semis cannot see the hooded taillights. Those extra grilles over the rear lamps act as effective visors, making the stop lights invisible to anyone approaching from the rear at an elevated angle.

The Limited's controls are scattered around the instrument panel. We get discouraged at the mandated sameness of today's cars, but a trip in a car of the

Fifties reminds one of why the mandates came. Even the power window switches are out of place, high up on the trailing edge of the instrument panel's cover.

The '58 Buicks had their fuel fillers mounted on the rear bumper, so Aaron Krueger has to unlatch and tip the tire rearward each time he slakes the big Buick's thirst.

Aaron drives his Limited as much as he can during nice weather. He took it to Chicago on an unforgettable cruise.

"Everyone wanted to buy it," he laughs. He has another Limited, a hardtop sedan, that he purchased as a parts car. It is just parked for now, while he fights the urge to restore it, too. Why, we asked Aaron, do you really like the 1958 Buick Limited so much? There was no hesitation in his answer: "Chrome." Then, after a meditative silence, "Yeah!" ஒ

1959 BUICK ELECTRA 225 CONVERTIBLE

by Tim Howley
photos by the author

For 1959 Buick had new styling, new engineering and new advertising. Everything looked right for the rebound that didn't happen.

In the late fifties, after enjoying two decades of growth which eventually brought it into third place, and annual sales reaching nearly three-quarter million in 1955, Buick began slipping on a whole bushel of banana peels. The star of Flint fell to fourth in 1957, fifth in 1958, seventh in 1959, and ninth in 1960. While Buick would rise back to fifth in the late sixties, it would never regain the position and prestige it enjoyed during its golden years under the guidance of Harlow Curtice and later Ivan Wiles. Historians often cite a combination of bad design, bad engineering, and bad management under Edward T. Ragsdale as the primary factors behind Buick's precipitous fall. These are only part of the story. The 1959-60 Buicks were excellent cars from both styling and engineering standpoints. In the end, Ragsdale took the fall for all that went wrong both within the Division and without during this uncertain period.

Even though Buick Centurys were performing impressively in NASCAR in 1955, and production that year reached an unprecedented 737,035, all was not well. Buick was moving ahead much too fast to maintain quality control. The 1956 models were riddled with engi-neering gremlins. This was followed by disastrous 1957 styling, and the brief but stinging Eisenhower recession which began in the fall of that year. Plus, as American cars grew bigger and thirstier, the American car-buying public began looking overseas for smaller, less fuel-addicted transportation.

However, you can't blame Buick completely for the 1957 models. Their bodies were shared with the Pontiac, Oldsmobile, and Cadillac dinosaurs. The basic design for all four makes was initiated by Harley Earl and enthusiastically approved by Harlow Curtice, who became General Motors President in 1953. The Buick Division only gave Buick identity to what John Keats, in his 1959 expose of Detroit, *The Insolent Chariots*, labeled as the height of Detroit excess. If Ragsdale is to be blamed at all, it is for not standing up to Curtice, a tough man to argue with, but a man who loved a good fight.

Ragsdale, who had only a high school education and learned automobile drafting and engineering at Maxwell and Pierce-Arrow, came to Buick in 1923 as a body draftsman. He became a body engineer in 1935, assistant chief engineer in 1939, and general manufacturing manager in 1949. He was well liked, innovative, and a hard worker, but somewhat lacking in the fine art of corporate smooth talk, which held sway at GM headquarters. His credits included designing the first Buick Estate Wagon (1940) and co-designing the 1949 Riviera hardtop convertible with Ned Nickles (See SIA #89).

Buick retained third place in the industry in 1956, the year that Ragsdale became division manager, with 635,158 units produced. He had little say about 1957 and 1958 design because plans were already locked in when he was appointed to the Division's top post. The 1958 may well have been the most ghastly Buick ever built, through little fault of his. It had the new and not necessarily improved Flight-Pitch Dynaflow, disastrous air-bag suspension on all four wheels (optional), and the most excessive use of chrome in Detroit history. There was one real improvement — air-cooled aluminum front brake drums with a radial fin design. Notwithstanding, the public said "yuk" to the 1957 and 1958 Buicks. Production plummeted to 404,049 for 1957 and 240,659 for 1958, the lowest point since 1948.

Even as the 1957 Buicks were dying on the showroom floors and while the 1958 was playing to an empty house, Ragsdale had his mind set on 1959 as the year of rebirth, with Buicks that would look nothing like Buicks. As the new 1959 models were nearing production, Buick management did what management always does when they're in trouble. They fired their advertising agency, the Arthur Kudner Company. Kudner was a pal of Harlow Curtice, and Curtice set him up with his own advertising agency when he launched the revolutionary 1936 models. During the late thirties and early forties Kudner created masterful Buick advertising. Kudner died in 1944, and Curtice moved up to the corporate vice president level in 1948. With a new generation of Buicks on the way for 1959, it was only customary ad practice to fire the old generation of hucksters. The account was turned over to McCann-Erickson, which has handled Buick advertising ever since. The new Delta Wing Buicks were named LeSabre, replacing the Special; Invicta,

Above: Windshield wraps up and over in typical GM fashion of the time.

replacing the Super and Century; Electra, replacing the Roadmaster; and Electra 225, replacing the Limited, which had reappeared only in 1958. The 364-c.i.d., ohv V-8, which had been the sole engine available for 1957 and 1958, was now the LeSabre engine only. All Invictas and Electras had the new 401, which gave improved performance plus better gas economy — about two mpg better than the 1958s (see sidebar, page 74). The new Buick engine was carefully teamed with the transmission and rear end to operate as a unit to give maximum torque at lower speeds. The standard 1959 rear axle was the economy 2.78:1, compared to the higher, 3.23:1 rear-end setup of 1958.

Stylingwise, the new Buicks not only had tail fins, but fins over the headlamps that swept all the way back to the rear bumper. The headlamps were slant-eyed, à la 1958 Lincoln, and the grille design was little chrome blocks, introduced in 1958. The windshield swept up into the roof. On the hardtop models the rear window made a full 90-degree turn, so you could hardly tell whether a new Buick was coming or going. Nor could you tell that it was a Buick. This was the most changed Buick since 1936. In fact, it was the looks that killed the car more

Above: At nearly 19 feet, the Electra occupied plenty of highway. **Below left:** Canted quad headlamps were unique '59 design feature. **Below right:** Like rest of car, wheel covers were all-new design. **Bottom:** Despite size and weight, 325-horse V-8 could move the car from zero to 60 in less than 10 seconds.

FLASH AND FINS

*Above: Buick knight's helmet and V-8 symbol combine on front fender flashes. **Below:** Dash design is pure late '50s flash. **Bottom left:** Big car means big trunk. **Right:** Inside handles are flip-up type. Vents crank open by hand.*

1959 Buick Performance Options

	Standard	Optional
LeSabre	364 engine, synchromesh transmission, 3.58 axle	Twin Turbine, 3.07 axle **Performance Package **Economy Package
Invicta	401 engine, Twin Turbine 3.23 axle	Dual exhausts **Economy Package ***Performance Package
Electra	401 engine, Twin Turbine 3.23 axle	**Economy Package

*Performance Package — Twin Turbine, 3.23 axle, 4-bbl carb, dual exhausts.
**Economy Package — Triple Turbine, 2.78 axle, 4-bbl carb, dual exhausts.
***Performance Package — Triple Turbine, 3.23 axle, dual exhausts.

than anything else. Buyers wanted their Buicks to look like Buicks, and this year Buicks definitely didn't, a major factor behind Buick dropping to seventh place in the industry, although production was up to 284,248. The engineering, which was excellent, still was overshadowed by the 1957-58 image and a recent history of recalls.

The swoopy new bodies were shared with Pontiac, Oldsmobile and, to a lesser extent, Cadillac, with each division incorporating its own distinctive body architecture. The greenhouses of all four makes were nearly identical.

Inside, the new Buicks had two huge instrument pods flanked by two smaller pods. The entire dash layout was very much a Chrysler variation. Even though the car was two inches lower, head room was about the same as the 1958, with 1½ inches stolen out of the seat cushions.

The frame was the new K-type, with boxed side rails, said to reduce longitudinal deflection two thirds over Buick's longstanding X-type frame. "Air Poise" air suspension was offered again as an option, but on the rear wheels only, which was a vast improvement both in ride and reliability from the '58 disaster. The front coils of previous years were returned, only now they allowed for nearly a half-inch more wheel travel. There was a wider and thicker front stabilizer, improved shocks and shock fluid, and the rear track bar was raised over three inches on the rear axle and frame mountings. Both front and rear wheels were set farther apart, but not quite as far as Pontiac's "wide track," which had one-inch-plus-wider track in the front and a four-inch-wider track in the rear than the Buick.

Finned aluminum drums up front were improved for better heat transfer, dimensional stability, and smoother braking surface. Now, finned cast-iron drums were added to the rear.

There were two types of automatic transmissions. Twin Turbine (called Variable Pitch Dynaflow in 1958) had a ratio of 4.7:1 at stall. The Triple Turbine transmission (introduced in 1958 as Flight Pitch Dynaflow) had a new second turbine blade to improve response, and had a maximum starting ratio of 4.75:1. Both transmissions for 1959 were vastly improved for smoothness, reliability, and economy. Flight Pitch Dynaflow, or "triple turbine," was actually a corporate development that Buick executed. It was not a bad transmission after 1958, just ungodly expensive to produce. Some would say the money that Buick spent tooling up for it and producing it contributed as much as any factor to the Division's problems during this period.

When *Motor Trend* asked Oliver "O.K." Kelly, Buick's new chief engineer, about Buick being a "changed" car for '59, he

Driving Impressions

Our driveReport car is a big, white whale of a 1959 Buick Electra 225 convertible, weighing in at 4,465 pounds, measuring 225.4 inches overall, and with a nice excessive 64.45 inches of rear overhang. It symbolizes the height of late fifties Detroit decadence, outfinned only by the 1959 Cadillac and outchromed only by the 1958 Oldsmobile 98 and Buick Limited. An endangered species ever since it hit the used car lots, even though 5,493 of these friendly dragons were built, this particular model represents a magnificent example of Buick's darkest hour. We found the car at Deer Park, an Escondido, California, winery and collection of mostly fifties chromemobiles. Bob Knapp, founder and owner of Deer Park, bought the Buick at Lake Tahoe in 1978. At the time he was driving a 1959 Buick LeSabre convertible. He pulled into a gas station, and the owner began admiring his car. He said he had one just like it for sale. Just like it turned out to be the far more desirable Electra 225, and this one was in fine condition, requiring only new leather seats, paint, and minor mechanical and trim work.

We approached the Buick with the skepticism of Richard Nixon on his 1959 trip to Poland. Could Buick really have made so much improvement in one year, and if they did then why did the car more or less bomb out? The utter nonsense of two sets of fins! The blinding reflections from all those instruments! You'd practically need a jet pilot's license to operate that thing. The speedometer stretches almost 20 inches across the dash, with a fat red line marking road speed.

But immediately the big Buick began winning us over. The instruments are all well placed and easy to read, and the controls are all quite easy to use once you become familiar with their locations and functions.

The shift indicator had vertical markings in 1959. The Twin Turbine is easy enough to read with the familiar PNDLR, which goes back to the original 1948 Dynaflow. But be careful if you change from a Twin Turbine to a Triple Turbine and back again. The patterns are almost backward, and on Triple jobs you pass through Reverse after leaving Park. Check your indicator before flooring the throttle or you could just find yourself backing up instead of making a sporty takeoff.

From the very first moment I took the wheel I found the Buick an utter pleasure to drive. Lots of low-speed torque carefully matched to the transmission provides plenty of smooth power up to around 35 miles an hour. Then acceleration flattens out a bit, but is very smooth all the way up to 60, which was as fast as we drove it. With today's crowded California driving conditions, it's hard to find a place where you can really put a machine like this through all of the paces.

We did observe a number of things from just driving around through the Escondido hill country. The car handled beautifully in the turns, considering its vintage and size. Body lean was not nearly as excessive as that of most big cars of the era. The steering was a bit slow, and you always tend to understeer on American cars of this vintage. The ride was predictably soft, but

overall the experience was extremely satisfying. The braking in the winding, mountainous roads was excellent, so good we would have thought the car had disc brakes if we didn't know better.

It would be interesting to run a comparison between this car and a 1958 Buick Roadmaster in comparable condition. We have no doubt that the '59 would win hands down, and for a lot of good reasons, especially in the handling department.

To sum it up, we were more impressed with this '59 Electra 225 than just about any fifties car we have ever driven: impressed with handling and ride, impressed with the quiet feeling for a convertible, impressed with the quality of construction. This car makes us wonder why anybody would have been foolish enough to shell out another $1,200-$1,300 for a Cadillac 62 convertible in 1959. Or for that matter why any collector would want to pay two or three times as much for a 1959 Cadillac convertible today. This Buick is, in our opinion, everything the '59 Cadillac is, plus it's a lot better looking. It took us a while to get used to the '59 Buick styling and personality, but by the end of our day with the car we were sold on it, and totally agree with the advertising that claimed it to be the most changed car of the year and the best Buick of the decade. Here is one top-down collectible that we feel is grossly underrated. Why didn't the car sell better when new? We can only conclude it was the market and the marketing. The vehicle itself had a lot going for it.

illustrations by Russell von Sauers, The Graphic Automobile Studio

specifications

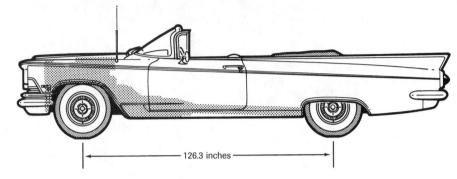

62.41 inches

126.3 inches

1959 Buick Electra 225 Convertible

Price	$4,192
Standard equipment:	Twin-Turbine Dynaflow, leather seats, power windows, safety group, deluxe wheel covers, outside rearview mirror, power steering, power brakes
Options on dR car:	Wonderbar signal seeking radio, electric antenna, speed control safety buzzer

ENGINE

Type	90 degree ohv V-8, cast-iron block
Bore/stroke	4.1875"x3.64"
Displacement	401 cubic inches
Compression ratio	10.5:1
Hp/rpm	325 @ 4,000
Taxable hp	56.11
Max torque/rpm	445 @ 2,800
No. main bearings	5
Lubrication system	Pressure
Induction system	One 4-bbl carburetor, camshaft-driven fuel pump
Exhaust system	Dual
Electrical system	12 volts
Valve lifters	Hydraulic

TRANSMISSION

Type	Twin-Turbine automatic torque converter with gears
Ratios: Drive	1 x converter ratio
Max ratio at stall	4.7:1

DIFFERENTIAL

Type	Hypoid
Ratio	3.23:1

STEERING

Type	Saginaw ball nut sector, hydraulic power
Turns lock-to-lock	4
Ratio	19.7:1
Turning diameter	44 feet

BRAKES

Type	Hydraulic with air-cooled aluminum front drums and air-cooled cast iron rear drums
Size	12 inches

CHASSIS & BODY

Frame	K-type with boxed side rails
Body construction	All steel
Body style	Convertible coupe

SUSPENSION

Front	Independent with coil springs and ball joints
Rear	Conventional helical coil springs
Tires	8.00/15 4-ply
Wheels	15-inch welded steel discs

WEIGHTS & MEASURES

Wheelbase	126.3"
Overall length	225.4"
Overall width	80.74"
Height	55.9"
Front tread	62.41"
Rear tread	60.00"
Shipping weight	4,465 pounds

CAPACITIES

Crankcase	6 quarts including filter
Cooling system	20 quarts
Fuel tank	21 gallons

PERFORMANCE

0-30 mph	3.4 seconds
0-50 mph	6.7 seconds
0-60 mph	9.5 seconds
0-70 mph	12.4 seconds
40-60 mph	5.3 seconds
Top speed	122 mph

Source, 1959 Invicta four-door hardtop tested by *Mechanix Illustrated.*

GAS MILEAGE

19.2	at a steady 30 mph
18.5	at a steady 40 mph
15.6	at a steady 60 mph

Source, 1959 Electra four-door hardtop tested by *Motor Trend.*

Above: *Rear seat room isn't bad.*
Right: *V in a circle moved from hood in '58 to grille in '59.*

Above Left: Doors open wide and are nicely trimmed. Left: Interior trim styling is linear and low-key. Above: Final '59 design is rather mild compared to some styling proposals. Below: Fin treatment was a radical breakaway for Buick's staid buyers, and they stayed away from showrooms in droves.

replied: "We spent a lot of time on things that may not show the first time you drive the car. For example. the roll center has been raised 1.4 inches in front, three inches at the rear wheels, so that weight is now suspended rather than pivoted, as before. As a result, we have a car that handles. Air suspension is used at the rear only, which gives us the air ride, plus the firm feel of steel coil front springs. Transmissions have been redesigned, and axle ratios changed for better matching to our new high-torque, low-rpm engine.

"Another thing you'll notice is that our '59 is quieter. [In addition to added soundproofing] we found that by moving the radiator and fan forward six inches, and throwing away the fan shroud, we reduced air turbulence under the hood and made the engine quieter."

Mechanix Illustrated's dean of automotive journalese, Tom McCahill, was so impressed with the new Invicta four-door hardtop he tested that at first he was almost at an unaccustomed loss for words, simply stating, "this '59 Buick is one hell of a road car." But knowing that his readers would expect more colorful prose, he went on to add... "with the traction of a leech. Many a lesser car on this wet road surface would have been off the shoulder like a French evening gown and sailing to parts unknown. You could no more have taken the bends at 60 mph with last year's Buick than you could sprout antlers on a rabbit. Oscar Kelly, the old fox, [he meant Oliver] knew all this beforehand or he wouldn't have been sitting there in the front seat with me.

McCahill didn't have a single unkind word for the '59 Buick. In his bald-headed opinion, the roadability was excellent" and performance was "fine." His zero to 60 time of 9.5 seconds was "brisk," and his top speed was 122 mph.

All of the motorbooks gave the '59 Buick rave reviews. *Motor Trend* named the Invicta four-door hardtop the best looking car of the year and the invicta wagon the best looking wagon. Buick

got the jump on everybody with a September 16 introduction. While early sales were encouraging, a steel strike slowed down the early momentum, followed by a year of buyer indifference to the new look and new image, proving that Buicks are supposed to look like Buicks, and a new advertising agency is hardly ever the answer.

By the end of the year, Ragsdale retired early and probably not voluntarily, ending a distinguished if not spectacular 36-year career with the Division. Curtice, who protected him and personally was willing to take much of the blame for the 1957 and '58 models, retired in 1958. Ragsdale did not hit it off at all well with the new corporate management.

The 1960 models received a minor facelift to give them more of a Buick identity. But sales continued to slip, and Buick moved down to ninth place in the industry. When you get to the bottom, there's no place left to go but out or up. With new styling, much downsizing, and the new compact Skylark in 1961, Buick began a long, slow recovery.

1959 Buicks were fantastic automobiles by any measure but "old guard" Buick standards. They were not popular used, which may explain why there are very few left to collect today. Our Electra 225 convertible driveReport car is one of

a handful left in the West.

A final note on the failure of the 1959 Buick concerns marketing follies. The 1958 Edsel was largely the product of consumer surveys. So was the 1959 Buick. The division asked buyers what they wanted, and so Buick built it in 1959. Longer, lower, futuristic looking, upwardly mobile looking, a soft ride, good handling, and quiet. A car for people who put on a lot of long, hard miles. Unfortunately, by the time it reached the showroom, those poor souls who had answered the surveys were out looking into Volkswagens. ᴓ

Acknowledgments and Bibliography

Buick, The Complete History, *by Terry B. Dunham and Lawrence R. Gustin with the staff of* Automobile Quarterly, *1980:1958 Air Suspension Buick road test,* Motor Trend, *May 1958; 1959 Buick engine analysis,* Motor Trend, *September 1958: 1959 Buick road test,* Motor Trend, *October 1958; Tom McCahill tests the '59 Buick,* Mechanix Illustrated, *October 1958;* Encyclopedia of American Cars, 1930-1980, *by the Editors of* Consumer Guide, *1984;* Standard Catalog of American Cars, 1946-1975, *by the editors of* Old Cars, *1984. Special thanks to Bob Knapp and the staff at Deer Park for furnishing our driveReport car.*

1962 BUICK SKYLARK

SCHOOL TEACHER'S HOT ROD

Originally published in Special Interest Autos #87, May-June 1985

SAID the editors of *Road & Track*, "There was a time, not too long ago, when we would have laughed if anyone had told us that Buick would one day build a car that we'd like to own.... But Buick's done it...." The car in question was the 1962 Skylark, which the magazine went on to describe as "one of the best all-around cars available today."

High praise, indeed, coming from that source!

Buick, taking account of the changing demands of the American motoring public, had entered the burgeoning compact-car market just the year before, with an aluminum-engined V-8 known by a familiar name: the Buick Special. George Romney (see *SIA* #66) had counseled some years earlier that most Americans simply have no need for a big car. Romney bolstered his argument with figures demonstrating that the average automobile trip in the United States is no more than 13 miles in length. Nobody, he pointed out, needs a "gas-guzzling dinosaur" for that kind of duty!

As the idea caught on, buyers for Romney's own Rambler rose dramatically until his little car held fourth place in US sales. A similar success was scored

by Arch Brown
photos by Vince Manocchi

by Germany's odd little Volkswagen, then just beginning to show its potential in the American market.

The other manufacturers watched with intense interest, then took appropriate steps on their own. Studebaker took the plunge in 1959 with its stubby, sturdy little Lark (see *SIA* #42), a chopped-off version of the car they had been peddling since 1953. Overnight, Studebaker sales nearly trebled!

By 1960 the Big Three had joined the fray, Chevrolet with the Corvair, Ford with the Falcon, Plymouth with the Valiant — all brand new designs, differing as markedly from their corporate ancestors as they did from one another.

But what about the upscale buyer, the motorist who wanted a car of modest dimensions but one with a little more performance, a lacing of luxury, a dash of panache? Rambler had its Ambassador, Studebaker its Lark Cruiser, but the Big Three literally had nothing to offer.

Until, that is, 1961, when General Motors' Buick, Oldsmobile, and Pontiac divisions fielded, respectively, the Special, the F-85, and the Tempest.

These were somewhat larger cars than the Big Three compacts — 8½ inches longer, for example, than the Corvair. But to present the matter in another light, the new, downsized Buick was more than two feet shorter and 1,500 pounds lighter than the base LeSabre series!

Powering the Junior Pontiac was a new, 194.5-cubic-inch four-banger, developed almost instantly by the simple expedient of sawing the division's big V-8 in half. Buick and Olds had something more sophisticated to offer: two 215-c.i.d. V-8s featuring aluminum blocks and cylinder heads.

The two engines were not identical. While sharing the same block casting, there were substantial differences between the powerplants in the design of their respective combustion chambers and sundry other components. Horsepower was identical between the two, at 155, but the Buick held a slight edge in torque output.

The new engines were the smallest and, of course, the lightest V-8s ever used in American production automo-

Table of Prices, Weights and Production
1962 Buick Special and Skylark

Model #	Body Style	Price	Weight	Production
	SPECIAL V-6			
4027	Coupe	$2,304	2,638	19,135
4019	Sedan, 4-door	$2,358	2,666	23,249
4067	Convertible*	$2,587	2,858	7,918
4035	Station Wagon, 2-seat	$2,655	2,878	7,382
4045	Station Wagon, 3-seat	$2,736	2,896	2,814
	SPECIAL DELUXE V-8			
4119	Sedan, 4-door	$2,593	2,648	31,660
4167	Convertible	$2,879	2,820	8,332
4135	Station Wagon, 2-seat	$2,890	2,845	10,380
	SKYLARK V-8			
4347	Sport Coupe	$2,787	2,707	34,060
4367	Convertible	$3,012	2,871	8,913

*Base convertible had a manual top. Other convertibles were equipped with power tops.

Right: A triple rendition of traditional Buick coat of arms forms centerpiece of Skylark's grille. Below: Dual headlamps were standard on all Specials. Facing page, top: Skylark convertible's styling still looks fresh and crisp nearly a quarter-century after it first debuted. Below: Buick's famous "portholes" became these little stampings on the Special.

biles. And they were sturdy! Iron cylinder sleeves were cast in place, alloy cast-iron valve seat inserts were installed by a shrink-fit process, and alloy iron valve guides were pressed into place. So premature wear due to the relatively soft block was never a problem; and its light weight and heat-conducting properties were important pluses.

Karl Ludvigsen, writing in *Sports Cars Illustrated*, predicted that the aluminum V-8s would be in great demand for engine-swaps, particularly for use in small imported cars. He noted, for instance, that "the 1.6-liter Volvo 'four' weighs almost exactly the same as this remarkable V-8, at less than half the displacement!" And there was some use of the new engines in such applications, though not as much as Ludvigsen evidently expected.

Styling of the new cars was fresh and very attractive. Some parts of the inner body and chassis structure were borrowed from the Corvair, but the styling themes were actually similar to the larger B-O-P cars. The little Buick, for instance, featured the same pointed front fenders as the senior series. Somewhat hazardous to pedestrians, perhaps, but the points did, at least, enhance the Buick's appearance of length.

Like the F-85, the Special employed a conventional front-engine, rear-drive layout. The standard transmission was a column-mounted three-speed manual gearbox supplied by GM's Chevrolet division. A floor-mounted four-speed from Warner Gear, basically the same as the unit used in the Corvette, was optional at $199.80. But by all odds the most popular choice was the $189.00 automatic transmission, known as the Dual Path Turbine Drive.

Here, by the way, was another respect in which the Buick Special differed from the Olds F-85. The Oldsmobile employed a small, three-speed, water-cooled version of the venerable Hydramatic, while Buick's Dual Path Turbine Drive was a combination of the Buick torque converter with two-speed plane-

1962 Buick Skylark vs. Competing Convertibles
Specifications and Performance Statistics

	Buick Skylark	Buick Spec. Dlx.	Chevrolet Impala	Chevrolet Nova 400	Ford Galaxie	Plymouth Fury	Pontiac Tempest	Studebaker Lark Daytona
Price*	$3,012	$2,879	$3,026	$2,475	$3,033	$2,924	$2,564	$2,814
Shipping weight	2,871	2,820	3,535	2,720	3,782	3,210	2,955	3,330
Wheelbase	112.1"	112.1"	119"	110"	119"	116"	112"	113"
Engine	V-8	V-a	V-8	L-6	V-8	V-8	L-4	V-8
C.I.D.	215	215	283	194	292	318	194.5	259.2
Hp/rpm	190/4,800	155/4,600	170/4,200	120/4,400	170/4,200	230/4,400	110/3,800	180/4,500
Compression ratio	11.0:1	9.0:1	8.5:1	8.5:1	8.8:1	9.0:1	8.6:1	8.5:1
Hp/c.i.d.	.884	.721	.601	.619	.582	.723	.566	.694
Pounds/hp	15.1	18.2	20.8	22.7	22.2	14.0	26.9	18.5

*f.o.b. factory, including federal excise tax

Note that when it came to extracting maximum horsepower from each cubic inch, the Skylark was in a class by itself. Note also that with the exception of the Plymouth, thhe Skylark was far ahead of its competition in terms of its power-to-weight ratio.

tary gearing. It was an air-cooled unit, so light in weight that Specials equipped with standard transmissions actually outweighed the automatic jobs by 15 pounds.

Introduced on October 5, 1960, the new Buick Special was initially offered only in two body styles: the four-door sedan and the station wagon, the latter being available with either two or three seats. It was a sparkling performer, capable of zero-to-60 in less than 15 seconds, and content to cruise all day long at 80 miles an hour. Gas mileage, in the 18-22 mpg range, wasn't quite as good as the Big Three compacts, yet it was substantially better than the full-sized versions of the low-priced three.

Riding comfort far surpassed that of the less expensive compacts, and the trim level, at least in the deluxe version, was clearly superior.

The little Buick demonstrated its frugal ways in the 1961 Mobilgas Economy Run, taking first place in its class, with an average of 24.7 miles to the gallon. Second place went to another Buick Special.

In March 1961 came a lovely variation on the Special theme. This was the Skylark, named for the exotic, limited production convertibles of 1953-54. This one, however, was initially offered only as a five-passenger coupe. A different grille, comprised of thin horizontal bars instead of a "waffle iron" casting, distinguished the new model from its stablemates, and under the hood was a high-performance version of the aluminum engine. Thanks to an increase in the compression ratio from 8.8 to 10.25:1, the Skylark boasted 85 horsepower — 30 more than the other Buick Specials.

When 1962 rolled around, the Buick Special — by now the best-seller among the B-O-P compacts — had some new models to display. In the base series there was an attractive coupe, and convertibles were offered in all three trim levels: base, deluxe and Skylark. In order to add rigidity to the unitized body/frame construction, the ragtops used a reinforced floor pan, increasing their weight by about 200 pounds as compared to the sedans.

Styling of the 1962 models was unchanged except that the handsome grille of the 1961½ Skylark was now used throughout the entire line. The Skylark's compression ratio was given another squeeze for 1962, raising it to 11.0:1 and elevating the horsepower rating to 190. It was a formidable performer, for even with the relatively heavy convertible body, it carried only 15.1 pounds per horsepower — compared, for instance, to 20.8 pounds for the Chevrolet Impala. And the Skylark matched the Impala's price almost dollar-for-dollar.

Naturally, a number of the car-enthu-

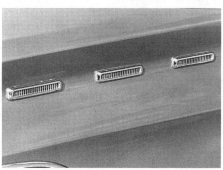

siast magazines undertook to road-test the high-stepping new Skylark. *Road & Track* recorded zero-to-60 in 10.2 seconds; the standing quarter mile in 17.9 seconds, with a recorded speed of 79 mph at the end; and an estimated top of 107 miles an hour. Their test was conducted with a coupe, equipped with the floor-mounted, four-speed manual gearbox. But the writer of *R & T*'s report noted that having spent considerable time behind the wheel of an automatic-equipped car, he had concluded that "there is not a great deal of difference (in performance) between the automatic and standard shift models." *Motor Trend*, recording almost identical times in a 1963 convertible, observed that "the Skylark has a lot to offer anyone who wants comfort and luxury as well as performance and sportiness in his family transportation."

Trouble was brewing, however, and in retrospect it appears that Buick's Special/Skylark series, as originally conceived, may have been doomed almost from the start. For one thing, the corporate bean-counters complained that the aluminum engine cost too much to produce. In response to this concern, a cast-iron V-6 was brought forth in record time — less than a year — to become the standard engine in the base 1962 Special series. And the public, evidently still equating size with

price (or quality, or prestige, or something), wanted something a little bigger than the B-O-P compacts. Or at least at that point they thought that's what they wanted. One anonymous Buick executive later observed, "If we had kept that little '62 Special and emphasized that small car, instead of letting it get big, Buick would be on top of the world today." It's an interesting thought.

The first response to this "bigger is better" urge came in 1963. The sculptured sides of the 1961-62 models were replaced by a new, smooth, slightly convex skin, its slab-sided look broken only by two accent lines. The car was stretched by some four inches, most of the growth taking place in the rear overhang. Norbye and Dunne, who — in *Buick the Postwar Years* — speak of the 1961-62 body side treatment as "overdone to say the least," view the 1963 styling effort as in improvement. But collectors nowadays put a premium on the original configuration — and so do we. Nor was the revision a smash hit at the time, for that matter. For while the full-sized Buick LeSabre for 1963 scored an impressive sales gain over the year before, production of the Special/Skylark leveled off.

And when the 1964 models were introduced, Buick's first true compact cars were gone, replaced by a pair of intermediates bearing the same Special and Skylark designations. Whatever the long-range implications may have been, at least for the short run Buick had evidently assessed the market correctly, for sales of the new models were up by more than 20 percent.

And the little aluminum engine, one of the most interesting pieces of machinery to come out of Detroit — or Flint — in a very long time, was shipped off to Britain. You'll find it there today, hiding beneath the bonnet of the excellent Rover 3500.

Right: Instrument panel is almost stark in its simplicity. **Below:** *Clock mounts on top of dash; is difficult to read from driver's seat.* **Facing page:** *Aluminum block V-8 was used for only three years in Special; it's the powerplant for a number of English cars today.*

Driving Impressions

As incredible as it may seem, Dave Higby rescued our driveReport car from the back of a junk dealer's truck, back in 1974, paying the man $50 for the privilege of hauling it away!

Once having brought the Buick home, Dave was delighted to discover that the little car was actually in running condition. The rear main bearing seal leaked, to be sure, but the more he examined the car the more convinced he became

that the 89,000-mile odometer reading was for real. Eight years would pass, in fact, before it was deemed necessary to overhaul the engine.

Along with the mechanical refurbishing, the 1982 project entailed considerable body work and, of course, new paint. A partial restoration of the vinyl interior was also required. New Old Stock parts, Dave learned, are all but impossible to find, but decent parts cars are available. (The latter serve double duty for the Higbys, by the way, since Mrs. Higby's daily transport is a '62 Skylark hardtop, lovingly maintained by her husband.)

The biggest problem involved in restoring and maintaining these cars, according to Dave. has to do with those pointed front fenders. They are easily damaged, he reports, and absolutely fiendish to repair.

We were delighted to have an opportunity to drive the Skylark, for we have particularly admired this model ever since its introduction. (Our lady, in fact, had been so taken with the little Buick

Jetfire: Turbo Much Too Soon
by Christopher G. Foster

Today "turbo" is a household word. It is considered sufficiently generic that no car maker has been able to copyright it, and it's applied recklessly to all manner of consumer goods from electric shavers to jogging shorts. The turbocharger, of course, is an adaptation of the age-old supercharger. But where the latter is either shaft or belt driven from the engine, the turbo is spun by a turbine located in the flow of the engine's exhaust, in effect capturing some energy that would otherwise go out the pipe. But turbocharging, as simple as it is, took a long time to come of age. General Motors was an early proponent of turbocharging, their first efforts hitting the market over 20 years ago, but the economics and mores of the time quickly relegated their efforts to the closet, to re-emerge only in the last few years.

The GM 215-cubic-inch aluminum V-8, while actually put into production by Buick, was used by each of the "middle divisions" in their upmarket compacts. The least successful of these was the Pontiac Tempest version, where the V-8 was actually *too light* for optimum balance; Pontiac's transaxle (see *SIA* #48) made the V-8 Tempest tail heavy. The V-8 was the sole powerplant used in Oldsmobile's F-85. Oldsmobile, always proud of their own engineering, accepted Buick's blocks, crankshafts and camshafts, but insisted on doing their own heads, manifolding, and final assembly.

The impetus for turbocharging came from Olds general manager Jack Wolfram. He wanted a gutsier F-85 Cutlass, and the chassis wouldn't take the larger cast-iron Rocket engine. The aluminum V-8 had some stretch left, but using it would require collusion with Buick manufacturing. Engineer Gil Burrell came across some early turbocharging studies in the company archives and, while the conclusions were generally negative, he continued to mull the idea over.

It took a lot of experimentation to get a system that even approached marketability. The blower itself came from Garrett AiResearch, whose turbochargers are found in most of today's turbocars. Mounted in the valley between the cylinder banks, it was plumbed to the right-hand exhaust manifold and featured a vacuum controlled gate, which acted to limit boost to 5 psi. It was fed by a single-throat sidedraft Rochester carburetor. The turbo came into play about 2,400 rpm, where the exhaust gases quickly sped it up to 83,000 rpm until the wastegate opened. Detonation has always been a foe of supercharging; today we operate with lowered compression ratios and microprocessor control, but Burrell wanted to keep compression up for greater efficiency. His remedy to the detonation problem was both novel and classical: water-alcohol injection; classical because the technique had been around for years, and novel because Olds christened the mundane medium "turbo rocket fluid."

Wolfram wanted a package deal, an exclusive

car model for this engine, but there wasn't money for anything extensive. Instead, the turbo became part and parcel of a "Jetfire" edition of the new-for-'62 hardtop coupe. The Jetfire bowed at the New York Auto Show in April 1962.

The engine in turbo trim turned out the magic one horsepower per cubic inch — 215 hp at 4,600 rpm. And the turbocharger did as it was supposed to, adding oomph at the top end without sacrificing low speed drivability or economy. There was just one hitch: The top end wasn't all that spectacular. *Motor Trend* tested the Jetfire with a three-speed Hydro and found that it was all right out of the gate, but that once the engine reached 4,600 revs it just died. They wound it to 5,500 without valve float, but there was just no energy left after the power peak. To compound things, the Hydro started to upshift at that point, and the car just stumbled through the rest of the quarter mile for an 18.7 elapsed time. That was a fraction of a second slower than their test of a '63 four-barrel car without the turbo. *Car Life* got a better quarter-mile time, 17.1 seconds, with a '63 jetfire with the four speed, and were impressed with the car's "flexibility." A docile engine "transformed into a powerhouse with a mere push of the pedal," they said, and waxed metaphorically: "With the Jetfire there's still a tiger at home — but it's housebroken." Both magazines, however, concluded that the Cutlass handling and brakes really weren't up to coping with that much power. Couple that with the fact that the water-alcohol injection smacked of a J.C. Whitney contraption, and it only added up to sales of 9,607 units over two years. The performance-car future at GM, of course, lay in the intermediate successors to the B-O-P compacts fitted with engines from the full-size lineup, but that's another story.

illustrations by Russell von Sauers, The Graphic Automobile Studio

specifications

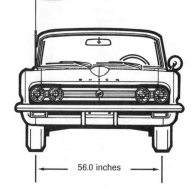

56.0 inches

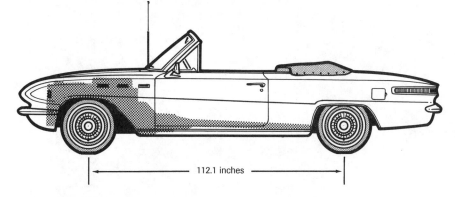

112.1 inches

1962 Buick Skylark

Price	$3,012 f.o.b. Flint, Michigan, with standard equipment. (Federal excise tax included.)
Standard equipment	Heater/defroster; electric windshield wipers; directional signals; dual sliding sun shades; all-vinyl bucket seats; foam-padded; cigarette lighter; padded instrument panel; wheel covers; rear passenger courtesy lights; glove compartment light; full carpeting; dual horns; special steering wheel; power top

ENGINE

Type	Ohv V-8; aluminum block and cylinder heads
Bore/stroke	3.5 inches x 2.8 inches
Displacement	215 cubic inches
Max bhp @ rpm	190 @ 4,800
Max torque @ rpm	235 @ 3,000
Compression ratio	11.0:1
Carburetor	Rochester 2GC 2-barrel
Electrical system	12 volt

TRANSMISSION

Type	Automatic; Dual Path Turbine Drive
Ratios: 1st	1.58:1
2nd	1.00:1
Reverse	N/a
Torque converter, max ratio at stall: 2.50:1	

DIFFERENTIAL

Type	Hypoid
Ratio	3.08:1
Drive axles	Semi-floating

STEERING

Type	Link, power-assisted
Turns, lock to lock	4
Ratio	17.5 gear; 20.8 overall
Turn circle	38 feet, 11 inches (wall-to-wall)

BRAKES

Type	4-wheel hydraulic drum, power assisted
Drum diameter	9 inches
Total swept area	224 square inches

CHASSIS AND BODY

Frame and body	Unitized, all-steel
Body style	Convertible coupe

SUSPENSION

Front	Independent, coil springs; link stabilizer
Rear	Coil springs; solid axle
Tires	6.50 x 13
Wheels	Pressed steel

WEIGHTS AND MEASURES

Wheelbase	112.1 inches
Overall length	188.4 inches
Overall height	54.2 inches (unloaded)
Overall width	71 inches
Front tread	56 inches
Rear tread	56 inches
Ground clearance	4.9 inches
Shipping weight	2,871 pounds

CAPACITIES

Crankcase	5 quarts (including filter)
Cooling system	13½ quarts (including filter)
Fuel tank	16 gallons
Automatic transmission	12 pints

PERFORMANCE FACTORS

Hp per c.i.d.	.884
Weight per hp	15.1 pounds
Weight per c.i.d.	13.4 pounds

PERFORMANCE STATISTICS*

Top speed (est)	107 mph
0-30	3.6 seconds
0-40	5.2 seconds
0-50	7.5 seconds
0-60	10.2 seconds
0-70	13.4 seconds
0-80	18.3 seconds
0-100	32.5 seconds
Standing ¼ mile	17.9 sec. (Speed at end: 79 mph)
Production (this model/body style): 8,913	

*From *Road & Track*, March 1962, using a Skylark coupe equipped with a 4-speed manual transmission. DriveReport car, being heavier and equipped with an automatic transmission, may be expected to be marginally slower.

---

that had our circumstances permitted it, back in 1962, we surely would have bought one.)

We weren't disappointed. It's a delightfully responsive car, quick and nimble, sheer joy to drive. The front seat is fairly erect, which suits our preference just fine, and plenty of front leg room is provided. The same cannot be said for the rear compartment, however. Nothing the matter with the back seat per se, and entry and egress are comparatively easy. But once seated, we found our knees tucked up under our chin.

Trunk space is ample — generous, in fact, for a compact convertible.

Higby's car is equipped with a full

*Above left: Door panels are very plush for a car that was so moderately priced. There's a reflector in the end of each armrest to help mark open doors to oncoming traffic at night. **Top and above right:** Up front there's lots of acreage to stretch out in, and rear seat room is adequate.*

bank of accessory gauges, a big improvement over the factory-supplied idiot lights. (Did somebody name them "idiot" lights in honor of the turkey who first thought of them, do you suppose?) And mounted atop the dashboard is a clock. We drove the Buick with the top down — the way a convertible ought to be driven — but when at our request Dave raised the lid we were impressed by the generous head room. Rather a surprise, given the car's low profile.

Years ago we owned a car with a two-speed automatic transmission. We didn't like it much. Not enough "punch" off the line, and there was an unpleasant lurch when it shifted to high gear. This one is of a different breed, however. It does its job smoothly, and evidently — as noted by *Road & Track* — with little penalty in performance, as compared with the stick shift.

Acceleration is really flashy; it's an exhilarating car to drive. Higby reports - and we can readily believe — that it will cruise hour after hour at speeds far in excess of the legal limit — and with very little sound coming from the engine compartment.

Norbye and Dunne have noted that the chassis of the small Buick is "not quite up to the performance levels of the engine," and perhaps they're right. At least, the car seems more at home on the boulevard than on irregular surfaces; and the 6.50 x 13 tires are clearly inadequate for their job. Nevertheless, we like the way the car handles. It goes where it's pointed, and it does what the driver tells it to do. Dave Higby reports that a pair of heavy-duty front shocks, installed when the engine was overhauled, resulted in a significant improvement in this respect.

The power steering, though very light, manages to avoid most of the numbness typical of many power steering mechanisms of the early sixties. We would prefer a somewhat quicker ratio for our own use; four full turns lock-to-lock seems excessive. But for its time, when most drivers had not yet become accustomed to the power assist, perhaps it was about right. Understeer, we noted, is moderate.

Motor Trend, in testing the 1963 Skylark, noted that its stopping distances were commendably shorter than average. We found, however, that the power brakes take some getting used to. Reac-

The First Skylarks

The smart little aluminum-engined coupes and convertibles of 1961-63 were not the first Buicks to bear the Skylark name. Nor, of course, the last.

The original Skylark (see SIA #5) was introduced in 1953 as part of Buick's fiftieth anniversary celebration. Buick's sensational V-8 engine was brand new that year (as was its 12-volt electrical system), but the styling of the entire line was warmed over from the year before, and it was rather less than inspiring. Hence the Skylark: something to stir up an air of excitement in Buick showrooms.

There was just a suggestion, in the appearance of that first Skylark, of the XP300, Buick's glamorous 1952 show car. But basically it was a Roadmaster convertible with some significant alterations. Under the direction of chief stylist Ned Nickles, the Buick crew had performed the kind of magic that might have taken place in a first-class custom body shop: The windshield was chopped; the belt line was lowered and notched; the traditional Buick "portholes" were eliminated; full, round, rear-wheel cutouts were fashioned and a set of gorgeous Kelsey-Hayes chromed wires — complete with fake knockoff hubs — was fitted. They even sealed the owner's signature into the Lucite hub at the center of the steering wheel.

Virtually every conceivable extra was included in the Skylark's $5,000 price tag (a hefty $1,500 premium over the tab for the Roadmaster ragtop, by the way): Twin-Turbine Dynaflow, for instance; Selectronic radio; and power *everything*!

The Skylark wasn't really intended to make money for Buick. Specialty cars seldom do, given the extra hours of skilled labor that go into their construction. It was intended, rather, to call the public's attention to Buick — and it can hardly have failed to do that.

Neither was the Skylark supposed to continue in production beyond the 1953 model year. But it did, for one more season — some say, because GM president Harlow "Red" Curtice liked it.

The 1954 Skylark was of another breed, however. Based this time on the newly reintroduced Century convertible, it was a little smaller, a little lighter, a tad more powerful (200 horsepower vs. 188 in the '53 car) — and doubtless marginally faster than the original. If that mattered very much.

Styling of the '54, with its sharply sloping rear deck and a pair of tacked-on "suspenders" running down the back, was controversial, but the price was cut to $4,355.

Probably Buick could have sold more '54 Skylarks if anyone had tried very hard, though its price was still well above the stock Century convertible. But since it was no moneymaker anyway, why bother? Production that year came to only 854 units, less than half the 1,690 turned out the year before.

And then the Skylark was laid to rest until the name, at least, was happily revived seven years later.

Above left: Turbine-style wheel covers were optional on rest of Special models, standard on Skylarks. Left: Power-operated top goes up and down quickly and easily. Above: Surely one of the handsomest profiles of any car of the early sixties, regardless of size.

tion to the pressure of the driver's foot is delayed, just for an instant, but when they take hold, these binders bring the car to a halt, stat!

We feel compelled to add, however, that on a well-balanced automobile of the Skylark's weight (2.871 pounds) both the power steering and power brakes may be unnecessary. We suspect that the car would handle better without them; and of course we'd love to drive a car like this, equipped with a four-speed transmission!

Buick buyers are presumed to demand a "Buick ride" — which of course requires relatively soft springing. The Skylark provides just that; it's amazing how gently and easily it carries its passengers, for so light a car — and despite a comparatively short wheelbase. Of course, that leads to a fair amount of heeling over during hard cornering. But despite the roll, control of the car is easy to maintain, even when the driver is pushing it pretty hard. There's not a lot of lateral support in the front bucket seats, though; a firm grip on the steering wheel is advisable.

The aluminum-engined Buick was only a year away from its demise when this delightful little ragtop was built. A pity; for it's a highly competent, thoroughly pleasant automobile — one that deserved a longer production life. 🜋

The 1962 90° V-6: An Engine for the Eighties

It was obvious early-on that Buick would need another engine to supplement (if not, indeed, to replace) the aluminum V-8 in its compact Special series. The light alloy block was just fine, but it cost too much to produce. Something else was needed if the little Buick was to become both profitable and competitive.

Buick engineers went to work in a hurry. Ed Rollert, the new general manager who had been brought in to stem Buick's disastrous slide of 1959-60, had been thinking in terms of slicing a V-8 in half — as Pontiac had done — in order to create a new four-cylinder engine for the purpose. But in the end he was persuaded by the division's chief engine designer, Joe Turlay, that carving a third off a V-8 engine block to create a V-6 was an equally feasible and much more desirable solution.

Thus was born, for the 1962 season, the first V-6 to appear in a modern American production car. It won for Buick Motor Trend's coveted *Car of the Year* award, for "pure progress in design, originative engineering excellence, and the power concept of the future...." One wonders whether the editors comprehended how prophetic they really were. Writing in *Stag*, Dale Show described the V-6-powered Buick Special as Detroit's best car in 30 years, noting that its power "is due partly to the fact that the V-6 — unlike the V-8 — fires on one side and then the other alternately, left bank then right bank, causing a ram effect when a cylinder takes in gas and air."

As introduced on the 1962 Buick Special, the new V-6 displaced 198 cubic inches and generated 135 horsepower at 4,600 revolutions per minute. Bore and stroke were 3.62 by 3.2 inches, and the compression ratio was 1.8:1. In action, it felt very nearly as powerful as the V-8, prompting Buick sales manager Roland Withers to comment, "That engine doesn't know it's not an eight!" Buick advertising stressed, "Six for Savings — V for voom!" About a third of all Specials were equipped with the V-6 that year, though its availability was restricted to the base series.

The new engine weighed about 50 pounds more than the aluminum V-8 — not enough, Buick calculated, to upset the excellent balance of the car. As predicted, it turned out to be somewhat more economical than the V-8. And to the bean-counters in the front office its big advantage was its substantially lower production cost. Buick could be competitive with this one.

By 1964 the Skylark/Special had grown bigger and heavier, and its two available engines had been correspondingly enlarged. The V-6 was bored and stroked to 225 cubic inches, and it shared its 3.75 by 3.4-inch cylinder dimensions with a new, cast-iron, 300-c.i.d. V-8.

But the V-6 was not without its critics. The 90-degree angle between the cylinder banks, taken together with a crankshaft whose throws were spaced 120 degrees apart, gave it firing impulses at 90 and 150 degrees. This produced a rough idle, sort of a "lope" that tended to be objectionable at low rpm's. This was particularly true of cars equipped with standard gearboxes; the fluid coupling in the automatic transmission tended to absorb some of the roughness. In any case, even its detractors admitted that the performance of the V-6 was, at highway speeds, as smooth as it was sprightly.

But fuel was cheap in those days, and demand for the V-6 slackened. After the 1967 model year, Buick discontinued it and sold the tooling to Kaiser Jeep. And that was that.

Well, almost. Early in 1974, with the fuel crunch placing a premium on good fuel mileage, Buick repurchased the old tooling, and once again the V-6 took its place in Buick's engine line-up. It was a resurrection without precedent in the industry; and starting with the 1975 model the standard powerplant for both the Skyhawk and Skylark series was the V-6 — bored, this time, to 231 cubic inches.

There have been further developments since that time, of course:

• In 1978, by means of splitting each crankpin by an included angle of 30 degrees, the throw was advanced by 15 degrees for the cylinders on the right bank and delayed 15 degrees for those on the left bank. Thus, the 90° V-6 was given an even, smooth firing pattern.

• That same year, a turbocharged V-6 made its appearance in the Regal Sport Coupe. (A prototype turbo unit had already served as the 1976 Indianapolis 500 pace car.)

• Two years later, bored this time to 252 cubic inches, the V-6 became the base engine of Buick's big Electra series.

The world had changed, and Buick's V-6 had at last come into its own. It had been just a little ahead of its time, back in 1962!

1962 BUICK WILDCAT

A BUICK WITH BITE

by Tim Howley
photos by Rick Lenz

DURING the fifties and sixties the most American of all automobiles emerged, the personal/luxury/performance car. It was a star-spangled cross between a large hardtop or convertible and performance car which took most of its performance honors from badges, bangles and beads, and was mechanically little or no different from Maude Frickert's four-door sedan with the standard but powerful V-8. It was a compromise between two extremes, yet it was wildly popular in its day and remains with us now in small numbers as a highly prized collectible. Among these fascinating mutants of the Eisenhower and Kennedy years, the '62 Buick Wildcat stands at or pretty close to the top. But for the Buick to become a Wildcat was a long process of evolution that would have staggered even Darwin's troubled psyche.

The origin of the species can probably be traced to the 1952-54-era Lincoln coupes (see *SIA* #128) which dominated the Mexican Road Races. These were followed by the early Chrysler 300s, with the Buick Centurys of the same mid-fifties period not far behind. In 1958 Ford threw a monkey wrench into the whole system by making the former semi-sport Thunderbird two-seater into a full-size personal luxury four-seater with front buckets and console, not yet with the shift mounted in the console. Nor was the body that of a standard passenger car. It was a low-slung futuristic "dream job" of unitized construc-

tion, sharing its unique style and shape with no other car in the Ford camp.

In that same year, 1958, Pontiac introduced bucket-style front seats into standard passenger-car bodies by making the seats an option on its fuel-injected Bonneville (see *SIA* #90). In 1959 Buick and Oldsmobile followed suit with optional front bucket-style seats. These seats were automatically adjustable, the Pontiac buckets were not; in fact the passenger seat was stationary.

The next stage of the personal luxury-car evolution occurred in 1962 when GM introduced the Pontiac Grand Prix hardtop, Oldsmobile Starfire hardtop and convertible, and Buick Wildcat hardtop. (The Chevrolet Super Sport was a slightly different breed, as it was not a separate model, remaining an Impala option package until 1964.) All of these were special trim jobs with bucket seats plus a center console including an

Originally published in Special Interest Autos #144, Nov.-Dec. 1994

Above: It looks like pure big Buick up front. **Below and below right:** But the Wildcat emblems and logo give the game away on the car's sides. **Bottom right:** Updated "portholes" look more like air conditioning outlets.

automatic shifter poking out of a fancy art deco aluminum and chrome console sheath. Ford and Chrysler had similar offerings that year. Some will say that the Wildcat was a forerunner to the Buick Riviera which came the next year.

The Buick Wildcat was a Spring 1962 offering introduced simultaneously with the compact Buick Skylark convertible. It was not a special model but was included in the Invicta series and shared the same model number, 4647, as the Invicta two-door hardtop.

A total of 12,355 of those Invictas were built, and there is no breakout of Wildcats from that figure, but best estimates put the number at around 2,000. What makes the Wildcat unique is the trim, which included:

Rear seat speaker
Foam padded vinyl front bucket seats
Shifter mounted in center console with storage box

Rear floor courtesy light mounted at rear of console
Tachometer
Electric clock
Deluxe steering wheel
Automatic trunk light
License plate frame
Electric windshield wipers
Step-on parking brake
Special acoustical ceiling material
Special custom vinyl roof in white or black
Wildcat identification on rear quarter roof panels
Special Wildcat hubcaps
Special Wildcat name identification
Dual exhaust
15-inch wheels
Custom bright exterior moldings

It is interesting to note that you could get bucket seats with console on other models for $229 extra in convertibles and $296 extra in coupes.

A Wildcat could be had with any of Buick's 15 body colors. There were blue, white, fawn, and red interior choices, but no black, Only two tops were offered, white or black vinyl in a very distinctive grain pattern unique to the Wildcat. The interiors were solid vinyls, no weaves, and you could not get leather surfaced seats.

While Oldsmobile opted to put a slightly modified Olds 394-c.i.d. engine in its Starfires to develop 345 horsepower, Buick decided to play it safe with the standard Invicta 401 with 10.25:1 compression ratio, four-barrel carburetor which developed 325 horsepower at 4,400 rpm. The 401, at 325 horsepower, had been the standard Buick Invicta and Electra engine since 1959. No manual transmission was offered on this or any full-sized Buick. Nonetheless, the Wildcat had more than enough wallop to smoke the rear tires while reaching 0-60

Origin of The Buick Wildcat Name

In the early and mid-fifties, the name "Wildcat" was synonymous with some of Buick's most famous and influential show cars. The first was Wildcat I, unveiled at the 1953 Motorama. The styling greatly influenced the 1954 Buick line. Then came Wildcat II for 1954, done primarily by Ned Nickles. The completely open front wheel cutouts immediately showed up on the 1954 Skylark (see this issue's drive-Report), and the front end ended up on the 1955 Buick. Both Wildcat I and II were fiberglass jobs. Wildcat III for 1955 was created by a lot of top GM designers. Homer LaGassey recalls contributing much to the design. Wildcat III looked something like the '56 Buick from the front, and the sweep spear on the side showed up in modified form on the ill-fated '57 Buick line. All of these advanced Buick designs were running models. Wildcat I is now in the Joe Bortz collection in Chicago. We suspect the others still survive, but we are not quite sure where. GM, unlike Ford, does not as a matter of policy butcher its star show cars after they reach the end of the show-circuit road.

The Wildcat name was given to the 401 engine when it came out in 1959, and finally made it to a Buick production car in 1962, but the styling of this car or any other Buick of the period was not the least influenced by the earlier Wildcat creations.

The Wildcat name was then applied to a super aerodynamic car created in the seventies by Homer LaGassey's students at the Center for Creative Studies in Detroit's College of Art and Design.

A note about LaGassey. He was such a dynamite young stylist in the fifties that even though he was assigned to the Olds and then the Pontiac studio, Buick kept "borrowing" him to work on many of their hallmark production cars and best advanced designs of the fifties. Disgusted with the '57 Buick, LaGassey went to Chrysler, then to Ford in 1964, and finally decided that the only worthwhile mission in life for a designer was to teach. So in the early seventies he started devoting all of his time to teaching automobile design. Today, some of the neatest cars on the road were done by "Homer's kids."

In 1987 LaGassey retired to painting World War II era ships and planes in the obscure berg of Greenbush, Michigan. In 1994 he, along with Nuccio Bertone, was inducted into the Automotive Hall of Fame. At age 70, LaGassey still paints with a fury, and the Wildcat legends live on.

1962 BUICK WILDCAT

mph in less than nine seconds, and hit over 100 in slightly under half a minute.

One of the things Buick boasted about with its Wildcat was a forward-mounted engine with "advanced thrust" for better handling. In reality, it doesn't appear to be mounted any further forward than other Buick models. What dreamers, these Buick copywriters! A forward-mounted engine theoretically results in slightly better high-speed stability but a tendency to really "plow" into the turns, making the Wildcat about as far from a true sports-type as Flint is from LeMans. But then, back in the early sixties, how many Buick buyers were interested in sports car handling? They were after straight line performance, and this is what the Wildcat, like all Buicks, delivered in spades.

The Wildcat of 1962 was derived from a new generation of full-sized Buicks introduced in 1961. Styling of the 1961-62 Buicks was considerably subdued from the winged phantoms of 1959-60. The '61-62 LeSabre and Invicta models remained on a 123-inch wheelbase and were about three inches shorter overall.

Left: *With bias-ply tires and cushy springing, Wildcat's handling doesn't match its power.* **Above:** *Wildcat uses special wheel cover inserts.* **Below:** *Traditional Buick coat of arms occupies center of grille.*

All Buicks had a totally new chassis for '61 with X frame, redesigned suspension and two-section, triple-jointed, open driveshaft in place of the familiar torque tube. All of this helped make even the lowest priced LeSabre a better handling car than the 1960 land yacht. The new driveshaft dictated suspension changes. Four coil springs, a Buick feature since 1938, now had a new system of control links for faster and flatter cornering than ever before.

The wraparound windshield was slightly subdued, and the bat wings were clipped. Both the windshield and the overall styling took their cues from the 1960 Cadillac Brougham, which influenced all 1961-62 GM cars. Buick instrument panels, which had been completely restyled for 1960, were again all new for '61. However one 1960 instrument oddity was retained. That was an "adjustable-tilt" speedometer which was actually a mirror reflecting a speedometer mounted backwards in the instrument panel. For '62 this little trick was eliminated.

Motor Trend noted, "...with all the power accessories, including windows and air conditioning, and in test trim carrying slightly over 4,600 pounds...we recorded 0-to-30, 0-to-45 and 0-60 mph

in 2.9, 5.2 and 8.1 seconds. The standing quarter-mile was reached in 17.1 seconds, with a top speed of 87 mph. Down the long Riverside back straight we observed an honest 115 mph."

Praising the Turbine-Drive automatic highly and claiming that "the standard Buick brakes are still the best being offered in this country," *MT* commented thus on the handling: "On tight corners or on loose surfaces the front end tends to plough, but there is always enough power available to keep all but the worst drivers out of trouble. At speeds through wide, sweeping turns, the understeer is not so noticeable, and the car's behavior is fairly predictable — except when the road surface is rough. Here the light shocks are at their worst and allow the wheels to tramp excessively. A hefty anti-roll bar is used at the front and this, in conjunction with the rear-end control arms and Panhard-type track bar, keeps the Wildcat surprisingly level in corners.... The Buick is probably at its best out on the open road where all-day, high-speed cruising is the order. It has excellent directional stability and is little affected by cross-winds. Noise levels, from the wind, the road or engine, are very low at high cruising speeds. A driver could put in a 12-hour, 600-mile

day in this car and still be fairly fresh at his destination."

There is some confusion about the Wildcat axle ratio. *Motor Trend* listed it as 3.42:1 compared to 3.23:1 as the standard Buick Invicta and Electra ratio. *Motor Life* listed it as 3.23:1, while noting that the performance was no different than on a standard Invicta previously tested. Interesting and a bit baffling.

Were cars of this ilk and era a trip down the road to nowhere? Hardly. They helped focus Detroit thinking, and paved the way to the totally integrated luxury/performance machines we drive today.

Driving Impressions

Finding a first year, 1962 Buick Wildcat to test drive was not easy. Their obscurity is compounded by the fact that the Buick Club of America Directory lists them under the 4647 model number of all 1962 Invicta two-door hardtops. It took us over a year to find a car, but when we did we really lucked out. The car we found is a senior first-place winner in both the BCA and AACA, and well could be the finest example of the first-year Buick Wildcat extant. It is owned by Wayne Yonce, a

illustrations by Russell von Sauers, The Graphic Automobile Studio

specifications

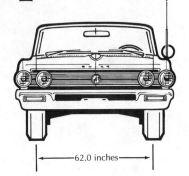
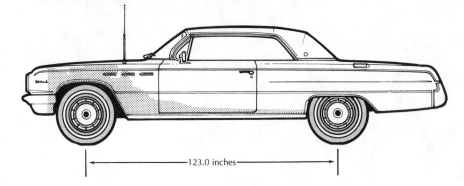

62.0 inches

123.0 inches

1962 Buick Wildcat two-door hardtop, Model 4647

Price when new	$3,927
Price as equipped	$4,800 approximately
Options on dR car	Seat belts, power steering, power windows, Sonomatic pushbutton radio with power antenna, windshield washer with dual speed wipers, soft ray tinted glass, custom padded cushions on the seats, air conditioning, power windows, remote control sideview mirrors; safety group of backup lamps, glare-proof mirror, parking brake warning light, safety buzzer and trip courtesy lights; accessory group of electric clock, license plate frame, trunk light; luggage compartment and ash tray light, remote control trunk release in the glove compartment, carpet covers, vanity mirror, super lift air shock absorbers, white sidewall tires

ENGINE
Type	90-degree ohv V-8, water-cooled, cast-iron block, 5 mains, full-pressure lubrication
Bore x stroke	4.1875 inches x 3.64 inches
Displacement	401 cubic inches
Max. bhp @ rpm	325 @ 4,400
Max. torque @ rpm	445 ft. lb.. @ 2,800
Compression ratio	10.25:1
Induction system	4-bbl Rochester downdraft carburetor, mechanical fuel pump
Exhaust system	Cast-iron manifolds, dual exhaust
Electrical system	6-volt battery/coil

TRANSMISSION
Type	Dual-range Turbo-Drive, console-mounted shift lever
Ratios: 1st	1.82 x 3.4:1
2nd	1.82:1
3rd	1.00:1

DIFFERENTIAL
Type	Hypoid
Ratio	3.23:1
Drive axles	Semi-floating

STEERING
Type	Recirculating ball and nut with integral power piston
Turns lock-to-lock	3.5
Ratio	19.1:1
Turn circle	45.9 feet

BRAKES
Type	Hydraulic, 4-wheel drums, internal expanding, power assist; finned aluminum front, cast iron rear
Drum diameter	12 inches
Total lining area	197.4 square inches

CHASSIS & BODY
Frame	X-type, boxed frame
Body construction	All steel
Body style	Two-door hardtop coupe

SUSPENSION
Front	Coil springs with upper and lower control arms, direct-acting telescopic shocks and anti-roll bar; gas air hydraulic shock absorbers
Rear	Solid axle, coil springs, leading control arms, track bar and direct-acting gas air hydraulic shock absorbers
Tires	7.60 x 15, 4-ply tube type, whitewalls
Wheels	Pressed steel, drop-center rims, lug-bolted to brake drums

WEIGHTS AND MEASURES
Wheelbase	123 inches
Overall length	214.1 inches
Overall width	78 inches
Overall height	56.3 inches
Front track	62 inches
Rear track	61 inches
Ground clearance	5.2 inches
Curb weight	4,360 pounds
Weight as tested	4,700 pounds, approximately

CAPACITIES
Crankcase	5 quarts
Cooling system	18.5 quarts
Fuel tank	20 gallons

FUEL CONSUMPTION
Best	16 mpg
Average	10.5 mpg

PERFORMANCE
Acceleration: 0-30	2.9 seconds
0-45 mph	5.2 seconds
0-60 mph	8.1 seconds
Standing 1/4 mile	17.1 seconds/87 mph
Stopping distance	from 38 mph: 38 feet; from 60 mph: 168 feet

(Source: *Motor Trend*, August 1962)

PERFORMANCE
Acceleration: 0-30 mph	3.1 seconds
0-40 mph	4.8 seconds
0-50 mph	6.8 seconds
0-60 mph	8.9 seconds
0-70 mph	12.2 seconds
0-80 mph	16.1 seconds
0-100 mph	27.5 seconds
Standing 1/4 mile	17 seconds/82 mph

(Source: *Car Life*, July 1962)

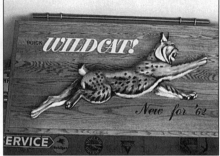

Above: Coat of arms also decorates trunk lid. **Below:** Buick has big, broad-shouldered appearance. **Top right:** Quad taillamps are separated by backup lamps. **Center:** Owner's garage is decorated with showroom sign promoting the model. **Bottom:** There's also i.d. on the dash.

1962 BUICK WILDCAT

retired electrician living in Fallbrook, California.

Wayne already owned a good but high-mileage 1962 Buick Wildcat when he chanced upon this one in a shopping center parking lot in Escondido, California, in 1991. The car had never strayed far from Escondido, where it had been sold new. Yonce arrived just at the right time, because the elderly original owner of this 75,000-mile car was now reluctantly ready to part with it for health reasons. Over a two-year period Yonce upgraded the car to concours condition. He did not take the body off the frame, nor did he need to rebuild the engine or transmission. But the interior was gutted, the body was stripped and repainted to Cardinal Red. All of the interior trim was brought up to showroom condition without ever replacing the original seat material or door panels. The engine compartment was incredibly well detailed by Yonce. Amazingly, Wayne was able to find the original vinyl top color and pattern.

Frequently, we do not get to drive a car a great distance; this one we did. We

drove it all around the serpentine hills in the Fallbrook area, plus out on Interstate 15 up to 80 mph. In the hills (easterners could call them mountains), the handling left a bit to be desired, which did not surprise us for a Buick of this vintage. The tires are the original 7.60 x 15 four-ply bias-type with the narrow whitewalls. He could have gone to radials that would have improved the handling a lot without disturbing the car's appearance, but he wanted to keep every aspect of this car original, which we commend. We were very disappointed with the brakes, and found ourselves using low range more than we should have for downhill braking. The floor shifter takes a little getting used to. It does not have the button found on most shifters of this vintage. Then, when going into reverse you have to notch the shifter to the left.

Despite what *MT* said years ago, this baby really heels in hard turns. The driver will not notice it nearly as much as the poor passenger, who has no dash-panel grab bar (like on the Grand Prix) or touring-designed grab-handle arm rest. On the plus side for handling, this car is equipped with air shocks which were a much needed option available on Buick in '62.

1961 Buick instrumentation was bizarre, as discussed earlier. The '62 instruments, much less tricky, are far more readable with nice crisp, white numerals on a black field. I just love that '61-62 Buick dash design, very similar to the '61 Lincoln, but in my opinion a bit nicer.

Upon entering the car you sink into the driver's bucket seat. The buckets sit much too low for the average-height driver, but just right for owner Wayne Yonce who is six feet four. At five feet eight, I could barely see over the steering wheel, and the only fender end visible was the left front. These seats cry for a power lift, an option that was not available on this model. The Electra had a power bucket option that year, on the driver's side only.

Buick's Turbo-Drive automatic is as smooth as a ten-gallon drum of yogurt. Due to the variable-pitch feature of the torque converter stator blades, gear changes are not noticed at all. If you've driven the old Dynaflow, this transmission is very un-Buick-like. The brakes are big 12-inch drums, finned aluminum on the front, cast iron on the rear. Beginning in 1958, Buick led the industry in brake improvement, but once you're used to today's front discs

1962 BUICK WILDCAT

you may not be satisfied with the '62 Buick setup, and we definitely were not.

It's in the performance department where this Wildcat sings. If you really want to punch it, stay in low up until over 30 and then slam it into drive. You will experience exhilarating performance all the way up to 70 mph and beyond. The Wildcat is a real thrill on the Interstate, guaranteed to leave everything but the CHP far behind. The air-conditioning at any speed will put icicles on Santa's beard while flying along any California interstate in midsummer. Unfortunately this car does not run very well on today's anemic premium, unleaded fuels, and octane booster is a must if you want the full experience of what the Wildcat was meant to be. Wind noise at high speeds is annoying, but that just may be windlace problems on this restoration, and not an inherent problem with the car. We did note that very little of the legendary solid

Buick road feel was transmitted through the very power steering, especially in the hills. In general we loved the car and hated to give it up. The greatest beauty of the car, however, is the meticulous detail in the upgrading of a fine original. Wayne has returned every little nut, bolt and washer to the original cadmium plating where originally specified, and put all of the little color code marks on engine accessories, wires and parts. It probably never left the showroom looking this good, but he has detailed the car to what Buick originally meant it to be. It is flawless, but not over-restored. This was a fairly well equipped car when new, and Wayne has added a lot of accessories. But we noted that it still lacks power bucket seats, Posi-Traction, Wonder Bar radio, and power door locks. Go for it, Wayne.

The Cardinal Red paint job with a matching red interior may not shave a tenth of a second off the 0-60 time, but it sure makes this Wildcat look like it's going 100 when stopped at the gas pump. And be assured, there will be plenty of gas stops, as this baby can guzzle gas like the Dallas Cowboys going

through Gatorade! However, at a steady 60 on the road, it can deliver up to 16 mpg, as the owner can attest having driven it to the 1993 Buick National Meet in Phoenix where the car won a first in class and senior award, the 1993 AACA Western National Fall Meet in Sunnyvale, California, where it was a junior first, and the 1994 AACA Western Spring Meet in Palm Springs — taking a senior award. ❑

Acknowledgments and Bibliography

"*Wildcat From Buick,*" Motor Trend, *August 1962;* "*Buick Wildcat,*" Car Life, *July 1962;* "*1,000 Mile Test Drive Compares T-Bird, Wildcat and Chrysler 333-H,*" Popular Science, *August 1962;* 1962 Buick Wildcat/Skylark Brochures and Buick Specifications Sheets, *Buick Motor Division, 1962;* Standard Catalog of Buick, 1903-1990, *by Mary Sieber and Ken Buttolph, Krause Publications, 1991;* Encyclopedia of American Cars, *1930-1980;* Consumer's Guide, *1984. Special thanks to Wayne Yonce, Fallbrook, California, for furnishing our driveReport car.*

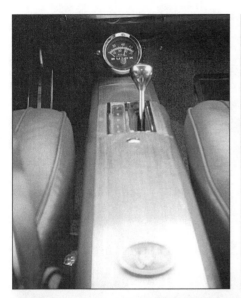

Early Sixties Buick Memories

In 1966 this author briefly owned a 1961 Buick Electra 225 convertible, white with a red interior. At the time I worked for McCann-Erickson Advertising in downtown Chicago. A woman working for McCann, knowing my love of cars, mentioned that her husband had died about six months earlier, and the Buick had not moved from the front of her home since. She said the battery was gone, she did not know the mechanical condition of the car, and I could have it "as is" for $800. I had the car towed to Park Ridge, where we were living, installed a new battery, changed the oil, cleaned the car and that was it. The mileage was then about 41,000, and the car was flawless. I soon sold it to an advertising art director friend, George Svestka, for about $1,600,

George paying me $400 down and $100 a month for a year. The widow was happy, George was happy, and after a year I was $800 ahead. But looking back now I realize that was one of the best ones that ever got away. I'll tell you one better. About this same time George found me a 1956 Olds 98 hardtop, 29,000 original miles and mint, still in the hands of the little-old-lady owner, for $250. I quickly turned that one for $500. Don't laugh. In those days suburban Chicago was crawling with cars like this, and I was turning them over at the rate of one or two a month, selling them to my advertising agency friends and earning about half again as much as I did at my copywriting job. Those were the days, and Chicago was the place!

*Facing page, top: Wildcat offers 0-60 in less than nine seconds. **Below:** Steering wheel appears quite delicate compared to rest of car. **This page, top:** Console with tachometer and floor shift is standard part of Wildcat package. **Above left:** Door trim is same as other Buicks. **Right:** Big car, big trunk. **Bottom:** There's that cat again, this time drawing attention to the engine's cubic-inch displacement.*

The Car You Wear

by **Michael Lamm,** *Editor*

1963 Buick Riviera

"It was first done as a La Salle, and that's [why we had] the two narrow grilles in the front fenders," recalls William L. (Bill) Mitchell, GM's design vice president and the father, so to speak, of the 1963 Riviera. "We originally did this study for Cadillac. The design, I felt, had to be razor sharp and very sheer.

"One night, while this was going on, I was over in England for the auto show, and I happened to be coming out of the Claridges on a damp, foggy evening. Here was this Rolls parked out front. I looked at those corners and sharp angles, and I thought, 'My God, if that car were just a foot lower—there's our silhouette.'"

At that time Ned Nickles was working under Mitchell in the confidential Special Projects studio where the Riviera-to-be first saw light. Nickles, who coincidentally fathered the 1953-54 Buick Skylark, says, "I believe I made the original sketch of the Riviera—a watercolor rendering in 3/4 front view at a high level. This

sketch was done as a 6-passenger convertible at first, and it had the two vertical fender nacelles with grilles...and concealed headlights behind those grilles. The idea was that the grilles were two La Salle noses, and at first we called this design *La Salle II*."

Bill Mitchell liked the car and the idea very much, and although it had no actual sponsor—no division behind it at that time—he ordered a full-sized clay model made. This clay came to be code-named XP-715, and the XP-715 had taken on a definite Riviera shape by early 1960. At that point, Mitchell began lobbying with GM's top management, trying to talk them into producing the XP-715.

Mr. Mitchell continues: "The car was intended, in my mind at least, as General Motors' answer to the Thunderbird. Ford was smarter than we were, because they came out with the 4-place T-Bird first. We used to display quite a few different close-coupled, 4-passenger idea cars in Motorama days, long before the 4-seater Thunderbird came out. The

Ford people would come over and take dimensions right off our cars. We saw them do it. So they made the Thunderbird using our show-cars, and we lust sat around and watched.

"So I took a private, separate studio and did this car. Mr. [John F.] Gordon, who was then GM president, took an interest in it, and he would sort of come in there and watch. Well, the clay was finally finished and put into the auditorium. I remember I showed it to Mr. Donner and Mr. Gordon after a board show one night. They liked it, but I remember them saying, 'Well, who's going to build it?'"

At first there was no guarantee that anyone would build it. Cadillac, the XP-715's first-intended, turned it down on grounds that they didn't need it. Cadillac was selling all the cars it could build at that time and didn't have the plant capacity to add another model. Chevrolet bowed out, too, for similar reasons. That left Pontiac, Oldsmobile, and Buick, all of whom wanted the XP-715 in varying degrees.

Corporate management decided that the only fair way to award the Riviera would be to hold a contest. Let the divisions compete, they suggested—let them present facts, figures, marketing strategy, manufacturing plans, research data, etc. Let them show how much they really wanted the new car. Pontiac, Olds, and Buick were initially allowed 60 days to prepare formal presentations.

Needless to say, Buick won. "I was at Buick at the time as assistant chief engineer in charge of everything except chassis and driveline," reminisces George Ryder, now director of engineering and product development for GM's overseas operations, "and I remember that by diligence, perseverance, hard work, motherhood, apple pie, and all that good stuff, we worked like s.o.b.'s and put together a pretty decent presentation."

Roland Withers, Buick's sales manager, puts it this way: "A lot of the men on the Executive Committee [to whom the presentations were made] had come from Cadillac, including Gordon, Cole, Roche, and several others. So Buick wasn't the committee's favorite division.

Well, we were told that whoever made the greatest presentation, with facts and research, and could prove they could do the best selling job.... So we made our presentation, and that day at lunch we were told by several executive vice presidents—they said, 'Why hell, you guys murdered them out there today, no question about it.' And they said we'd get the Riviera when it came to a vote. But you never can tell, because sure enough, later that afternoon some of our 'friends' decided to give everyone another chance. They said to come back in about three weeks, and they wanted this and that and the other thing answered. Which was a bunch of bull, because they were just telling these other divisions that they'd better beef it up or they'd lost the car. Well, we came back the second time, and that time we were awarded the car."

George Moon, the Riviera's chief interior designer and presently executive in charge of all GM passenger-car interiors, adds, "Buick had just taken on the McCann-Erickson ad agency at that time. It was very exciting for the designers, both exterior and interior, to be working with them on a program to sell Buick's need for this car to the corporation. Never before and never since has a division brought in advertising people to help promote and 'sell' a car to management. It was a very unusual thing.

"McCann-Erickson helped with the presentation...gave it a sophistication and professionalism that we normally didn't get. Buick was able to come up with the economics on how to build the car, how to merchandise it, and so forth, but I really think the McCann-Erickson/Buick design staff presentation had a great deal to do with influencing the corporate people. A lot was going on that I wasn't privy to, but I am aware that Marion Harper, who

Work on La Salle II began in Special Projects studio under Bill Mitchell in early 1960. First clays had twin-bladed La Salle bumpers.

Ned Nickles's original convertible sketch rests on easel at right. It had fender nacelles emulating earlier La Salle grille treatment.

PHOTOS COURTESY GM DESIGN STAFF

Four-door La Salle II was also contemplated at a time when Mitchell hoped Cadillac would buy the car. Air intake rested beneath bumper.

By August '60, Mitchell had fiberglass mockup with full interior but still no division to build it. At this point, GM held the contest.

Buick won, and early Buick clay used single headlamps, auxiliary beams below bumper.

By April 1961, Riviera needed only detailing and ornamentation: wheelcovers, fender scoops, insignia, etc. It was decided production would be held to 40,000 a year to buoy up demand.

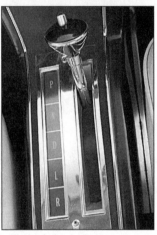

BUICK MOTOR DIV.

Riviera borrows gauges from '63 senior Buicks, and tilt wheel gives seven settings. Shift quadrant uses old-style PNDLR sequence.

Planned as a 4-passenger personal car, Riviera uses cruciform frame that gives a high driveshaft tunnel and recessed floor wells, so each seat is isolated. Crash

was then the chairman of McCann-Erickson and a very dynamic advertising man, lent great credence and weight to getting this car for Buick—establishing the image. His work is best summarized by the photo that Irving Penn made of the rear quarter window with the elegant-looking girl inside. You could see just her profile. It was the first attempt by Buick to reach the Rolls-Royce, Mercedes, elegant, sophisticated market with this new, very elite car."

Looking back today, there's no doubt that Buick needed the Riviera. Buick was fighting for its economic life, and more desperately

than insiders care to admit even now. Buick production had fallen by over half a million cars between 1955 and 1959—down from 738,814 to 232,579 respectively. The Eisenhower recession of 1958-59 came down especially hard on Buick.

General Motors brought seven key people into Buick during 1959-60, including a new general manager. These men had successes behind them in other GM divisions. They were brought to Buick to work miracles, and they did.

Edward D. Rollert, Buick's new general manager, arrived from Harrison Radiator Division, where he'd put that house in order.

But his most memorable triumph (before Buick) had been to save the Elgin Watch Co. in 1946-51. Ed Rollert streamlined Elgin's operations so that production rose 90% during his tenure. Hawkish, a mover of men, Rollert worked a similar feat at Buick.

Another Buick newcomer was chief engineer Lowell A. Kintigh (rhymes with minty), who replaced Oliver K. (Okay) Kelley, previously of GM Engineering Staff. Kintigh began his auto career at GM Research in 1929 as a junior engineer, moving to Olds in 1930. He rose to dyno room foreman in 1935, Olds staff engineer in 1940, experimental engineer in 1945, assistant chief Olds engineer in 1949,

Gentle ride, fine handling, quiet road manners, and plenty of punch make the Riviera a pleasure on any surface. Mileage averages 11 mpg.

Mrs. Hazel Daggett, who's GM v.p. Bill Mitchell's mother, prefers her silver-leathered, 45,000-mile 1964 Riviera to newer models.

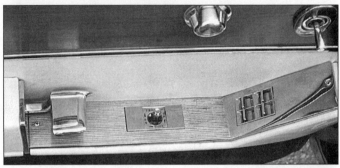

program to develop a 3-man rear bench died aborning. Leather was optional only in '63. Huge doors make back-seat entry easy, but they're heavy when tilt-parked.

Vacuum trunk release (top) rests in smallish glovebox. Doors have twin handles, the rear ones so back-seat passengers aren't trapped.

and he took Buick's top engineering spot in 1959.

Roland S. (Rollie) Withers began with GM on their customer research staff in 1933. He toured with GM's Parade of Progress during 1936-39; then throughout WW-II he documented GM's war effort. Owlish and a super salesman, Withers moved to AC Div. after the war and later became general manager of GM's United Motors Service Div. In 1961, he was named Buick's general sales manager.

George Ryder comments: "We had one of the most phenomenal teams at Buick at this time that you ever wanted to see. Ed Rollert, Rollie Withers, Lowell Kintigh—then Chuck

Chapman had the engine and transmission; Phil Bowser was engineer in charge of brakes, rear axle, and suspension. Rollert, because of his super effectiveness, welded this bunch together as a team in a phenomenal way that's really hard to duplicate. It was Rollert's personal effort, personal dedication, and his fantastic leadership ability that did it."

The new seven plus capable members of the old regime began turning Buick around in amazingly short order. It was as Ryder said: diligence, hard work, perseverance, motherhood, and apple pie. Buick's new team: 1) programmed total restyles for the 1961 big cars, 2) added the Special and Skylark that year, 3)

offered the new V-6, and 4) outbid Pontiac and Olds for the 1963 Riviera.

George Ryder continues, "And now we were doing the Riv, too—a very unusual thing. There was tremendous overlap at the time we were doing the Riviera. We were finishing up the Y-job [the code name for the Special]; we were in the middle of the B-C-jobs [full-sized Buicks]; and we were beginning the E-job [Riviera] all at the same time. It was difficult to keep changing hats, not just from a work standpoint but also because we were designing for divverent objectives. We had to analyze our design problems differently in the Riviera than in the next job we'd have to pick up two minutes later."

Buick 401 was Riv's standard V-8, with 425 optional. The '65 GS had twin 4s, 360 bhp.

Lined, roomy trunk tucks covered spare out of the way, giving Riviera perfectly flat floor.

Effortless speed is one of Riviera's problems. Optional speed minder helps prevent tickets.

Bill Mitchell's personal Riviera, the Silver Arrow I, sports extended front and rear fenders, chopped top, wire wheels, no ventipanes.

Basically a '63, Mitchell's Silver Arrow I puts headlights into glass fender nacelles. This car now makes its home in Flint museum.

Owen Owens demonstrates ample rear leg room. Rear of console holds lighter and ashtray, while radio speaker rests inside seat divider.

Razor-edge roof's inspiration came from Rolls Mitchell saw in England.

Comparative Specifications

	Thunderbird			Riviera		
	1963	1964	1965	1963	1964	1965
Base price, coupe	$4,065	$4,026	$4,394	$3,864	$3,914	$4,318
Total production	63,313	92,465	74,972	40,000	37,658	34,586
Wheelbase, inches		113.2			117.0	
Overall length, inches		205.4			208.0	
Shipping wt., lb., cpe.	4,195	3,825	4,470	4,025	4,025	4,063
Basic V-8, cid		390			401	
Basic bhp @ rpm		300 @ 4,600			325 @ 4,400	
Optional bhp @ rpm		400 @ 5,000*			340 & 360 @ 4,400	

*Ford offered the 400-bhp V-8 in 1962-63 only; for 1965 it was rated 340 bhp @ 5,000 rpm.

Chief engineer Lowell Kintigh now looks back at the 1963 Riviera with these words: "It's the kind of car you wear and not have to drive. Our whole objective was to make an outstanding handling and riding car out of what Bill Mitchell and his staff handed us. And based on a lot of sweat and tears, I feel we accomplished that."

The Riviera's cruciform frame looked similar to the big Buick's, yet it was totally different dimensionally. The X junction had a massive saddle that wrapped right around the driveline. The cruciform idea gave maximum floor depth and foot space, and since this was to be a 4-passenger car, the high driveshaft tunnel didn't bother anyone.

Except for the new body and frame, all other components were adaptations of standard Buick parts. Modified Electra 225 brakes and suspension included Al-Fin drums up front—finned aluminum drum shells bonded around cast-iron liners. The Riviera's standard engine was Buick's 401, with a 425-incher optional (325 and 340 bhp respectively). Dual Path Turbine Drive was the only transmission available, but it shifted more smoothly and had more positive action than in other Buicks.

The Riviera's toughest engineering challenge was to blend a high combination of ride and handling. *Road & Track* publisher John R. Bond, writing in *Car Life* for October 1962, made this interesting and unusual comparison of the Riviera and the then-new Mercedes 230-SL sports car.

"The Buick approach is different from that employed at Mercedes, but not diametrically opposed. The Mercedes engineers stated that some sacrifice in ride was acceptable (to them) if it proved necessary in order to get first-class handling qualities.

"Buick engineers wanted their traditional soft ride with sports-car-like roadability. In other words, they were not willing to sacrifice any ride to get what they wanted....

"The Riviera uses standard passenger-car suspension components, but with minor geometry changes. The front roll center is high for a Buick, but at 1.63 in. it is only 30% as high as the 230-SL. However, the Riviera's roll center at the rear is 12.6 in., or about 20% higher than the German sports car.

"Buick engineers believe in roll steer to increase understeer. The front end has 20% roll steer, the rear end 14%. Where Mercedes puts 75% of the total anti-roll force in front, Buick distributes the force 40/60, front to rear.

"Like Mercedes, Buick and tire company engineers cooperated to develop a special tire. The Riviera tire is a fairly conventional low-profile type, but it has a different cord angle, a wider tread and rounded-off tire shoulders instead of the usual sharp buttress. Buick engineers would not accept the belted tires' poor enveloping power, which causes some ride harshness."

John Bond's comment about custom-engineered tires for the Riviera shows how far Buick was willing to go to get good handling at little sacrifice in ride. Mr. Bond concludes, "The Riviera gives a luxury ride with better than average handling. The Mercedes-Benz gives superb handling with a slightly harsher ride than found in M-B sedans. But neither car begins to approach the roadability and adhesiveness of the modern European road racing car." (Buick, of course, wasn't trying to build a racing car.)

The name Riviera had been used for Buick hardtops since 1949, and it continued uninterrupted as a model designation through 1962. In 1963, of course, it denoted a separate and unique Buick line.

The Riviera's marketing philosophy held

specifications

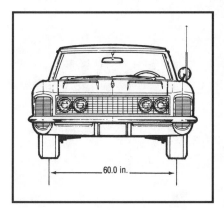

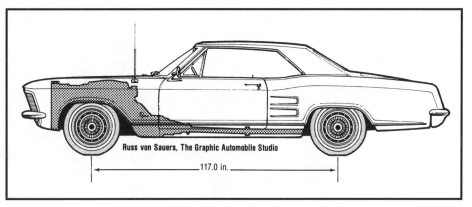

Russ von Sauers, The Graphic Automobile Studio

60.0 in.

117.0 in.

1963 Buick Riviera coupe

Price when new	$4333 f.o.b. Flint, Mich. (1963).
Standard equipment	Automatic transmission, power steering, power brakes, con-sole, bucket seats.
ENGINE	
Type	Ohv V-8, water-cooled, cast-iron block, 5 mains, full pressure lubrication.
Bore & stroke	4.3125 3.64 in.
Displacement	425 cid.
Max. bhp @ rpm	325 W 4400.
Man. torque @ rpm	445 W 2800.
Compression ratio	10.25:1.
Induction system	Single 4-barrel carburetor, mechanical fuel pump.
Exhaust system	Cast-iron manifolds, twin muf-flers with resonators.
Electrical system	12-volt battery/coil.
CLUTCH	
Type	None.
TRANSMISSION	
Type	Dual Path Turbine Drive 2-speed automatic with 5-element torque converter, console selector.
Ratios: Low	1.82:1 x 6.19 stall.
Drive	1.00:1 x 3.40 stall.
Reverse	1.82:1 x 6.19 stall.

DIFFERENTIAL	
Type	Spiral-bevel gears.
Ratio	3.23:1.
Drive axles	Semi-floating.
STEERING	
Type	Recirculating ball & nut with integral power assist.
Turns lock to lock	3.5.
Ratio	20.5:1.
Turn circle	43.6ft.
BRAKES	
Type	4-wheel hydraulic drums, internal expanding, vacuum assist.
Drum diameter	12.0 in.
Total swept area	320.5 sq. in.
CHASSIS & BODY	
Frame	Cruciform box-section frame X saddle, 3 crossmembers.
Body construction	All steel.
Body style	2-door, 4/ 5-passenger hardtop coupe.
SUSPENSION	
Front	Independent, unequal A-arms, coil springs. hydraulic tubular shocks, anti-roll bar.
Rear	Solid axle, coil springs, radius arms and one upper torque arm, hydraulic tubular shocks.
Tires	7.10 x 15 tubeless whitewalls.

Wheels	Welded steel discs, drop-center rims, lug-bolted to brake drums.
WEIGHTS & MEASURES	
Wheelbase	117.0 in.
Overall length	208.0 in.
Overall height	53.2 in.
Overall width	74.6 in.
Front tread	60.0 in.
Rear tread	59.0 in.
Ground clearance	5.5 in.
Curb weight	4100 lb.
CAPACITIES	
Crankcase	5 qt.
Cooling system	17 qt.
Fuel tank	20 gal.
FUEL CONSUMPTION	
Best	14-16mpg.
Average	10-12 mpg.

PERFORMANCE (from Car Life, Oct.1962):

0-30 mph	3.1 sec.
0-40 mph	4.3 sec.
0-50 mph	5.8 sec.
0-60 mph	7.7 sec.
0-70 mph	10.0 sec.
0-80mph	13.6 sec.
Standing 1/4 mile	16.2 sec. & 86 mph.
Top speed (av.)	123.0 mph.

BUICK MOTOR DIV.

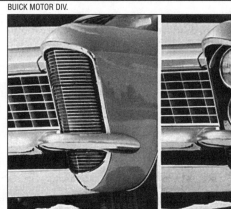

For the first two years, Riviera's headlights remained exposed, because management deemed hiding them too expensive. But for 1965, they mounted behind vacu-um-operated clamshells. Thus, they returned to the way Mitchell and Nickles wanted them to be in the first place.

some interesting twists, as Roland Withers explains. "I figured we could sell 50,000-55,000 Rivieras a year, but I told Management I wanted to go with only 40,000 a year for three years. I knew that Buick had gotten past its troubles of 1958-59, but even the dealers and customers didn't realize it. We needed a car to build showroom floor traffic, so what I wanted to do was take the Riviera and make a hot car out of it—keep it in short supply. People would want it and yet would have to wait for it. So we held to that, trying not to sell over 40,000 for three years running.

"There were some people who didn't agree with this, but it turned out to be the smart thing to do, because it made a helluva hot automobile, got us a tremendous amount of floor traffic and, of course, it made for a very good used car for those who bought it new and then traded it back a few years later."

Withers's idea of limiting production made sense in another way, too. The Riviera body was built in Fisher's Cleveland plant only—nowhere else—and on a single shift. Some people within Buick and GM urged putting on a double shift to increase production, but Withers pointed to Ford's Thunderbird experience. Thunderbirds, he reminded critics, were being built at the rate of over 10,000 a month for the first four months of the model year (October through January). After that, Ford would cut back to 3000 units per month for the rest of the year. That meant worker layoffs and disruption of plant routine—something Withers considered poor policy.

As it turned out, Buick produced and sold exactly 40,000 Rivieras that first year—1963—but slightly fewer for 1964 and '65 (see chart, p. 98). Thunderbirds, as you see, outsold Rivieras by considerable margins each year between 1963 and '65. And although Thunderbird had the advantage of two additional body styles (convertible and roadster), these accounted for very few actual sales.

As originally conceived, the 1963 Riviera was intended to come out with headlights concealed inside the fender nacelles. Management decided this would be too expensive, so for 1963-64, quad lamps were mounted in the grille.

Only connoisseurs can tell the 1964 from the '63 Riviera. Little chromed Circle R's were added to the taillights, wheelcovers, and hood ornament. There were also a few minor instrument panel changes for 1964. And a 360-bhp V-8 option arrived that year, with twin 4-barrel Carter carbs and finned aluminum rocker covers.

For 1965, the Riviera did get its disappearing headlights. George Ryder, the engineer, nearly lost his life over those. Seems they were testing the vacuum clamshell mechanism for the hidden lights. One snowy Saturday morning between Cripple Creek and Colorado Springs, at 13,000 feet and 270 below zero, Ryder and two others piled their experimental 1965 Riviera into a snowbank and got it hopelessly stuck. They had to walk out 15 miles. (The vacuum headlights, by the way, worked even in the stuck car.)

Other 1965 styling changes included re-

Another version of Mr. Mitchell's Silver Arrow had thermostatically controlled grille doors.

moval of the chrome scoop trim from the rear fenders, setting the taillights into the rear bumper, and ribbed rocker trim. A new 1965 Gran Sport package ($219) topped the line and included the 360-bhp V-8.

Owen Owens, the irrepressible Orinda, California, collector and prime mover of the Silverado Concours, invited me to drive two of his six 1963-65 Rivieras. I did, and it confirmed my opinion that except in brakes, no major improvements have been made in American luxury cars these past dozen or 50 years.

We drove Owen's twin 1963 Rivieras through the winding hills behind Berkeley, where suspensions, brakes, and engines got a considerable workout. The white car ran standard tire pressures (24/26 psi), whereas we pumped up the grey car's tires to 34/32 psi.

What a difference! Tire scrub and squeal in the white car held it to 35 mph through banked 180° U-bends, while the grey Riv sailed through at an easy, comfortable 45. With proper tire pressure, the Riviera can hold its own against any full-sized 1976 American car on the road.

Yet the grey car's taut tires make for a slightly jiggly ride. The white car feels much smoother. Both drive in extreme silence at any speed. Steering is quick and perhaps a trifle light. Brakes feel fine once I got used to their touchiness, but I do admit that discs outstop the Al-Fin drums, because after taking our high-speed photos, Owen and I could smell quite a bit of burned asbestos. Even so, there was no fade at that point. We didn't push the brakes to a fade condition, but I felt we were right on the edge.

Seating is superb, with the driver's leather bucket adjustable six ways, including for height and rake. Everything's in easy reach, yet I do admit that the instrument panel is a bit plain for a car of this type. George Moon, the man who designed this car's interior, says he had to work with the 1963 Buick sedan's dashboard. The only modification is some reworked sheet metal on each end. Dials, con-

trols, etc., are directly from the big 1963 Buicks.

The back seat is intended for two people, but I'd heard a tale from designer Ned Nickles that Buick sales execs had last-minute thoughts about the split rear bench and insisted on space for a center rider. Moon put through a crash program just before intro time but missed the deadline, so the first Rivs arrived in showrooms with the split rear seats. To everyone's surprise, no customers objected, and it wasn't unusual for a fifth passenger to straddle the driveshaft hump in the back. I tried it myself, and while it's not the height of comfort, I've sat on worse.

The big, 425-cid, 325-bhp V-8 puts out tremendous torque, and it lazes along so effortlessly at speed that the warning buzzer in both of Owen's cars came in very handy. With these, you set a movable needle in the speedometer to the speed you want to stay below, and when you hit that, a buzzer buzzes. Without it, you find yourself cruising 80 before you know it.

The Riviera, along with the Thunderbird, gave rise to what we today call personal luxury cars. For 1976, these include Monte Carlo, Grand Prix, Cordoba, Charger, Eldorado, Riviera, and T-Bird. Bill Mitchell mentioned recently that the 1977 or 1978 (he wasn't specific) Eldorado/Toronado/Riviera will get back more to the size of the 1963 Riv, and that's as it should be, he feels. Looking at his own customized 1963 Riviera, Mitchell says, "Doggone it, if we hadn't already done that car, I'd steal the idea today!" ☜

Our thanks to William L. Mitchell, Tom Christiansen, Drew Hare, George Moon, George Ryder, Cliff Merriott, Joe Karschner, and Gerry Rideout, all of General Motors; Ned Nickles, St. Clair Shores, Michigan; Lowell A. Kintigh and Forest R. McFarland, Flint, Michigan; Roland Withers, Boca Raton, Florida; Dick Nesbitt, Dearborn, Michigan; John R. Bond, Escondido, California; Terry Dunham, Fresno, California; and Owen Owens, Orinda, California.

1967 Buick GS 400
The Image Changer

by John F. Katz
photos by VInce Wright

THIS is not your father's Oldsmobile, but it isn't his Pontiac GTO either. It's a Buick, and in the sixties, at least, Buick waltzed to the conservative beat of its own easy-listening band. So when the boys from Flint finally joined in the rowdy, mid-size muscle-car mambo, they still played the tune with a distinctly Buick sound.

Even the look of Buick's GS 400, while lean and aggressive, left no doubt about its parentage: It was a near-perfect, 9/10-scale re-bop of a '65–66 Wildcat. Parked solo for photography, with no other vehicles around for reference, our driveReport car could just as easily be its own full-size sister. That's partly because all Buicks, great and small, still shared a visual link to the '63–65 Riviera. Notice particularly the horizontal break along the side of the body, level with the top of the grille, with rounded sheet metal above it and more sheer surfaces below. Notice, also, the sharp-edged roofline. Then come on inside and see how a Buick muscle car drives.

Start her up and listen to the idle. Pay careful attention, and you can hear/feel the syncopated lope of a high-overlap cam. But the sound is subtle and distant, not thrust crudely in your face. Not in a Buick.

Now let back the clutch. It chatters a bit, no matter how much gas you give it, but the rhythm of the cam smooths over as the big V-8 applies its maritime

Above left: *GS 400 presents a clean frontal appearance.* **Top right:** *Airscoops enhance muscle image.* **Above right:** *Model i.d. is also found on rear fenders.*

torque to the unyielding pavement. The long, stout Hurst shifter rows some distance through the air but still clicks tightly from cog to cog, as the GS hustles with muscle-car urgency toward the next suburban obstacle. Now the engine speaks with deep, V-8 thunder, but softly—so softly, it is nearly drowned out by the turbine-like whine of the transmission. A few years later, Buick would bill itself as "something to believe in," but clearly this one already believed that it shouldn't ruffle its passengers, not even while shutting down the hot rod in the next lane over.

I had noticed that owner Louis Serra winds the engine out just a little further in the tall 2.20:1 first gear and then shifts directly into third. I tried this myself and found it worked fairly well. The ratios are so close, in fact, that the brawny V-8 can leap from first directly into fourth—with an obvious sacrifice in performance.

But an unhurried driving style makes more sense around suburban Philadelphia, where perpetually dense traffic discouraged us from exploring the upper registers of the GS 400's repertoire. Louis told us that the thrust kicks in as low as 2,000 rpm anyway, but it was difficult to tell. A tach was an option, and the original owner didn't order one. So there's just a huge, bright bauble in the console where the rpm-o-meter would have gone. I did notice that I could back down to 25 mph in third, slam the gas without shifting, and still launch like a small Hebrew slingshot aimed at a large, loathsome Philistine. But even then, there's as much *whoosh* as rumble in the Buick's soundtrack. Louis men-

tioned that his modern-car friends find the old GS pretty noisy. Compared to what? After loafing around in your Lexus, the GS is noisy. Next to a '67 GTO, it's as quiet as a Puritan village on a summer Sunday.

Of course the Buick image demanded effortless driving, and the GS 400's steering and brakes are boosted more than most enthusiasts would like. The steering returns very little road feel, but responds accurately and predictably. There are just over four turns from lock-to-lock, so the ratio isn't too fast, either. And if the big-block 400 weighs heavily on the Buick's nose, then the strong steering servo masks it. The GS corners flat and confident, and changes direction with the nimbleness of a compact.

Similarly, the finned aluminum drum brakes modulate easily in spite of the power boost, and they perform extremely well. We didn't stomp them repeatedly, but Louis said they resist fade well for their time. Even the clutch doesn't seem too stiff—until you've pumped it up and down in traffic for a while.

Surprisingly, then, the GS rides on the fine line between comfortably controlled and uncomfortably stiff. Shock control is actually better than the mid-sixties average, but overall the GS delivers a very un-Buick ride. Undoubtedly, at least some of the harshness can be blamed on the repro tires, which Louis chose for their accurate placement of the original Firestone red stripe. At least the body remains tight and solid, squeaking only a little over those infamous Philadelphia cobblestones.

What it lacks in ride, however, the GS makes up in interior comfort. The all-

vinyl front bucket seats look great and work better, leaning back at just the right angle and wrapping around the lower spine for long-term comfort. (*Motor Trend* griped that they "cradle the driver too much," which is kind of like complaining that your girlfriend is too pretty.) The hard and skinny-rimmed steering wheel juts up *a little* high and close, but this is 1967, and overall the driving position feels natural. The somewhat odd-looking wheel has one huge, flat spoke at six o'clock (designed as a crash pad, according to contemporary reports) and two more thin ones comfortably positioned at nine and three.

The gauge (singular) is huge and readily readable. That's all the info Buick offered, though: just one big, rectangular speedometer with a tiny vertical fuel gauge tucked, like an afterthought, at its extreme left end. A tach, as we said, cost extra, and no other dials were even offered. Look-alike knobs for the lights, wipers, cigarette lighter, and radio spread out across a bright panel at the bottom of the dash, and the slightly oblique angle of the panel doesn't make them any easier to reach. Switches and sliders for the heater and defroster sit higher and handier. Louis's car has factory air, but the only visible evidence of it are two air outlets and an extra position on the heater/defroster selector.

Visibility isn't too bad. That long, sharp hood actually looks shorter when you're sitting behind it, and the wide sail panels block less of the rear-quarter view than I expected. The rear seating area is fine for kids and adequate for adults, its worst shortcoming being a low and skimpy lower cushion. Whatever the Buick's interior deficiencies, however, they are typical of its time. On the whole, Flint created a competitive musclecar, as fast as most of its peers, yet sufficiently quiet and comfortable to merit that triple-shield badge.

Fifth place and trying harder

Buick certainly knew how to build big, fast, comfortable cars. The division proclaimed its supremacy in mid-'65 with the Riviera Gran Sport, a special edition, full-size freeway-gobbler packing a twin-carb, 425-c.i.d. V-8; specially tuned exhausts; high-performance automatic transmission; and a limited-slip rear.

But Buick General Manager Ed Rollert had watched the sales figures roll up for the Ford Mustang and Pontiac GTO, and he felt that Flint should share a slice of the youth market, too. So sometime after the hot Rivvie appeared, Buick leaped into the mid-size muscle wars with a Gran Sport edition of the Skylark.

Like the Pontiac GTO and Olds 4-4-2 before it, the Skylark GS stuffed a full-size engine into a mid-size body shell—in this case Buick's 401-c.i.d. V-8, producing the same 325 bhp at 4,600 rpm that it developed in Buick's 3,753-pound Wildcat.

(Technically, this should not have happened. The General's Engineering Policy Committee did not allow engines displacing more than 400 cubic inches to be installed in mid-size cars—and with a bore and stroke of 4.1875 x 3.640 inches, the Buick V-8 displaced almost *exactly* 401 cubes. But the committee agreed to wink at the single offending inch as long as Buick advertised the

Above left: *Front seat passengers have a reminder of what they're riding in on dashboard.* **Right:** *Stainless trim on and around front fenders adds just the right amount of flash.* **Below:** *Doors have typical late sixties GM appearance.*

engine as a "400" in the Skylark. Buick continued to list the same engine as a "401" in full-size models, and historians have been trying to sort out the inevitable confusion ever since.)

Buick offered the Skylark GS in three two-door body styles—sedan, hardtop, and convertible—but all three rode on the ragtop's box-section frame. Heavy-duty brakes and suspension and a

deluxe bucket-seat interior completed the package; Positraction was sorely needed but offered only as an option. Exterior identification was kept to a minimum.

Buick said the hot Skylark could scat from standstill to sixty in seven seconds, which independent road testers showed to be at least a half-second optimistic. Nonetheless, *Motor Trend* pro-

Buick vs. the Competition, 1967

	Buick GS 400	Chevelle SS 396*	Pontiac GTO*	Oldsmobile 4-4-2	Dodge Coronet R/T	Ford Fairlane GTA
Base price	$3,019	$2,875	$2,935	$3,015	$3,199	$3,064
C.i.d.	400	396	400	400	440	390
Bore x stroke, inches	4.04x3.90	4.09x3.76	4.12x3.75	4.00x3.98	4.32x3.75	4.05x3.78
Compression	10.25:1	11.0:1	10.75:1	10.5:1	10.1:1	10.5:1
Bhp @ rpm	340 @ 5,000	350 @ 5,200	360 @ 5,400	350 @ 5,000	375 @ 4,600	320 @ 4,800
Torque (lb-ft) @ rpm	440 @ 3,200	415 @ 3,400	438 @ 3,800	440 @ 3,600	480 @ 3,200	427 @ 3,200
Transmission	3-sp. auto	4-sp. manual	3-sp. auto	3-sp. auto	3-sp. auto	3-sp auto
Axle ratio	3.90:1	3.73:1	3.90:1	3.08:1	3.23:1	2.75:1
Wheelbase, inches	115	115	115	115	117	116
Curb weight, lb.	3,817	3,415	3,490	3,850	3,860	3,607
Stroke/bore	0.96	0.92	0.91	0.99	0.87	0.93
Bhp/c.i.d.	0.85	0.88	0.90	0.88	0.85	0.82
Lb/bhp	11.2	9.8	9.7	11.0	10.3	11.3
Performance						
0-60 mph, seconds	6.9	6.5	5.2	7.1	7.2	8.4
40-60 mph, seconds	3.2	4.0	2.0	4.2	3.0	4.2
50-70 mph, seconds	4.0	4.7	2.0	4.3	3.6	5.1
1/4 mile @ mph	15.2 @ 93	14.9 @ 96	14.1 @ 101	15.5 @ 91	15.4 @ 94	16.2 @ 89

*with dealer-installed kit that boosted horsepower to 375 @ 5,200.
**with Royal Bobcat modifications and Hurst headers; horsepower increase not specified.
All test results are from various contemporary issues of *Motor Trend*. All test cars were two-door hardtops except for the Fairlane, which was a convertible; the hardtop model would have cost $2,839 and weighed 3,301 pounds. Passing times for the Chevelle seem slow relative to its standing-start quarter mile; we can only guess that *MT* tried to lug it through the passing test without shifting.

specifications

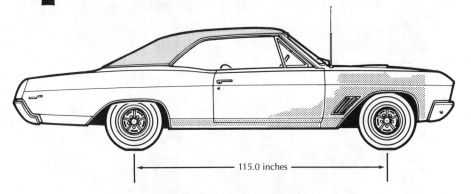

←—— 115.0 inches ——→   ←— 58.0 inches —→

1967 Buick GS 400

Price	$3,019
Std. equipment incl.	400-c.i.d. V-8; hood scoops, Wide Oval red-stripe tires; vinyl bucket seats, carpeting, deluxe steering wheel, dual horns
Options on dR car	4-speed transmission, power steering, power brakes, air conditioning, Positraction, chrome wheels, vinyl top, console, radio, rear speaker, custom seat belts, tinted glass, tilt wheel, California air injector
Price as equipped	$4,335

ENGINE

Type	V-8
Bore x stroke	4.04 inches x 3.90 inches
Displacement	400 cubic inches
Compression ratio	10.25:1
Horsepower @ rpm	340 @ 5,000 (gross)
Torque @ rpm	440 @ 3,200 (gross)
Taxable horsepower	55.9
Valve configuration	Ohv
Valve lifters	Hydraulic
Main bearings	5
Induction system	1 Rochester 4-bbl
Fuel system	Mechanical pump
Lubrication system	Pressure, gear pump
Cooling system	Pressure
Exhaust system	Dual, reverse flow
Electrical system	12-volts

TRANSMISSION

Type	4-speed manual, all synchro

Ratios:	1st	2.20:1
	2nd	1.64:1
	3rd	1.28:1
	4th	1.00:1
	Reverse	2.27:1

CLUTCH

Type	Single dry disc
Diameter	11.0 inches

DIFFERENTIAL

Type	Rear; hypoid, with clutch-type limited-slip differential
Ratio	3.36:1

STEERING

Type	Saginaw recirculating ball with integral hydraulic servo
Turns lock-to-lock	4.1
Ratios	17.5:1 gear; 20.9:1 overall
Turning circle	40.6 feet

BRAKES

Type	4-wheel hydraulic with dual circuits and vacuum servo
Type and size	Front: 9.5-inch finned aluminum drum. Rear: 9.5-inch iron drum
Swept area	268.6 square inches
Parking brake	Mechanical, on rear drums

CHASSIS & BODY

Construction	Semi-unit body on box-section perimeter frame

SUSPENSION

Front	Independent, upper and lower control arms, coil springs, link-type anti-roll bar
Rear	Live axle, two lower trailing links, two upper semi-trailing anti-torque links, coil springs
Shock absorbers	Telescopic hydraulic
Tires	Firestone Wide Oval F70x14
Wheels	Stamped steel 6JKx14

WEIGHTS AND MEASURES

Wheelbase	115.0 inches
Overall length	205.0 inches
Overall width	75.4 inches
Overall height	53.1 inches
Front track	58.0 inches
Rear track	59.0 inches
Min. road clearance	6.9 inches
Curb weight	3,765 pounds
Distribution, f/r	56.3/43.7

CAPACITIES

Crankcase	5.0 quarts (with filter)
Cooling system	16.6 quarts
Fuel tank	20 gallons
Transmission	22 pints
Drive axle	2.75 pints

CALCULATED DATA

Horsepower per c.i.d.	0.85
Weight per hp	11.1 pounds
P.S.I. (brakes)	14.0
Stroke/bore ratio	0.965

Left: Round cove in transmission tunnel is just begging for a tachometer. *Right:* Hurst shifter helps assure fast action through the gears.

claimed their smooth-riding Skylark GS "another winner" as well as proof "that a performance machine doesn't have to have a harsh ride to handle well."

Rollert departed in June '65 to take over as vice president of the Car and Truck Group, but his successor, General Manufacturing Manager Bob Kessler, continued his policy of model proliferation and youth-oriented marketing. All Buick intermediates rolled into '66 with all-new and softer-looking sheet metal, clearly influenced by the direction of Buick's full-size line. Base-model Specials retained their traditional Buick "VentiPorts," but Skylarks now sported fake air outlets behind the front wheel wells instead. Gran Sports strutted more confidently this year, with blacked-out trim, subtle stripes, and twin ersatz air intakes on top of the hood. Inside, a bench seat was now available.

Motor Trend tested a Skylark Gran Sport in July '66, and measured a 0-60 time of 7.6 seconds, and a 90.54-mph quarter-mile in 15.47. Assistant Editor Steve Kelly described the Buick as "an automobile of many virtues and very few vices."

Earlier that year, however, *Car and Driver* had hired racer Masten Gregory to wring out all the hot mid-size cars at Bridgehampton. Chrysler opted out (they feared that Ford and GM might—imagine such a thing—*cheat*), leaving the General's four intermediates vs. the Ford Fairlane GTA and Mercury Cyclone GT. The Skylark GS finished dead last, both at Bridgehampton (with a lap time of 2:08.5) and in quarter-mile acceleration (14.92 seconds at 95.13 mph). Still, the Buick scored the quickest stops from 80 mph, and Gregory gave it high

marks as the most "forgiving" car of the six, despite its having the softest suspension.

Further, the *C/D* staff conceded that the Buick's two-speed automatic transmission hamstrung it in a field of four-speed manual competitors (except for the three-speed automatic Fairlane). They also allowed that the GS was the most "stock" of the six cars (meaning Buick had cheated the least), and in a subjective evaluation rated it fourth, behind its three GM cousins but ahead of both Dearborn products. "It is too bad Buick doesn't really pay some close attention to the demands of this super-car market," they concluded, "because the Gran Sport has tremendous potential. If they ever decide to go to work, look out."

In the more critical sales race, Buick moved only 13,816 Gran Sport Skylarks

for '66, finishing fifth behind the Pontiac GTO (96,946), Chevelle SS (72,272), Ford Fairlane GT/GTA (37,342), and Oldsmobile 4-4-2 (21,997). *Car Life* blamed the Buick's conservative styling and high price relative to its performance, citing a "design/specification philosophy...more nearly suit[ed]...to sporting Gran-daddies than to Gran young sports."

But Buick did go to work for '67, with a new GS designed to turn that image around.

Flint Lock

For one thing, Buick changed the name of its hot mid-size from "Skylark Gran Sport" to "GS 400"—officially recognizing the abbreviation that everyone was using anyway, while separating the performance model from the increasing-

Top: *GS 400 combines a superior ride with good braking and handling.* ***Above:*** *Although body shell was shared among several GM divisions, the GS 400 manages to be readily recognized as a Buick and nothing but a Buick.*

*Above left: Front end styling is all sharp angles. **Top right:** Dashboard and steering wheel are decidedly non-sporty. **Above right:** Driving position is just right for sanctioned or impromptu drags.*

ly luxury-oriented Skylark. For additional distinction, the GS wore the simpler grille from the base-line Special, spruced up with a red accent, and its hood-top air inlets evolved into a pair of low-profile scoops that were painted black regardless of body color. The GS shared its more boldly pointed front end and somewhat softened hindquarters with all '67 Buick intermediates. The front-fender air outlets of both the Skylark and GS evolved into two bright-metal fish gills, while Specials kept their VentiPorts. Little was changed inside, except for an odd-looking steering wheel with one broad vertical spoke and two slim horizontal ones, a design said to reduce injuries if impacted.

Under the hood, however, was a totally new and more modern engine. In *The Buick: A Complete History*, authors Dunham and Gustin credit the new mill chiefly to engineer Cliff Studaker, who told them how hard it had been to sell the total, expensive overhaul to the front office. But Buick's big V-8 dated from 1953 and had reached the limit of its development.

The problem with the old "vertical valve" or "nailhead" V-8 was that it crowded both intake and exhaust valves, plus the lifter bosses, onto the inboard sides of its pent-roof heads. This layout did keep the valve linkage short and stiff, and the combustion chambers admirably compact (with domed pistons), while minimizing the overall width of the unit. The intake ports traced a gentle S-curve, and by 1953 standards the engine developed a fairly high specific output (.583 bhp/c.i.d.), with abundant low-end torque and exceptionally quiet running. But the configuration also limited the size of the valves and forced the exhaust through a tight, tortuous path over the top of the head—characteristics which had grown increasingly troublesome as the engineers pushed for more peak ponies at higher rpm.

Buick had already taken a different direction with the design of its little aluminum V-8 in 1961, and of the iron V-6 and 300-c.i.d. V-8 that derived from it. The replacement for the big V-8 would more closely resemble these newer engines.

Engineer Joe Turlay, a veteran of the original V-8 program, developed a combustion chamber that combined a dish in the piston crown with a saucer shape in the head. The saucer was tilted, so the chamber resembled a wedge in cross section, with only 15 degrees between the axes of the valves and the cylinders. Still, the saucer shape provided a better ratio of volume to surface area than would be possible with a conventional wedge head. This gave the new Buick superior thermal efficiency, for improved fuel economy and lower hydrocarbon emissions.

Detail improvements simplified head assembly. Where Buick had used dual valve springs previously, now each valve had only a single spring with an internal, flat-wound damper. Valve guides were no longer pressed in but were cast integral with the head, as were the rocker-shaft stands.

Studaker's engineers decided that the big-bore, short-stroke ideal had reached its limit as well. They salvaged as much block tooling as possible by keeping the 4.75-inch bore spacing of the old 425 and 401. But where these older engines had shared a 3.64-inch crank, Buick now stretched their common stroke to 3.90 inches, while decreasing bore

Petit Sport

Alongside the 1967 GS 400, Buick released the baby-brother GS 340, "a brand-new offering that puts performance within the range of budget car buyers." Available only as a two-door hardtop, its list price of just $2,845 undercut even the Chevelle SS by $30. In many ways the 340 anticipated Plymouth's economy-muscle Road Runner by a full model year, while in others it missed the point entirely.

Lift the hood, and you'd find an engine that strongly resembled the big-block 400, with the same square-shouldered valve covers, and all the accessory drives in nearly the same places. The most obvious external difference was a round, open air cleaner, dressed up in chrome, in place of the 400's spacey, molded-plastic unit. But the 340 engine was in fact a small-block, a direct descendant of the aluminum 215 and iron 300. Buick had stroked the 300 to 340 cubic inches for the '66 LeSabre and mid-size wagons, and for '67 installed a 220-bhp 340 two-barrel in Skylark four-door hardtops as well.

The GS 340 added a four-barrel carb for 260 bhp at 4,200 rpm, and 365 foot pounds of torque at 2,800—more than enough power for any public road, but still well short of the price of admission to the authentic muscle-car club. (For perspective, Pontiac offered a 250-bhp 326 as a $95 option in any Tempest.) Transmission

choices were limited to a three-speed manual or two-speed automatic, with Positraction available at extra cost.

Buick sales literature listed "specific" springs, shocks, and front anti-roll bar as GS 340 features, but the real heavy-duty pieces, including a rear sway bar and fast-ratio manual steering, were part of an optional "Sport Pac."

Tires were standard-size 7.75 x 14s, and brakes were standard-issue Skylark drums; rather than the wide ovals and finned drums of the GS 400. Front discs were, again, listed on the option sheet.

But what the 340 lacked in content, Buick tried to make up in appearance. The baby GS shared its big brother's hood scoops, only painted red instead of black, and wore broad red stripes on its lower body. For suitably striking contrast, exterior colors were limited to white or "platinum mist." Inside, the GS 340 came with rather stark-looking black-vinyl bench seats; if buckets were even offered, the brochure doesn't mention them.

Despite sales of only 3,692 GS 340s in '67, Buick persisted with the concept, releasing a slightly bored-out GS 350 version of the re-designed '68. In fact, Flint continued to offer a junior-edition GS of some form until the Century replaced the Skylark in '73. Sales were always uneven, at best.

Above: *Massive air cleaner lifts to reveal massive 340-bhp engine.*

dimensions from 4.3125 and 4.1875, respectively, to 4.1875 and 4.04. This yielded new cubic capacities of 429.7 (call it 430) and 399.7 (400) cubic inches. The nut-and-bolt Nostradamuses at both *Motor Trend* and *Car Life* quickly crunched some numbers and noticed that, by combining the old 425's bore with the new 3.90 stroke, Buick could painlessly produce an engine of 455 cubic inches.

Despite industry trends, this was not a "thin-wall" block, and it weighed pretty much the same as the old one. Main bearings grew from 2.499 inches to 3.25, to tie with Pontiac's as the largest in the industry. The crank kept the same 2.25-inch pins as before, but was now cast from nodular iron, rather than forged. The engineers also shortened and stiffened the entire structure by moving the water, fuel, and oil pumps, along with the distributor drive and oil filter, to a die-cast aluminum housing at the front of the block—although this

also left the distributor vulnerable to splashing water. At the same time, however, the pan gasket rail crept up to just 1/4-inch below the crankshaft centerline—a change which, *MT* pointed out, could only simplify installation of a Toronado-style front drive.

With 10.5:1 heads and 360 bhp at 5,000 rpm, the 430 was now the standard engine in the Wildcat, Electra, and Riviera, while the new 400 replaced the 401 (which Buick had been calling a 400) in the GS. Compression with the smaller engine was only 10.25:1, but the camshaft, said *Car Life*, was "one of the hottest... installed in a regular production car," with 298 degrees of intake, 315 degrees of exhaust, and 61 degrees of overlap. Quick-bleed lifters allowed 5,800-rpm operation. With the new head design, valves grew to 2.00 inches on the intake side, and to 1.625 on the exhausts, with lifts of .4124 and .449, respectively.

Feeding these hungry heads was a

dual-plane intake manifold topped by a Rochester Quadrajet with 1.375-inch primaries and 2.25-inch secondaries; on top of that was a unique red plastic air cleaner with twin side scoops leading into a chamber of stationary spiral vanes said to improve swirl and turbulence in the intake charge. At least it looked really cool.

As with the other GM mid-size musclecars, a heavy-duty three-speed manual transmission remained as standard, with a close-ratio four-speed as an option. But while civilian Skylarks retained their two-speed "Super Turbine 200" automatic, shiftless GS 400's now shared Buick's three-speed Super Turbine 300 with their full-size bunkmates. Olds and Pontiac arranged similar upgrades for the 4-4-2 and GTO, while Chevy stuck with the old Powerglide for the Chevelle SS.

But Buick automatics—even the two-speed—featured a variable-pitch torque converter; by switching the angle of the

Wouldn't you really rather have...

Louis Serra's father owned a GS 400 very much like our driveReport car. It, too, was gold, with a black vinyl top, but it was equipped with the Super Turbine 300 automatic transmission. Louis's brother still has it, and plans to restore it someday.

Louis, on the other hand, has always driven Corvettes. "But in the late eighties, I got interested in muscle cars," he told us. "I looked at a couple of 4-4-2 convertibles and a couple of GTO's, but when I saw this car it naturally piqued my interest."

Our driveReport car was assembled in Fremont, California, and delivered to Rollos Beckham Motors in Victorville. Its first owner was an Air Force captain who brought his Buick to Germany with him, and then back again to California. By then a colonel, he sold the car to his best friend, a man named Tom Marlette.

Marlette performed a complete, frame-off restoration but saved as many original pieces as he could, including all of the ex-

terior emblems. He also re-installed most of the original interior, replacing only the carpet. Similarly, the transmission and Positraction axle went back into the car having never been disassembled. Marlette did tear down the engine but instantly regretted his decision, for even at 80,000 miles he found almost no sign of wear.

Marlette sold the car to Louis, who has driven it only about 2,000 miles since. A copy of the window sticker confirms that it has been restored exactly as it left the factory. The combination of air conditioning and the close-ratio four speed is very rare, and was not offered with axle ratios shorter than the standard 3.36.

Louis readily admits that, even today, his Buick doesn't grab the same kind of attention as a contemporary Chevelle SS or Pontiac GTO. In fact, GS 400s are *still* losing the sales race to their GM stablemates. Louis figures his car would sell somewhere "in the high teens" (were he ever inclined to

sell it), while an equally well-restored '67 GTO or SS might command $20,000-$25,000. The Buick appeals to a smaller audience. They are a dedicated bunch, however, as GS values fluctuate less than those of the Chevelle SS, GTO, or 4-4-2.

The fact that the GS 400 shares so many parts with the other GM intermediates certainly simplifies restoration. Unfortunately, the Buick also suffers the same vulnerability to tinworm as its more collectible cousins. "The back windows leak into the trunk," Louis explained, "and so the trunk and quarter panels rust out. Then, if they are really bad, the floor rusts out. Fortunately, my car was in California most of the time, so it wasn't exposed to any of that."

Another problem is unique to the '67 GS: Its ten-bolt rear end was used for that year only ('68 and later cars ride on a wider axle), so good luck finding one if it breaks. A Chevelle 12-bolt rear will fit, if you're not too fussy about authenticity.

Above: *Air cleaner's design gives engine a well-finished look.* **Below:** *Valve cover decals proclaim number of cubes found in those eight cylinders.*

stator blades, the Super Turbines could vary the "gear" ratio of the converter from a low of 2.25:1, for a rapid launch off the line; to a high of 1.80:1 for better freeway efficiency. These transmissions also switched into "high" at idle to discourage creep.

As installed in the GS, the Super Turbine 300 would shift up from first to second at 4,600 rpm, and then hold out until 4,800 before slipping into third. *Car Life* recorded better acceleration times by shifting it manually at 5,600, but still called the Super Turbine "the best compromise for all-around performance." Remarkably, the three-speed automatic weighed a mere 58 pounds more than the close-ratio four-speed.

Curiously, Buick offered different optional consoles with the two different transmissions. GS automatics got a relatively conventional, bright metal console that reached back between the seats and provided a storage compartment, while stick-shift cars had only an odd, black-plastic apron that floated between the dash and the transmission tunnel. Either design provided space for a tach, but the tach itself was a separate option.

Regardless of the transmission you ordered, however, every GS 400 came with the toughest rear axle installed in any GM intermediate: a unique unit with oversized half-shafts and phosphate-coated gears. Still no Positraction, however, except as an extra-cost option. Final-drive ratios ranged from 4.30 to 2.73, which yielded theoretical maximum speeds ranging from 89 to 137

mph. Standard ratios were 3.36 with manual transmission and 2.93 with the automatic. *Car Life* pointed out that anything numerically higher than 3.90 was pointless on street tires, anyway.

Tires had gotten better in '67, however, with the introduction of Firestone "Wide Ovals" and "Speedway Wide Treads" by Goodyear. Buick installed both, according to availability, on the GS 400. These were the first street tires shaped with a low, 0.70 ("70-series") aspect ratio, and the improvements they wrought in both straight-line traction and cornering power were regarded then as revolutionary.

Standard Special/Skylark brakes were still cast-iron drums all around, but on the GS 400 (and on the long-wheelbase Sportwagon) the front drums were now cooled by aluminum fins—an idea Buick had introduced to its big cars back in '58. Most GM cars could be ordered with front disc brakes by then anyway, and the GS was no exception. With their four-piston calipers, the 11-inch vented discs drew raves from everyone who tested them. *Motor Trend* stopped a disc-brake GS from 60 mph in just 155 feet.

Of course, the GS retained its stiff convertible frame, which *Car Life* credited with the Buick's superior directional stability (better, said the scribes, than the Chevelle, GTO, or 4-4-2). Spring rates of 133 lb./in. in front and 116 lb./in. in back (both measured at the wheel) were softer than the magazine would have liked, but still plenty stiff by Buick standards.

In fact, the previously scornful *Car Life* now offered enthusiastic accolades. The GS 400 "follows the accepted 'Supercar' format with an unexpected excellence," wrote the editors. "The whole character of the car has undergone a transformation." *Motor Trend* cited "handling prowess that would make a dyed-in-the-wool sports car buff green with envy." Their test GS ran the quarter mile in 15.2 seconds at 93 mph—quicker than *any* factory-stock muscle car the magazine tested that year (see GS vs. the Competition, page 103).

But GS sales only held steady, at 13,813.

They would never be better. A shortened wheelbase and bold new body style arrived for '68; then the 455-c.i.d. engine came on board for 1970, heralded by the billboard-bold GS-X option package (see *SIA #146*). But the GS remained a minor player in the muscle-car league, until it was finally demoted to a mere handling package in 1973. ᏰᏕ

Bibliography and Acknowledgments

Terry B. Dunham and Lawrence R. Gustin, The Buick; *John A. Gunnell (editor)* Standard Catalog of American Cars 1946-1975; *Arch Brown, "1970 Buick GSX Stage 1,"* SIA #146; *John Ethridge, "Engine Evolution,"* Motor Trend, *September 1966; Bob McVay, "Skylark Gran Sport,"* Motor Trend, *May 1965; Steve Kelly, "Skylark & GS 400,"* Motor Trend, *April 1967; Martyn L. Schorr, "1,000 Miles in a Skylark GS-400,"* Cars, *date unknown; "6 Super Cars!"* Car and Driver, *March 1966; "GS 400,"* Car Life, *January 1967.*

Thanks to Kim M. Miller of the AACA Library and Research Center; Martyn L. Schorr of PMPR Inc; Joe Pauwels of Buick Motor Division; Mark Stevens of the Buick GS Club of America; Henry Siegle; special thanks to owner Louis Serra.

Above: *Distinctive seat design for the GS.* **Bottom:** *It looks like a regular Buick in the back.* **Below left:** *Rear seat room is o.k. for short trips.* **Below right:** *There's generous trunk room.*

1970 BUICK GSX STAGE I

THE VELVET HAMMER

by Arch Brown
photos by Rick Lenz

WHEN people talk about "Muscle" cars, more often than not they speak of the GTO, the "440" or hemi-powered MoPars, the Cyclone GT, or perhaps the 4-4-2. Or maybe, for the hairy-chested few, the Chevelle LS-6. In the mind of the average motorist, however, Buick has always been identified much more with luxury than with high performance.

But consider the Gran Sport. Not the Riviera Gran Sport of 1965-66; that was another breed altogether. We're talking here about what was originally called the Buick Skylark Gran Sport, the mid-sized hotshot, introduced in mid-1965

in response to the surprising popularity of Pontiac's GTO option.

And since the GTO is the car that started the "muscle car" thing in the first place, perhaps it would be appropriate to briefly review how it all came about.

In January 1963, General Motors president James Roche, in what passed for his infinite wisdom, had issued a decree

to the effect that all divisions were to withdraw from competitive events. Furthermore, engines in the forthcoming GM intermediates — the Buick Skylark/Special, Chevrolet Chevelle, Oldsmobile Cutlass and Pontiac Tempest — were to be limited, for some unfathomable reason, to 330 cubic inches' displacement. Either Roche had been looking the other way while the 1962 Dodges and Plymouths, powered by 413-c.i.d. "Max Wedge" engines, were romping all over the competition in National Hot Rod Association events; or else he simply failed to appreciate the publicity value to be derived from such records.

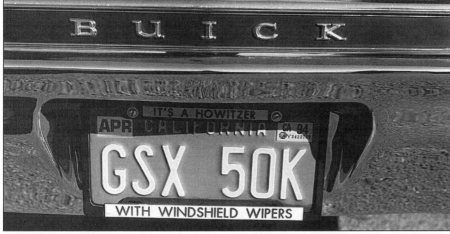

All this apparently amounted to no more than a challenge, as far as Pontiac chief engineer John Z. DeLorean was concerned. Determined to set performance, as well as sales records with his new intermediate-size Tempest, he combed through the corporate policy manual in search of a loophole.

He found one. No doubt Jim Roche hadn't intended it to be this way, but DeLorean learned that there was nothing in the policy manual to forbid the use of larger engines, provided they were carried on the option list, and not offered as standard equipment.

Hence the GTO option, a $295 pack-age, available to the buyer of any Tempest LeMans hardtop, pillared coupe or convertible. (GTO: "Gran Turismo Omologato," meaning a "sanctioned high-performance touring" machine. Only it sounds better in Italian, and was origi-nally applied to a particularly potent Ferrari model.)

Since the 326-c.i.d. Tempest engine used the same basic block as the 389 employed by the senior Pontiacs, it was no trick at all to pop the Bonneville engine into the intermediate-sized Tem-pest. Except it wasn't quite the same as the Bonneville mill, either, for as sup-plied with the GTO option, it was jazzed up with a high-performance camshaft and dual exhausts, together with freer-breathing heads borrowed from the divi-sion's 421-c.i.d. engine. In combination, these modifications raised the horse-power from 303 in the Bonneville to a scorching 325 in the GTO — with 348 available, if the buyer specified triple two-barrel carburetion. Beyond that, the GTO was supplied with specially valved shocks, heavy duty springs and stabilizer bar, and wide-rim wheels.

The GTO proved to be a hot ticket on Pontiac's sales floors from coast to coast, which caused a lot of people, apparently including Roche, to re-think

GSX badges abound in metal and decal form on the grille, sides and, shown here, the rear spoiler.

1970 BUICK GSX

their earlier positions. Sales of the GTO-equipped Tempests came to 32,450 that first year, and it was evident that twice that many could have found buyers, had they been available.

The other GM divisions were quick to play catch-up. For 1965 Oldsmobile dropped a 400-c.i.d. block into the Cutlass, to create the 4-4-2. Chevelle came up with the soon-to-be famous SS-396, and Buick introduced the Skylark Gran Sport.

At its debut in mid-1965, the Gran Sport was powered by a 401.2-c.i.d.

engine, first seen in the 1959 Electra and Invicta models. Since this fudged a bit on the corporation's 400-cubic-inch limit, Buick simply advertised it as a 400-cubic-inch powerplant. Horsepower was rated at 325, compared to 210 for the standard 300-c.i.d. V-8, which of course supplied excellent straight-line performance.

Other modifications included in the Gran Sport package were a beefed-up convertible frame, a stronger rear axle, revised springs and shocks, an all-synchro three-speed transmission, oversize tires on six-inch rims, and some special trim items.

According to *Car Life*, a Skylark GS with automatic transmission and 3.08:1 final drive had a top speed of 121 miles per hour, and did the standing quarter-mile in 15.3 seconds at 88 miles per hour. Creditable performance, this, compared to the standard Skylarks; and quite out of keeping with Buick's traditional, conservative image. But not yet in the same class as that of a four-speed GTO, tested by the same magazine. Running with 3.23:1 gears, the little Pontiac covered the quarter-mile in 14.8 seconds, at 99 miles per hour, and had a top speed of 135 mph.

Motor Trend gave the Skylark GS high marks, but *Car Life*'s editors expressed a couple of serious reservations about it. Weight distribution, for one thing: 58.3 percent of the car's heft was over the front wheels. And brakes. The Gran Sport was provided with a tougher lining material, thicker than that of the standard shoes. But it used the 9.5-inch drums of the garden-variety Skylark/Special models, and the lining area was actually less than that of the Chevy II. *Car Life* noted that the diminutive drums "can't dissipate heat fast enough to keep up with the load imposed upon them. Olds and Pontiac offer finned drums and metallic lining options, which alleviate this problem, but not Buick."

(The reader may recall that Buick drew a lot of fire for the mediocre brakes on its full-sized cars, back in the mid-fifties. It would have been reasonable to expect that the engineers would have learned a lesson from that, but evidently they hadn't.)

Only minor mechanical modifications were undertaken for 1966, and this time even *Motor Trend* was moved to comment that "The brakes aren't as good as they could be. The 9.5-inch drums front and rear do not provide the desirable braking power for a car capable of over 90 mph in a quarter-mile. This may be fine for the smaller-powered Specials with V-6s, but some addition should be made, or offered, on the performance models."

Corrective steps with respect to the binders were finally undertaken for 1967. Standard drum brakes still mea-

GSX Versus The Competition

Here's how Buick's 1970 GSX Stage I stacked up against some of its major competitors in the "Muscle Car" field:

	Buick GSX Stage I	Dodge Charger R/T	Mercury Cyclone GT	Oldsmobile Cutlass SX
Wheelbase	112″	117″	117″	112″
Overall length	202.0″	209.2″	209.9″	203.2″
Shipping wgt (hardtop)	3,582	3,390	3,434	3,659
Construction	Body/frame	Unit	Unit*	Body/frame
Engine c.i.d.	455.7	440.7	428.8	454.4
Stroke/bore ratio	0.905:1	0.868:1	0.823:1	1.029:1
Compression ratio	10.5:1	9.7:1	11.3:1	10.5:1
Rated horsepower/rpm	360/4,600	375/4,600	370/5,400	365/5,000
Rated torque/rpm	510/2,800	480/3,200	450/3,400	510/3,000
Transmission	Automatic	Automatic	Automatic	Automatic
Final drive ratio	3.42:1	3.55:1	3.50:1	3.08:1
Brakes (power)	Disc/drum	Disc/drum	Disc/drum	Disc/drum
Horsepower/c.i.d.	.790	.851	.863	.803
Weight (lb.)/hp**	9.95	9.04	9.28	10.02
Weight/c.i.d.	7.86	7.69	8.01	8.05
Performance*				
Standing 1/4 mile	14.4 sec.	14.9 sec.	14.5 sec.	14.8 sec.
Speed	96 mph	98 mph	99 mph	95 mph
Acceleration				
0-30 mph	2.7 sec.	2.7 sec.	2.7 sec.	2.6 sec.
0-45 mph	4.5 sec.	4.2 sec.	4.3 sec.	4.5 sec.
0-60 mph	6.4 sec.	6.4 sec.	6.4 sec.	6.6 sec.
0-75 mph	9.4 sec.	9.3 sec.	8.8 sec.	9.4 sec.
Passing				
40-60 mph	3.1 sec.	3.0 sec.	3.1 sec.	3.3 sec.
50-70 mph	3.5 sec.	3.2 sec.	3.3 sec.	3.8 sec.

* Unit with steel front frame
** Based on shipping weight of hardtop coupe
*** Buick statistics from *Hot Rod*, November 1969; others from *Motor Trend*, April 1970

Note: The reader is cautioned not to take horsepower readings too literally; for as noted in the text, with respect to "Muscle Cars" these figures were often understated for reasons having to do with insurance.

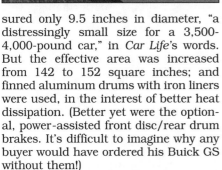

Above: *Accent stripe flows smoothly into spoiler.* Below left: *Two hood scoops help the 455 V-8 breathe easy.* Right: *Chromed styled steel wheels are part of the GSX package.*

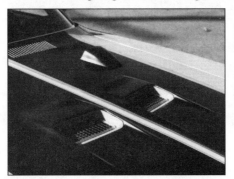

sured only 9.5 inches in diameter, "a distressingly small size for a 3,500-4,000-pound car," in *Car Life's* words. But the effective area was increased from 142 to 152 square inches; and finned aluminum drums with iron liners were used, in the interest of better heat dissipation. (Better yet were the optional, power-assisted front disc/rear drum brakes. It's difficult to imagine why any buyer would have ordered his Buick GS without them!)

There were two versions of the Gran Sport for 1967. The GS-340, offered only as a hardtop coupe, used a 260-horsepower, 340.2-c.i.d. engine, inherited from the previous year's full-sized LeSabre series. Unlike most of the overhead valve V-8s of the time, this one was slightly under-square, that is, the stroke was just a trifle greater than the bore.

Outselling the GS-340 by a margin of nearly four-to-one was the GS-400. Available in coupe and convertible, as well as hardtop form, it was powered by a new, 340-horsepower, 399.748-cubic-inch V-8, derived from the 429.7-c.i.d. mill employed by the new Buick Wildcat. This engine differed from 1966's 401-c.i.d. mill in at least one important respect: Its stroke/bore ratio was 0.965:1, compared to the previous 0.869:1. Evidently this change was undertaken in the interest of reducing exhaust emissions, though it resulted in improved performance as well. Horsepower was increased from 325 to 340, but torque was reduced just slightly, from 445 to 440.

Acceleration was sparkling. *Car Life* did the standing quarter-mile in 14.7 seconds, at 97 miles per hour. This didn't quite match the 14.5 sec./102 mph recorded by the same magazine with a ram-air GTO, but it was clearly a step toward establishing a new, high-performance image for Buick.

All of the General Motors intermediates were stunningly restyled for 1968.

1970 Buick Prices, Weights and Production
Intermediate Models:

	Price	Weight	Production
Skylark Series, 6-cylinder			
Coupe, 2-door	$2,685	3,155 lb.	18,620
Sedan, 4-door	$2,736	3,214 lb.	13,420
Skylark 350 Series, 6-cylinder			
Hardtop Coupe, 2-door	$2,859	3,180 lb.	70,918
Sedan, 4-door	$2,838	3,223 lb.	30,281
Skylark Custom Series, V-8			
Hardtop Coupe, 2-door	$3,132	3,435 lb.	36,367
Sedan, 4-door	$3,101	3,499 lb.	7,113
Hardtop Sedan, 4-door	$3,220	3,565 lb.	12,411
Convertible Coupe	$3,275	3,499 lb.	4,954
Gran Sport Series, V-8			
Hardtop Coupe, 2-door	$3,098	3,434 lb.	9,948
Gran Sport 455 Series, V-8			
Hardtop Coupe, 2-door	$3,283	3,562 lb.	8,732
Convertible Coupe	$3,469	3,619 lb.	1,416
Sportwagon Series, V-8			
Station Wagon, 2-seat	$3,210	3,775 lb.	2,239
Station Wagon, dual tailgate	$3,242	3,898 lb.	10,002

Notes:
1. Add $111 and 195 lb. for Skylark and Skylark 350 V-8s
2. The GSX was an option package, rather than a distinct series. Production is included in the Gran Sport 455 figures.

TOTAL PRODUCTION, INTERMEDIATE MODELS: 226,421

specifications

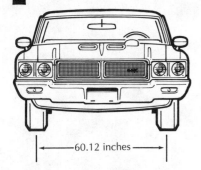

← 60.12 inches →

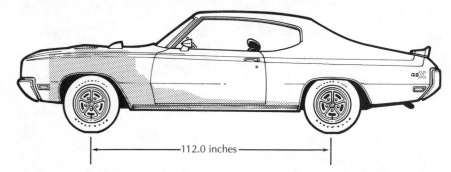

← 112.0 inches →

1970 Buick GSX

Base price (GS 455)	$3,283 f.o.b. factory, federal excise tax and preparation charges included
Price as equipped	$5,015.72 delivered in Santa Ana, California
Special equip./dR car	GSX package, including GSX hood, body and rocker panel stripes; molded plastic front and rear spoilers; right and left racing mirrors; hood tachometer; GSX headlamp bezels and additional GSX ornamentation; heavy duty cooling; 4-speed close-ratio transmission w/Hurst shifter; power front disc brakes; chromed styled steel wheels with 7-inch rims; super G60/15 wide oval, white-letter tires; Rallye Ride control package consisting of heavy duty wheels, rear stabilizer bar, front and rear firm ride tuned shocks, rear firm ride springs and rear lower control arm assembly; instrument gauges and rallye clock; consolette; black vinyl bucket seats with GSX ornamentation; Stage I package, including 360-hp high-performance 455-c.i.d. modified V-8 engine with high-lift camshaft, 10.5:1 compression pistons, special 4-bbl carburetor and low-restriction dual exhausts; 3.42:1 Positraction axle
Other options	Fast variable ratio power steering, Sonomatic radio with rear speaker, Soft-Ray tinted glass, carpet savers and handy maps; convenience group consisting of trunk light and mirror map light

ENGINE

Type	90-degree overhead-valve V-8
Bore x stroke	4.31 inches x 3.90 inches
Displacement	455.7 cubic inches
Compression ratio	10.5:1
Horsepower @ rpm	360 @ 4,600
Torque @ rpm	510 @ 2,800
Taxable horsepower	59.5
Valve diameter	Intake, 2.125 inches; exhaust, 1.750 inches
Camshaft	.490-inch lift, 316-degree duration intake, 340-degree exhaust, 90-degree overlap
Valve lifters	Hydraulic
Main bearings	5

Carburetion	Single Rochester Quadrajet; vacuum-operated secondary opening
Exhaust system	Dual; low-restriction

TRANSMISSION

Type	Muncie M21 4-speed manual, Hurst shifter
Ratios: 1st	2.20:1
2nd	1.64:1
3rd	1.28:1
4th	1.00:1
Reverse	2.27:1

CLUTCH

Diameter	11 inches
Actuation	Mechanical, foot pedal

DIFFERENTIAL

Type	Hypoid, Positraction
Ratio	3.42:1
Drive axles	Semi-floating

STEERING

Type	Saginaw recirculating ball nut, fast ratio, variable ratio, power-assisted
Turns lock-to-lock	4.5
Ratios	gear, 14.6 center, 11.0 at ends of travel; overall, 17.0 center, 13.6 at ends
Turning diameter	39.9 feet (curb/curb)

BRAKES

Type	Front disc, rear drum, power assisted
Disc diameter	11.0 inches
Drum diameter	9.5 inches
Effective area	104.2 square inches

CHASSIS & BODY

Construction	Body-on-frame
Frame	Perimeter type
Body construction	All steel
Body type	Sport coupe (hardtop)

SUSPENSION

Front	Independent, coil springs, ball joints
Rear	One-piece housing, coil springs, upper and lower torque arm location
Shock absorbers	Tuned, Firm-Ride direct-acting tubular, 1-inch diameter piston

Stabilizers	Front, link type, .970-inch diameter; rear, linkless, .875-inch diameter
Tires	G78/14 wide-oval
Wheels	Heavy duty styled steel, chrome plated, 7-inch rims

WEIGHTS AND MEASURES

Wheelbase	112.0 inches
Overall length	202.0 inches
Overall width	77.3 inches
Overall height	53.0 inches
Front track	60.12 inches
Rear track	59.0 inches
Min. road clearance	6.25 inches
Luggage capacity	16.4 cubic feet
Road weight	3,835 pounds (per *Road Test* magazine)

CAPACITIES

Crankcase	4 quarts (less filter)
Cooling system	19.2 quarts (with heater)
Fuel tank	20 gallons
Transmission	3 pounds
Rear axle	4.25 pounds

CALCULATED DATA

Horsepower per c.i.d.	.790
Weight per hp	10.7 pounds
Weight per c.i.d.	10.8 pounds

PERFORMANCE

PERFORMANCE	(from *Road Test*, 3/70, using a GS455 with Stage I equipment and 4-speed manual transmission
Standing 1/4 mile	14.26 seconds/101.12 mph
Braking (from 60 mph)	148 feet (drum brakes

PERFORMANCE	(from *Road Test*, 9/70, using a GSX with Stage I equipment and Turbo-HydraMatic transmission)
Standing 1/4 mile	13.95 seconds/ 100.5 mph
Braking (from 60 mph)	144-150 feet (front disc brakes)

PERFORMANCE	(From *Hot Rod*, 11/69, using a GS455 with Stage I equipment and Turbo-HydraMatic transmission
Standing 1/4 mile	14.4 seconds/96 mph
0-30 mph	2.7 seconds
0-45 mph	4.5 seconds
0-60 mph	6.4 seconds
0-75 mph	9.4 seconds
40-60 mph	3.1 seconds (229.9 feet)
50-70 mph	3.5 seconds (308.0 feet)

1970 BUICK GSX

Above: *Analog gauges and a "rallye" clock are also part of a GSX's standard equipment.* **Below left:** *Delco tar-top provides the juice.* **Below right:** *It wouldn't be GM muscle without a Hurst shifter.*

Four-door models employed a 116-inch wheelbase, an inch longer than before, while the two-door types were fitted to a bobtail, 112-inch chassis. No doubt styling was a consideration here, but oddly enough, the shorter wheelbase did good things for the ride, at least in freeway travel. *Hot Rod* magazine, in road-testing the earlier GM intermediates, had complained of a disconcerting, rhythmic pitch as first the front and then the rear wheels hit the joints in the cement. But as reported by that magazine's Eric Dahlquist, research revealed that "wheelbases of 112 inches (and 116 inches) were the magic sizes in seriously reducing the 'hop' condition, and that their 115-inch 1967 jobs were tuned smack in the middle of the wrong frequency band."

Once again there were two versions of the Gran Sport, known this time as the GS-350 and GS-400. A slight increase in the bore raised the displacement of the smaller engine to 349.3 cubic inches, boosting the horsepower to 280. Torque was similarly increased, from 365 to 375 foot pounds. Performance was enhanced correspondingly. This model came only as a two-door hardtop.

An interesting variant on the GS-350 was the California GS. Introduced only on the West Coast in 1967, it was offered nationally for 1968. Basically, it was the Special Deluxe (which is to say, bare bones) pillared coupe, equipped with the GS package, vinyl top, deluxe steering wheel and chromed wheels. A two-speed Super Turbine transmission, optional on the other GS-350s, was standard issue for the California GS.

But once again it was the GS-400 that was the hot ticket on the sales floor. It came, this time, as either a hardtop or a convertible, the pillared coupe having been dropped. Horsepower was listed at 340, same as before. Optional equipment included a three-speed version of the Super Turbine automatic transmission.

(Incidentally, one might expect that the shorter wheelbase of the 1968 GS models would have led to a reduction in weight, but things didn't work out that way. The 1968 models were actually heavier than their predecessors, by as much as 92 pounds in the case of the GS-350. Presumably the difference had to do with the stout convertible frame on which these cars were built.)

Among the dealer-installed options for the GS-400 was a new Stage I package which included 11.0:1 heads, solid skirt forged pistons with 0.007-inch clearance, high-lift camshaft, stronger valve springs, a revised lubrication system, and changes in the spark advance curve and carburetor calibration. The optional

automatic transmission, as combined with the Stage I equipment, was another three-speed job, with a 5,200 rpm governor for shift changes, to prevent over-revving. On paper, the Stage I package raised the GS-400's horsepower from 340 to 345, but 400 bhp is believed to be a more realistic figure.

Changes for 1969 were minimal, though a more aggressive-appearing grille was fitted to the GS models. A new, flow-through ventilation system led to the elimination of vent panes; and a new hood with functional air intakes was a GS exclusive. Two new automatic transmissions were introduced, the Turbo-HydraMatic 350 for the GS-350, and the Turbo-HydraMatic 400 — borrowed from the full-sized Buicks — for the GS-400. When combined with the Stage I package, this transmission had shift points specially calibrated for maximum performance.

The Stage I equipment, now a factory option, included Positraction, a heavy-duty cooling system, special mufflers and 2.5-inch tail pipes. *Motor Trend's* test crew was enthusiastic about their Stage I test car, noting that "The Stage I engine feels like a good supercar compromise. Power is there for street running, especially when you put your foot in it and open up all four barrels. Downshifting acceleration puts you back in your seat. One distinct characteristic of the engine seems to be its smoother idle with a big cam. It's not nearly as rough as similar supercars with similar grind cams."

The "Muscle Car" era was about to draw to a close when the 1970 models were introduced, but Buick used the

occasion to give the effort its best shot.

As before, there were two versions of the Gran Sport, both substantially more powerful than their predecessors. The GS-350, while unchanged with respect to engine displacement and compression ratio, was now rated at 315 horsepower, up from 280 in 1969. By the same token, torque was increased from 375 to 410 foot-pounds. While no match for the big-block GS, this car was no slug, either. *Road Test* did the standing quarter-mile in 17.4 seconds, at 88 miles per hour, which isn't too shabby except perhaps in comparison with the 15.27 sec./94.33 mph scored by *Car Life's* Olds Rallye 350.

From 1967 through '69, the big Buicks had been powered by a 429.7-c.i.d. V-8, basically a bored version of the engine employed by the GS-400. For 1970, this engine, bored this time to 455.7 cubes, was employed for the newly christened GS-455, as well as for the Riviera, Electra, Wildcat and LeSabre Custom models. The GS-455's compression ratio was reduced from 10.25:1 to 10.00:1, but horsepower edged up from 340 to 350. Torque was a healthy 510 foot pounds.

Stage I equipment was available once again, consisting this time of 10.50:1 heads, high-performance camshaft, heavy duty valve springs, low pressure dual exhausts, G60/15 wide-oval tires, and a 3.64:1 Positraction axle. Horsepower was advertised at 360, just ten more than the base GS-455. But that figure is purely fictional, presumably intended to help the insurance people sleep more soundly. The actual figure is surely well in excess of 400 bhp, gross.

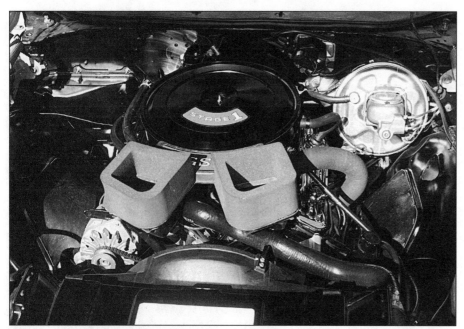

*Above and below left: Air cleaner makes sure you know what's under the hood. **Below right:** Trunk space is limited by placement of spare.*

1970 BUICK GSX

Performance was totally out of keeping with Buick's conservative image. According to *Road Test* magazine, the GS-455 Stage I would do the standing quarter mile in 14.26 seconds, at 101.12 miles per hour, which put it just a tad ahead of most of the competition. By way of comparison, *Car and Driver* (January 1970) reported 15.0 sec./96.5 mph for the Pontiac GTO-455; while the Mercury Cyclone, as tested by *Car Life* (March 1970) took 14.61 seconds to reach 99.22 miles per hour. Seemingly, about the only car that could edge the Stage I GS-455 — and that only slightly — was Plymouth's Super Bird (see *SIA* #100), clocked in a similar run by *Road Test* at 14.26 sec./103.7 mph.

But still, as *Automobile Quarterly* observed, the Buicks' rather traditional styling made them resemble "Flint stones." That situation was rectified with the introduction of the GSX, for this car, a sub-series of the GS-455, offered the ultimate in both luxury and performance. Available in only two colors, Saturn Yellow or Apollo White, this upscale model came with bucket seats, instrument gauges and rallye clock, a

unique GSX hood with tachometer, and a number of other performance and cosmetic items (see chart, page 113). A four-speed, close-ratio gearbox with Hurst shifter was standard, while the Turbo-HydraMatic transmission was optional at no additional charge. In combination with the Stage I package, this car left nothing to be desired in the performance realm.

Driving Impressions

The GSX Stage I displayed on these pages is probably the finest example to be found anywhere. A California car all of its life, it was purchased in September 1989 by the mother-and-son team of June Cecil and Sam Davis, of Garden Grove, California. At that time the odometer showed 41,255 miles, believed to be the correct, original figure. (Even at the time of our February 1994 test drive, it had logged only 45,880 miles!)

Almost immediately, the GSX was sent to Dave Kleiner, of GS Enterprises, Potosi, Wisconsin, where it received a full, frame-off restoration. The engine, meanwhile, was meticulously rebuilt and balanced by Dave Smith, of Corona, California. The quality of Kleiner's work — and Smith's — was demonstrated

when, in October 1990, the car took First Place at the Muscle Car Nationals. It captured another "First" the following May, at the GS Nationals in Bowling Green, Kentucky; and at the Buick Club of America's 1991 national meet, it scored 397 out of a possible 400 points.

And here's the kicker: Each year Sam Davis and June Cecil attend the GS Nationals, and for the past three years our driveReport car has accompanied them. Drag races are always a feature of that gathering, and each year it is June Cecil, now approaching her eightieth birthday, who races this car! A former logistics supervisor at Rockwell, June got into the muscle car hobby following her retirement, ten years ago. And a more knowledgeable enthusiast would be difficult to find. June and Sam own another 1970 GSX, that one fitted with the Turbo-HydraMatic transmission. But it's the four-speed job that is June's favorite.

We've driven a number of high-performance automobiles in recent years. Some of them — an LS-6 Chevelle comes to mind — are a bit of a handful. The GSX, however, is as docile as one could possibly wish, despite its tremendous power. Sam Davis refers to it as "the velvet hammer." The engine, which is fitted with hydraulic lifters, is smooth and quiet. The clutch, which requires only moderate pedal pressure, is equally smooth. Shifts are crisp and clean. The quick-ratio, variable-ratio power steering is easier to become accustomed to than we expected. The ride, while firm, is quite comfortable to our way of thinking, though we admit to something of a bias in that respect, for we detest soggy suspension. We had only a limited opportunity to test the brakes, of course, but we found them to be excellent. *Road Test*, which was able to wring out their GSX much more thoroughly than we could do, called the binders "good to excellent." And of course, acceleration is nothing short of fantastic.

There was one more Buick GSX, the 1971 model. But by that time it was a dealer-installed package, and it was mostly cosmetic in nature. Basically, there was only one Buick GS that year, powered by a detuned small-block engine, rated at 260 horsepower. The 455 mill was optional at extra cost, but it too had been tamed down in order to run on low-lead fuel. Its rating, this time, was 315 horsepower, or 345 with Stage I modifications.

Thus equipped, Buick's Gran Sport was still a creditably fast automobile, but it was no match for what had gone before. *Motor Trend*, road-testing a Stage I car, did the standing quarter-mile in 14.7 seconds, at 92.5 miles per hour, significantly slower than the 1970 model.

It's ironic. No sooner had Buick established itself as one of the fastest of the "muscle" cars — as well as the most luxurious — than the era of the high-performance intermediate came all too quickly to a close. ❑

Acknowledgments and Bibliography

Automotive Industries, *various issues*; *Dammann, George H.*, Seventy Years of Buick; *Dunham, Terry B. and Lawrence R. Gustin*, The Buick: A Complete History; *Gunnell, John (ed.)*, Standard Catalog of American Cars, 1946-1975; *Kelly, Steve*, "Mister Muscle of 1970," Hot Rod, *November 1969*; *McVay, Bob*, "Skylark Gran Sport Road Test," Motor Trend, *May 1965*; *Norbye, Jan P. and Jim Dunne*, Buick: The Postwar Years; *"Road Test: Buick Skylark Gran Sport,"* Car Life, *May 1965*; *"Freeway Flyer,"* Road Test, *September 1970* "Buick GS 455 Stage I," Road Test, *March 1970*; *"Buick — The 70s,"* Car Life, *October 1969*.

Our thanks to Helen Hutchings, Buick Club of America, Garden Grove, California. Special thanks to Sam Davis and June Cecil, Garden Grove, California.

A Buick that could crack 100 mph in the standing start/quarter mile is a far cry from the dignified banker-mobiles normally associated with the big B from Flint.

1970

To some of us, 1970 seems almost like yesterday. Yet nearly a quarter-century has passed, and 1970 was a significant year in a number of respects.

Those who follow the market will want to know that the Dow, that year, ranged from a low of 669 to a high of 842. What a pity we weren't buying stocks at prices like that. IBM perhaps; for 1970 was the year that company introduced the "floppy disc" on which this article will be submitted to *SIA*. The gross national product was up by five percent, inflation by 6.5 percent, while unemployment stood at a modest 4.9 percent.

History was being made in the area of race relations. On January 14th the United States Supreme Court set February 1, 1970, as the deadline for desegregating the public schools, and on August 31st more than 200 school districts throughout the South opened quietly with newly desegregated classes. The nation's concern in this area was underscored on April 8 when the Senate rejected, by a vote of 51 to 45, President Nixon's nomination of Judge G. Harrold Carswell to become an Associate Justice of the Supreme Court. Judge Carswell's "racist views" were cited as the reason for this action.

Women were commencing to flex their political muscles. On August 26, feminist Betty Friedan led a "Women's Strike for Equality," commemorating the 50th anniversary of the 19th Amendment, granting women the right to vote. Five months earlier, the Senate voted 64 to 17 to lower the voting age to 18. President Nixon signed the bill on June 22, calling for an immediate court test to determine the constitutionality of taking such action by statute rather than by constitutional amendment. And on December 21 the Supreme Court settled the issue once and for all, by ruling that 18-year-olds do indeed have the right to vote.

The Vietnam War, fated to rage for another five years, was already drawing numerous protests, some of them violent; and on May 4, four student demonstrators at Kent State University (Ohio) were shot and killed by National Guardsman. A subsequent investigation by a commission headed by former Pennsylvania governor William Scranton declared this action to have been "unnecessary, unwarranted and inexcusable."

Other deaths of the year included mystery novelist Erle Stanley Gardner, striptease artist Gypsy Rose Lee, screen comedian Charlie Ruggles, rock stars Janis Joplin and Jimi Hendrix and symphony conductor George Szell.

On the lighter side, Baltimore beat Cincinnati 4-0 in the World Series. Johnny Bush, of the Cincinnati team, was voted the National League's Most Valuable Player, while the corresponding American League recognition went to Baltimore's John "Boog" Powell.

The fashion world permitted unprecedented freedom during 1970. Skirts of all lengths were acceptable; pants could be worn on any occasion. Ethnic and "folksy" dress was O.K. Hair "teasing" was out, but Afro was in, among whites as well as blacks.

There was lots of good reading available. Among the best-selling works of fiction were Erich Segal's *Love Story*, John Fowles's *The French Lieutenant's Woman*, Mary Stewart's *The Crystal Cave*, Jimmy Breslin's *The Gang that Couldn't Shoot Straight* — and this writer's favorite, R. F. Delderfield's *God Is an Englishman*. Top selling non-fiction ranged from the *New English Bible* to *Everything You Always Wanted to Know About Sex but Were Afraid to Ask*. Other popular volumes included Robert Townsend's *Up the Organization*, Nancy Mitford's *Zelda* and Julius Fast's *Body Language*.

There was lots of good music that year. The Carpenters— Richard and Karen — had rocketed to fame; and for 1970 they had two major (and memorable) hits, both featuring arrangements by Richard Carpenter: "Close to You" and "We've Only Just Begun." (Regular readers of this publication may recall that 1970 was also the time when Richard Carpenter bought his first brand new automobile, a 'Cuda 440 Six-Pack. That car, which is still a treasured member of Richard's "Yesterday Once More" collection, is the subject of a drive-Report in *SIA* #98.) Other hit singles included "Let It Be" (The Beatles), "Bridge Over Troubled Water" (Simon and Garfunkel) and "Everything Is Beautiful" (Ray Stevens).

At the movies we saw *Love Story* (Ali McGraw and Ryan O'Neal), *Patton* (George C. Scott and Karl Malden), *Airport* (Burt Lancaster and Helen Hayes), and *M*A*S*H* (Elliott Gould and Donald Sutherland). Academy Awards went to *Patton* (Best Picture) and Glenda Jackson (Best Actress, for her role in *Women In Love*). George C. Scott was named Best Actor for his title role in *Patton*, but he refused the award.

But it was a different group that ranked as the top box office stars: The familiar names included Paul Newman, Clint Eastwood, Steve McQueen, John Wayne, Elliott Gould, Dustin Hoffman — and Barbra Streisand. Note, only one woman in the lot! Yet leading the list of "Stars of Tomorrow" were Liza Minelli, Goldie Hawn, Dyan Cannon and Marlo Thomas.

Television was enormously popular, of course. Top shows included *Marcus Welby M.D.*, *The Flip Wilson Show*, *Here's Lucy*, *Ironside*, *Gunsmoke*, *Hawaii Five-O* and the *ABC Movie of the Week*. And when ABC's Monday Night Football became TV's first prime-time football event, it captured 33 percent of the viewing audience.

Buick Model Year Production, 1903-2000

Year	Production Totals	Year	Production Totals	Year	Production Totals
1903	6	1936	179,533	1969	713,832
1904	37	1937	227,038	1970	459,931
1905	750	1938	173,905	1971	551,186
1906	1,400	1939	213,219	1972	679,641
1907	4,641	1940	310,995	1973	726,191
1908	8,820	1941	316,251	1974	400,262
1909	14,606	1942	16,601	1975	545,820
1910	30,525	1943	0	1976	706,249
1911	13,389	1944	0	1977	845,234
1912	19,812	1945	2,482	1978	776,515
1913	26,666	1946	156,080	1979	754,619
1914	32,889	1947	267,830	1980	854,011
1915	43,946	1948	275,504	1981	856,996
1916	124,834	1949	398,482	1982	739,984
1917	115,176	1950	552,827	1983	808,415
1918	77,691	1951	404,657	1984	906,626
1919	119,310	1952	321,048	**1985**	**1,002,906***
1920	115,176	1953	485,353	1986	850,103
1921	82,930	1954	531,463	1987	659,141
1922	123,152	1955	781,296	1988	484,764
1923	201,572	1956	535,364	1989	542,917
1924	160,411	1957	407,271	1990	321,918
1925	192,100	1958	257,124	1991	544,325
1926	266,753	1959	232,579	1992	580,154
1927	255,160	1960	307,804	1993	500,691
1928	221,758	1961	291,895	1994	546,836
1929	196,104	1962	415,892	1995	471,819
1930	119,165	1963	479,399	1996	427,316
1931	88,417	1964	482,685	1997	438,064
1932	41,522	1965	653,838	1998	431,142
1933	40,620	1966	580,421	1999	406,474
1934	78,757	1967	573,866	2000	476,343
1935	107,611	1968	652,047		

*Buick's biggest year ever

Buick Engines, 1904-1980

Year	Cylinders	Displacement	Bore x Stroke	Output (Gross HP)	Year	Cylinders	Displacement	Bore x Stroke	Output (Gross HP)
1904	O-2	159-cu.in.	4.50 x 5.00 in.	15, 22 (BHP)	1914	I-4	221-cu.in.	3.75 x 5.00 in.	35 (BHP)
1905	I-2	159-cu.in.	4.50 x 5.00 in.	22 (BHP)	1914	I-6	331-cu.in.	3.75 x 5.00 in.	48 (BHP)
1906	I-2	159-cu.in.	4.50 x 5.00 in.	22 (BHP)	1915	I-4	165-cu.in.	3.75 x 3.75 in.	22.5 (NACCHP)
1907	I-2	159-cu.in.	4.50 x 5.00 in.	22 (BHP)	1915	I-4	221-cu.in.	3.75 x 5.00 in.	37 (BHP)
1907	I-4	255-cu.in.	4.25 x 4.50 in.	30 (BHP)	1915	I-6	331-cu.in.	3.75 x 5.00 in.	55 (BHP)
1908	I-2	159-cu.in.	4.50 x 5.00 in.	22 (BHP)	1916	I-6	225-cu.in.	3.25 x 4.50 in.	45 (BHP)
1908	I-4	165-cu.in.	3.75 x 3.75 in.	22.5 (BHP)	1916	I-6	331-cu.in.	3.75 x 5.00 in.	55 (BHP)
1908	I-4	255-cu.in.	4.25 x 4.50 in.	30 (BHP)	1917	I-6	170-cu.in.	3.375 x 4.75 in.	35 (BHP)
1908	I-4	336-cu.in.	4.625 x 5.00 in.	40 (BHP)	1917	I-6	225-cu.in.	3.25 x 4.50 in.	45 (BHP)
1909	I-2	159-cu.in.	4.50 x 5.00 in.	22 (BHP)	1918	I-6	170-cu.in.	3.375 x 4.75 in.	35 (BHP)
1909	I-4	165-cu.in.	3.75 x 3.75 in.	22.5 (BHP)	1918	I-6	242-cu.in.	3.375 x 4.50 in.	60 (BHP)
1909	I-4	318-cu.in.	4. 50 x 5.00 in.	32.4 (SAE)	1919	I-6	242-cu.in.	3.375 x 4.50 in.	60 (BHP)
1909	I-4	336-cu.in.	4.625 x 5.00 in.	40 (BHP)					
1910	I-2	159-cu.in.	4.50 x 5.00 in.	22 (BHP)	1920	I-6	242-cu.in.	3.375 x 4.50 in.	60 (BHP)
1910	I-4	165-cu.in.	3.75 x 3.75 in.	22.5 (BHP)	1921	I-6	242-cu.in.	3.375 x 4.50 in.	60 (BHP)
1910	I-4	255-cu.in.	4.25 x 4.50 in.	28.9 (BHP)	1922	I-4	170-cu.in.	3.375 x 4.75 in.	35 (BHP)
1910	I-4	318-cu.in.	4. 50 x 5.00 in.	32.4 (BHP)	1922	I-6	242-cu.in.	3.375 x 4.50 in.	60 (BHP)
1910	I-4	336-cu.in.	4.625 x 5.00 in.	40 (BHP)	1923	I-4	170-cu.in.	3.375 x 4.75 in.	35 (BHP)
1911	I-2	127-cu.in.	4.50 x 4.00 in.	14.2 (SAE)	1923	I-6	242-cu.in.	3.375 x 4.50 in.	60 (BHP)
1911	I-4	165-cu.in.	3.75 x 3.75 in.	22.5 (SAE)	1924	I-4	170-cu.in.	3.375 x 4.75 in.	35 (BHP)
1911	I-4	201-cu.in.	3.75 x 3.75 in.	25.6 (SAE)	1924	I-6	255-cu.in.	3.375 x 4.75 in.	70 (BHP)
1911	I-4	255-cu.in.	4.25 x 4.50 in.	40 (BHP)	1925	I-6	191-cu.in.	3.00 x 4.50 in.	50 (BHP)
1911	I-4	318-cu.in.	4.50 x 5.00 in.	32.4 (SAE)	1925	I-6	255-cu.in.	3.375 x 4.75 in.	70 (BHP)
1912	I-4	165-cu.in.	3.75 x 3.75 in.	22.5 (SAE)	1926	I-6	207-cu.in.	3.125 x 4.50 in.	60 (BHP)
1912	I-4	201-cu.in.	3.75 x 3.75 in.	25.5 (SAE)	1926	I-6	274-cu.in.	3.50 x 4.75 in.	75 (BHP)
1912	I-4	318-cu.in.	4.50 x 5.00 in.	48 (BHP)	1927	I-6	207-cu.in.	3.125 x 4.50 in.	63 (BHP)
1913	I-4	165-cu.in.	3.75 x 3.75 in.	22.5 (NACCHP)	1927	I-6	274-cu.in.	3.50 x 4.75 in.	75 (BHP)
1913	I-4	201-cu.in.	3.75 x 3.75 in.	25.6 (NACCHP)	1928	I-6	207-cu.in.	3.125 x 4.50 in.	63 (BHP)
1913	I-4	255-cu.in.	3.75 x 3.75 in.	28.9 (NACCHP)	1928	I-6	274-cu.in.	3.50 x 4.75 in.	77 (BHP)
1914	I-4	165-cu.in.	3.75 x 3.75 in.	22 (SAE)	1929	I-6	239.1-cu.in.	3.312 x 4.625 in.	74 (BHP)
					1929	I-6	309.6-cu.in.	3.625 x 5.00 in.	31.5 (NACCHP)

Year	Cylinders	Displacement	Bore x Stroke	Output (Gross HP)

Starting in 1930, all power ratings are measured as brake horsepower

Year	Cylinders	Displacement	Bore x Stroke	Output (Gross HP)
1930	I-6	212.8-cu.in.	3.125 x 4.625 in.	67.5
1930	I-6	257.5-cu.in.	3.438 x 4.625 in.	80.5
1930	I-6	331.4-cu.in.	3.75 x 5.00 in.	99
1931	I-8	220.7-cu.in.	2.875 x 4.25 in.	77
1931	I-8	272.6-cu.in.	3.063 x 4.625 in.	90
1931	I-8	344.8-cu.in.	3.313 x 5.00 in.	104
1932	I-8	230.4-cu.in.	2.94 x 4.25 in.	82.5
1932	I-8	272.6-cu.in.	3.063 x 4.625 in.	90
1932	I-8	344.8-cu.in.	3.313 x 5.00 in.	104, 113
1933	I-8	230.4-cu.in.	2.94 x 4.25 in.	86
1933	I-8	272.6-cu.in.	3.063 x 4.625 in.	97
1933	I-8	344.8-cu.in.	3.313 x 5.00 in.	104
1934	I-8	233-cu.in.	3.094 x 3.875 in.	93
1934	I-8	235-cu.in.	2.97 x 4.25 in.	88
1934	I-8	278-cu.in.	3.094 x 4.625 in.	100
1934	I-8	344.8-cu.in.	3.313 x 5.00 in.	116
1935	I-8	233-cu.in.	3.094 x 3.875 in.	93
1935	I-8	235-cu.in.	2.97 x 4.25 in.	88
1935	I-8	278-cu.in.	3.094 x 4.625 in.	100
1935	I-8	344.8-cu.in.	3.313 x 5.00 in.	116
1936	I-8	233-cu.in.	3.094 x 3.875 in.	93
1936	I-8	320.2-cu.in.	3.44 x 4.31 in.	120
1937	I-8	248-cu.in.	3.094 x 4.125 in.	100
1937	I-8	320.2-cu.in.	3.44 x 4.31 in.	130
1938	I-8	248-cu.in.	3.094 x 4.125 in.	100
1938	I-8	320.2-cu.in.	3.44 x 4.31 in.	130
1939	I-8	248-cu.in.	3.094 x 4.125 in.	107
1939	I-8	320.2-cu.in.	3.44 x 4.31 in.	141
1940	I-8	248-cu.in.	3.094 x 4.125 in.	107
1940	I-8	320.2-cu.in.	3.44 x 4.31 in.	141
1941	I-8	248-cu.in.	3.094 x 4.125 in.	115, 125
1941	I-8	320.2-cu.in.	3.44 x 4.31 in.	165
1942	I-8	248-cu.in.	3.094 x 4.125 in.	110, 118
1942	I-8	320.2-cu.in.	3.44 x 4.31 in.	165
1946	I-8	320.2-cu.in.	3.44 x 4.31 in.	144
1947	I-8	248-cu.in.	3.094 x 4.125 in.	110
1947	I-8	320.2-cu.in.	3.44 x 4.31 in.	144
1948	I-8	248-cu.in.	3.094 x 4.125 in.	110
1948	I-8	320.2-cu.in.	3.44 x 4.31 in.	144, 150
1949	I-8	248-cu.in.	3.094 x 4.125 in.	110
1949	I-8	320.2-cu.in.	3.44 x 4.31 in.	120, 150
1950	I-8	263.3-cu.in.	3.188 x 4.125 in.	120, 124
1950	I-8	320.2-cu.in.	3.44 x 4.31 in.	128, 152
1951	I-8	263.3-cu.in.	3.188 x 4.125 in.	120, 124
1951	I-8	320.2-cu.in.	3.44 x 4.31 in.	128, 152
1952	I-8	263.3-cu.in.	3.188 x 4.125 in.	120, 124
1952	I-8	320.2-cu.in.	3.44 x 4.31 in.	128, 170
1953	I-8	263.3-cu.in.	3.188 x 4.125 in.	125, 130
1953	V-8	322-cu.in.	4.00 x 3.20 in.	164, 170, 188
1954	V-8	264-cu.in.	3.625 x 3.20 in.	143, 150
1954	V-8	322-cu.in.	4.00 x 3.20 in.	177, 195, 200
1955	V-8	264-cu.in.	3.625 x 3.20 in.	188
1955	V-8	322-cu.in.	4.00 x 3.20 in.	236
1956	V-8	322-cu.in.	4.00 x 3.20 in.	220, 255
1957	V-8	364-cu.in.	4.125 x 3.40 in.	250, 300, 330
1958	V-8	364-cu.in.	4.125 x 3.40 in.	250, 300
1959	V-8	364-cu.in.	4.125 x 3.40 in.	250, 300
1959	V-8	401-cu.in.	4.188 x 3.64 in.	325
1960	V-8	364-cu.in.	4.125 x 3.40 in.	250
1960	V-8	401-cu.in.	4.188 x 3.64 in.	325
1961	V-8	215-cu.in.	3.50 x 2.80 in.	155
1961	V-8	364-cu.in.	4.125 x 3.40 in.	235, 250
1961	V-8	401-cu.in.	4.188 x 3.64 in.	325
1962	V-6	198-cu.in.	3.625 x 3.20 in.	135
1962	V-8	215-cu.in.	3.50 x 2.80 in.	155, 190
1962	V-8	401-cu.in.	4.188 x 3.64 in.	265, 280, 325
1963	V-6	198-cu.in.	3.625 x 3.20 in.	135
1963	V-8	215-cu.in.	3.50 x 2.80 in.	155, 200
1963	V-8	401-cu.in.	4.188 x 3.64 in.	265, 280, 325
1963	V-8	425-cu.in.	4.313 x 3.64 in.	340
1964	V-6	225-cu.in.	3.75 x 3.40 in.	155
1964	V-8	300-cu.in.	3.75 x 3.40 in.	210, 250
1964	V-8	401-cu.in.	4.188 x 3.64 in.	325
1964	V-8	425-cu.in.	4.313 x 3.64 in.	340, 360
1965	V-6	225-cu.in.	3.75 x 3.40 in.	155
1965	V-8	300-cu.in.	3.75 x 3.40 in.	210
1965	V-8	401-cu.in.	4.188 x 3.64 in.	325
1965	V-8	425-cu.in.	4.313 x 3.64 in.	340, 360
1966	V-6	225-cu.in.	3.75 x 3.40 in.	160
1966	V-8	300-cu.in.	3.75 x 3.40 in.	210, 250
1966	V-8	340-cu.in.	3.75 x 3.85 in.	220, 260
1966	V-8	401-cu.in.	4.188 x 3.64 in.	325
1966	V-8	425-cu.in.	4.313 x 3.64 in.	340, 360
1967	V-6	225-cu.in.	3.75 x 3.40 in.	160
1967	V-8	300-cu.in.	3.75 x 3.40 in.	210, 250
1967	V-8	340-cu.in.	3.75 x 3.85 in.	220, 260
1967	V-8	400-cu.in.	4.04 x 3.90 in.	325
1967	V-8	430-cu.in.	4.313 x 3.90 in.	340, 360
1968	I-6	250-cu.in.	3.875 x 3.53 in.	155
1968	V-8	350-cu.in.	3.80 x 3.85 in.	230, 280
1968	V-8	400-cu.in.	4.04 x 3.90 in.	340
1968	V-8	430-cu.in.	4.313 x 3.90 in.	360
1969	I-6	250-cu.in.	3.875 x 3.53 in.	155
1969	V-8	350-cu.in.	3.80 x 3.85 in.	230, 280
1969	V-8	400-cu.in.	4.04 x 3.90 in.	340
1969	V-8	430-cu.in.	4.313 x 3.90 in.	360
1970	I-6	250-cu.in.	3.875 x 3.53 in.	155
1970	V-8	350-cu.in.	3.80 x 3.85 in.	260, 285, 315
1970	V-8	455-cu.in.	4.32 x 3.90 in.	350, 360, 370
1971	I-6	250-cu.in.	3.875 x 3.53 in.	145
1971	V-8	350-cu.in.	3.80 x 3.85 in.	230, 285
1971	V-8	455-cu.in.	4.32 x 3.90 in.	315, 330, 345

Starting in 1972, horsepower figures are "Net" ratings.

Year	Cylinders	Displacement	Bore x Stroke	Output (Gross HP)
1972	V-8	350-cu.in.	3.80 x 3.85 in.	150, 190
1972	V-8	455-cu.in.	4.32 x 3.90 in.	225, 260, 270
1973	I-6	250-cu.in.	3.875 x 3.50 in.	100
1973	V-8	350-cu.in.	3.80 x 3.85 in.	150, 175
1973	V-8	455-cu.in.	4.32 x 3.90 in.	225, 250, 260, 270
1974	I-6	250-cu.in.	3.875 x 3.50 in.	100
1974	V-8	350-cu.in.	3.80 x 3.85 in.	150, 175
1974	V-8	455-cu.in.	4.32 x 3.90 in.	210
1975	V-6	231-cu.in.	3.80 x 3.40 in.	110
1975	I-6	250-cu.in.	3.875 x 3.50 in.	105
1975	V-8	260-cu.in.	3.50 x 3.385 in.	110
1975	V-8	350-cu.in.	3.80 x 3.85 in.	145, 165
1975	V-8	455-cu.in.	4.32 x 3.90 in.	205
1976	V-6	231-cu.in.	3.80 x 3.40 in.	105
1976	V-8	260-cu.in.	3.50 x 3.385 in.	110
1976	V-8	350-cu.in.	3.80 x 3.85 in.	140, 155
1976	V-8	455-cu.in.	4.32 x 3.90 in.	205
1977	V-6	231-cu.in.	3.80 x 3.40 in.	105
1977 P	V-8	301-cu.in.	4.00 x 3.00 in.	135
1977 C	V-8	305-cu.in.	3.74 x 3.48 in.	145
1977	V-8	350-cu.in.	3.80 x 3.85 in.	140, 155
1977 O	V-8	350-cu.in.	4.06 x 3.385 in.	170
1977 C	V-8	350-cu.in.	4.00 x 3.48 in.	170
1977 O	V-8	403-cu.in.	4.32 x 3.90 in.	185
1978	V-6	196-cu.in.	3.80 x 3.40 in.	90
1978	V-6	231-cu.in.	3.80 x 3.40 in.	105, 150, 165
1978 P	V-8	301-cu.in.	4.00 x 3.00 in.	140
1978 C	V-8	305-cu.in.	3.74 x 3.48 in.	160
1978	V-8	350-cu.in.	3.80 x 3.85 in.	155
1978 O	V-8	350-cu.in.	4.06 x 3.385 in.	170
1978 C	V-8	350-cu.in.	4.00 x 3.48 in.	170
1978 O	V-8	403-cu.in.	4.32 x 3.90 in.	185

Buick Clubs & Specialists

For a complete list of all regional Buick clubs and national clubs' chapters, visit **Car Club Central** at **www.hemmings.com.** With nearly 10,000 car clubs listed, it's the largest car club site in the world! Not wired? For the most up-to-date information, consult the latest issue of *Hemmings Motor News* and or *Hemmings' Collector Car Almanac.* Call toll free, 1-800-CAR-HERE, Ext. 550.

BUICK CLUBS

1929 Silver Anniversary Buick Club
75 Oriole Pkwy.
Toronto, ON, Canada M4V 2E3
416-487-9522

Buick Club of America
P.O. Box 401927
Hesperia, CA 92340-1927
760-947-2485
(68 regional chapters)

Buick Club of Germany
AM Wimmerberg 55
Erkrath D-40699 Germany
+49 (211) 9007383

Buick GS Club of America
625 Pine Point Cir.
Valdosta, GA 31602
912-244-0577

New Zealand Buick Enthusiasts Club
26 Dunraven Pl
Torbay
North Shore City 1310
New Zealand
011-649-473-6856

Riviera Owners Association
P.O. Box 26344
Lakewood, CO 80226
303-987-3712

Other Important Clubs

Antique Automobile Club of America
501 W. Governor Road
Hershey, PA 17033
717-534-1910
(311 regional chapters, 7 international chapters)

Horseless Carriage Club of America
3311 Fairhaven Dr.
Orange, CA 92866-1357
661-326-1023
(91 regional chapters, 7 international chapters)

Veteran Motor Car Club of America
4441 W. Altadena Ave.
Glendale, AZ 85304-3526
800-428-7327
(82 regional chapters)

BUICK SPECIALISTS

Bob's Automobilia
P.O. Box 2119
Atascadero, CA 93423
805-434-2963
Reproduction trim and new mechanical parts

CARS Inc.
P.O. Box 5
Neshanic Station, NJ 08853
908-369-3666
New, used and reproduction parts for all 1936-1987 models

Classic Buicks
4632 Riverside Drive
Chino, CA 91701
909-591-0283
Body panels and interior trim

Kanter Auto Products
76 Monroe St
Boonton, NJ 07005
800-526-1096
New engine, suspension and electrical components

Poston Enterprises
206-N. Main St.
Atmore, AL 36502
800-635-9781
Mechanical, body and interior parts for GS and Skylarks

Pro Antique Auto parts
50 King Spring Rd.
Windsor Locks, CT 06096
860-623-8275
New and reproduction parts for all 1929-1964 models

Steele Rubber Products
6180 Hwy 150 East
Denver, NC 28037-9735
800-544-8665
Weatherstripping and bushings

Swanson's Vintage Buick parts
3574 Western Ave.
Sacramento, CA 95838
916-646-0430
Engine parts for 1938-1948 models

TA Performance
16167 N. 81st Street
Scottsdale, AZ 85260
480-922-6811
High-performance engine parts

Terrill Machine Inc.
Rt. 2 Box 61
DeLeon, TX 76444
254-893-2610
New engine parts